Complete Guide to Digital Project Management

From Pre-Sales to Post-Production

D1530083

Shailesh Kumar Shivakumar

Apress®

Complete Guide to Digital Project Management: From Pre-Sales to Post-Production

Shailesh Kumar Shivakumar
Bangalore, Karnataka, India

ISBN-13 (pbk): 978-1-4842-3416-7
https://doi.org/10.1007/978-1-4842-3417-4

ISBN-13 (electronic): 978-1-4842-3417-4

Library of Congress Control Number: 2018934388

Managing Director, Apress Media LLC: Welmoed Spahr
Acquisitions Editor: Shiva Ramachandran
Development Editor: Laura Berendson
Coordinating Editor: Rita Fernando

Cover designed by eStudioCalamar

Cover image designed by Freepik (www.freepik.com)

Distributed to the book trade worldwide by Springer Science+Business Media New York, 233 Spring Street, 6th Floor, New York, NY 10013. Phone 1-800-SPRINGER, fax (201) 348-4505, e-mail orders-ny@springer-sbm.com, or visit www.springeronline.com. Apress Media, LLC is a California LLC and the sole member (owner) is Springer Science + Business Media Finance Inc (SSBM Finance Inc). SSBM Finance Inc is a **Delaware** corporation.

For information on translations, please e-mail rights@apress.com, or visit http://www.apress.com/rights-permissions.

Apress titles may be purchased in bulk for academic, corporate, or promotional use. eBook versions and licenses are also available for most titles. For more information, reference our Print and eBook Bulk Sales web page at http://www.apress.com/bulk-sales.

Any source code or other supplementary material referenced by the author in this book is available to readers on GitHub via the book's product page, located at www.apress.com/9781484234167. For more detailed information, please visit http://www.apress.com/source-code.

Printed on acid-free paper

I would like to dedicate this book to:

*My parents, Shivakumara Setty V and Anasuya T M,
from whom I loaned love and strength,*

*My wife Chaitra Prabhudeva and my son Shishir from
whom I loaned time and support,*

*My in-laws, Prabhudeva T M and Krishnaveni B,
from whom I loaned help and courage.*

And

*To all my schoolteachers who bestowed lots of love and
knowledge upon me.*

Table of Contents

About the Author

Shailesh Kumar Shivakumar is a Practice Lead and Senior Technology Architect at Infosys Technologies. He is an award-winning digital technology practitioner with skills in technology and practice management. Shailesh is an experienced enterprise architect skilled in the wide spectrum of digital technologies, including enterprise portals, content systems, enterprise search, web analytics, cloud technologies, and other digital technologies. He has over 16 years of industry experience and was the chief architect in building a digital platform that won the "Best Web Support Site 2013" global award. His areas of expertise include digital technologies, software engineering, performance engineering, and digital program management. He is a Guinness world record holder of participation for successfully developing a mobile application during a coding marathon.

Shailesh is deeply focused on enterprise architecture, building alliance partnerships with product vendors, and has a proven track record of executing complex, large-scale programs. He successfully architected and led many engagements for Fortune 500 clients of Infosys and built globally deployed enterprise applications. He also headed a center-of-excellence for digital practice. He has created multiple IPs related to digital technologies at Infosys that can be used as solution accelerators. He led multiple thought-leadership and productivity improvement initiatives and was part of special interest groups (SIG) related to emerging web technologies at his organization.

Shailesh is listed in the "Marquis Who's Who in the World 2018" and is a 2018 Albert Nelson Marquis Lifetime Achievement Award Winner. He won prestigious awards such as Infosys Awards for Excellence 2013-14: "Multi-Talented Thought Leader" under the "Innovation – Thought leadership" category, the "Brand Ambassador Award 2013", the "Best Employee Award 2015," the delivery excellency award 2012, Unit champion award, Pinnacle award and multiple spot awards. He also received an honor from the executive vice chairman of his organization. He is featured as an "Infy star" in the Infosys

Hall of Fame and recently led a delivery team that won the "Best Project Team" award at his organization.

Shailesh holds numerous professional certifications, such as the TOGAF 9 certification, Oracle Certified Master (OCM) in Java EE5 Enterprise Architect certification, IBM Certified SOA Solution Designer, and IBM Certified Solution Architect Cloud Computing Infrastructure. He has authored three technical books on digital technologies and has published twelve technical whitepapers related to digital technologies. Shailesh has one granted US patent and three patent applications and is a frequent speaker at events such as IEEE conferences and Oracle JavaOne conference.

About the Technical Reviewer

George Koelsch is a system engineer who resides in Northern Virginia, within the DC metro area. He started system engineering 41 years ago while in the US Army and has continued that work for the last 31 years as a contractor for the Federal Government. With a five-year stint as an Industrial Engineer at Michelin Tire Corporation, he learned to become an efficiency expert, which he then applied to system engineering and project management to tailor the lifecycle development process before his contemporaries in the DC area were doing so. In his spare time, he has authored ten non-fiction articles on computers, coin collecting, stamp collecting, and high-energy physics.

Acknowledgments

I would like to convey my sincere and heart-felt thanks to Verma VSSRK, Rahul Krishan, Saumitra Bhatnagar, Sarbeswar Panda, Shankar Bhat, Nitin Saini and Sreenivas Kashyap at Infosys who encouraged me in all my initiatives.

My sincere thanks to Professor Dr. Viraj Kumar for his constant encouragement and patience. He has been a constant inspiration to me.

I would also like to recognize and thank Dr. P. V. Suresh for his constant encouragement and immense support.

My special thanks to the A team at Apress consisting of Susan McDermott, Rita Fernando, Shivangi Ramachandran, and Laura Berendson, for all their timely support and review help. The team is highly proactive and super responsive in planning and execution. I would also like to thank the editorial team and design team at Apress for the beautiful book design. I owe much of the book's success to the Apress team.

I would also like to sincerely thank George Koelsch for his valuable feedback comments and timely technical review, which has added lot of value to the book.

Introduction

Digital technologies are disrupting the way business is done and redefining the end user experience. As digital technologies are constantly evolving, a digital project manager should continuously seek to learn and understand the impact of digital technologies and thrive to constantly improve upon the project management practices. Continuous improvement is a never-ending endeavor for the project managers in digital project engagements. Digital project managers need to achieve a fine balance between high expectations from end users and business stakeholders and project constraints such as cost, quality, and schedule.

In this book, we explore the digital project management from a holistic perspective: from consulting until post-production maintenance. Having this 360-degree view can immensely benefit the digital project manager to proactively plan and successfully execute the program while minimizing the known risks.

Digital projects have their own set of unique challenges due to the niche technological skills, faster release plans, and continuous changes. We have tried to address these digital project-specific challenges.

Key Highlights of the Book

Here are some of the key value differentiators of this book:

- A focus on digital consulting and pre-sales (proof-of-concept, articulation of win themes) with detailed consulting case studies.

- Wide coverage of estimation models and pricing models, including modern estimation models such as user story based estimation used in modern digital projects.

- A focus on practical, proven, and usable project management artefacts/tools/frameworks such as:

  - Models such as the digital maturity model, the continuous execution model, and the quantitative risk management model

  - Templates such as the RACI template, the resource induction template, and the requirement elaboration template

- Frameworks such as the migration framework, digital product evaluation, and knowledge transition

- Tools related to DevOps, project planning, collaboration, Agile project management, test management, and project planning

- In-depth coverage of the Agile execution model along with its metrics, best practices, and applicability scenarios.

- Dedicated and in-depth coverage for achieving high quality in digital projects through a quality framework with a detailed case study.

- In-depth coverage of known anti-patterns and failure factors in digital projects along with lead indicators and mitigation strategies.

- Chapter dedicated to cover the proven best practices related to digital project management from various dimensions.

- In-depth focus on real-world project management scenarios and case studies, with three book chapters covering these topics.

- Exclusive chapter covering recent trends and innovations in digital space and its impact on digital project management.

Book's Organization

The book is organized into 17 chapters and 6 appendixes, wherein the 17 chapters are categorized into four parts. The first three parts covers three main phases of the project—project initiation, project execution, and project maintenance—and the last part is exclusively dedicated to project management scenarios and case studies. The next sections describe high-level summaries of each of the parts.

Part I: Initiation of Digital Projects

This part contains topics that are related to digital project initiation, consulting, and pre-sales. Chapter 1 introduces project management concepts such as project phases, governance, execution models, and more. Chapter 2 covers various topics related to digital project consulting, such as consulting frameworks, pre-sales activities along with a detailed digital consulting case study. Chapter 3 introduces various project management related plans such as project plan, collaboration plan, quality management plan, staffing plan, training plan, and risk management plan that a project manager would define during the initiation phase. Chapter 4 discusses various estimation models, such as function point estimation, SMC estimation, use case based estimation, and various pricing models.

Part II: Execution of Digital Projects

This part covers various topics related to project execution. Chapter 5 provides detailed insights into various models (such as earned value management and the digital maturity models), templates (such as the RACI template and the requirements template), and tools that a digital project manager can use during project execution. Chapter 6 details various project execution models such as the waterfall model and the iterative model, with special focus on the Agile model and its variants. Chapter 7 covers various aspects of project quality across project phases, along with a case study. Chapter 8 elaborates on various project management functions such as requirements management, stakeholder management, knowledge transition planning, project governance, and auditing. Chapter 9 covers people management topics such as coaching, feedback management, competency development, and such.

Part III: Monitoring and Maintenance of Digital Projects

The chapters in this part cover maintenance, monitoring, and post-production related topics. The main topics in this part are focused on the "continuous improvement" principle, which we adopt during the maintenance phase. We will initially look at the common lessons, best practices, and failure scenarios based on our experience from various digital projects. These insights will help digital project managers take proactive measures to identify and address known problem patterns in the early stages. Chapter 10 covers common reasons for failure in digital projects, along with a best practices-based approach to avoid failures. Chapter 11 covers various best practices that can be adopted at different phases of digital project management. Chapter 12 covers product evaluation framework, migration framework, and digital product governance. Chapter 13 covers the emerging trends and innovations in the digital space. Chapter 14 covers various project management activities during maintenance phase, such as incident management, production maintenance, knowledge transition, and more.

Part IV: Digital Project Management Scenarios and Case Studies

The chapters in this part are dedicated to the real-world project management scenarios and case studies so that project managers can gain insights from these scenarios and case studies and apply the insights to their current engagements. Chapter 15 covers various digital project management scenarios, such as scope creep handling, change request handling, etc.; each scenario is explained with its challenges, root causes, and handling methods. Chapter 16 discuses four detailed case studies related to digital project management. Chapter 17 discusses an elaborate digital transformation case study related to a digital bank.

Appendixes

Six appendixes complement the topics discussed in the book. Appendix A briefly discusses the cloud adoption strategy; Appendix B compiles the domain-specific use cases and business drivers; Appendix C provides the acceptance criteria for various testing phases; Appendix D provides a project scope template document; Appendix E provides a template for a product evaluation score card; and Appendix F compiles best practices in digital project governance.

Target Audience

The primary target audience of this book is the digital project manager and program manager who can use the insights, tools, frameworks, and models described here. The book will also be useful to self-driven Agile team members who can use the lessons from this book to efficiently execute Agile projects. Account managers, business sponsors, technical managers, and digital practitioners will also find useful information in relevant book chapters.

PART I

Initiation of Digital Projects

CHAPTER 1

Introduction to Digital Project Management

Project management aims to utilize resources across all technology tracks to achieve the intended goals within a set schedule. Managing digital projects involves managing various digital technologies (e.g., content management systems, portals, search, analytics, etc.) to achieve high-quality deliverables.

The vast majority of project management failures we see can be traced back to requirements management, scope creep, change request handling, adoption failures, or sustained maintenance—all activities that are in the realm of project management. Therefore, it is very important to understand the critical aspects of project management and its related challenges and to be aware of the best project management techniques.

This chapter introduces the key concepts in digital project management. The first section discusses digital project phases and project governance activities. The next section looks at various execution models, such as the iterative and Agile models with case studies. Subsequent sections cover risk management, change management, and release management for digital projects.

Project managers, project managers, account managers, business executives, and enterprise architects will find the content in this chapter useful.

What Are Digital Projects?

Digital projects in the context of this book refer mainly to modern day software projects that predominantly use digital technologies such as experience platforms, enterprise portals, content systems, commerce platforms, user experience technologies, mobile technologies, search, and collaboration.

© Shailesh Kumar Shivakumar 2018
S. K. Shivakumar, *Complete Guide to Digital Project Management*,
https://doi.org/10.1007/978-1-4842-3417-4_1

The Key Tenets of Digital Projects

Here are the key tenets of a typical digital project are as follows:

- The project uses modern day technologies such as experience platforms, commerce products, API platforms, Big Data technologies, AI technologies, and so on.

- The project releases are mainly executed through an Agile methodology or in iterations to attain faster time to market.

- The primary success metrics are user engagement, performance, responsiveness, agility, and user conversion.

- The solutions mainly cater to Internet users and provide omni-channel capabilities.

Regular Software Projects vs. Digital Projects

While digital projects have the fundamentally same features of any regular software projects, they have their own set of unique features and challenges as well. Table 1-1 provides the key differences between a regular software project and a digital project.

Table 1-1. *Digital Projects vs. Regular Software Projects*

	Digital Projects	Regular Software Projects
Primary technology	Modern digital technologies such as portals, CMS, and search	Proven matured technologies such as legacy technologies and legacy web frameworks
Execution methodology	Mostly Agile or iterative	Mostly waterfall
Resource Needs	Needs niche skillset with limited availability	Rich availability of resources
Target audience	Mainly Internet (B2C) audience	Targeted to B2B and B2C audience

As the definition of "digital technologies" is continuously evolving, in the context of this book, we refer to any project using modern digital technology (such as digital commerce, experience platforms, responsive UI frameworks, mobile applications, analytics, cloud technologies etc.) as a digital project.

Project Management of Digital Projects

This section discusses the various phases and activities in each phase of typical digital projects.

Mapping Digital Capabilities Across a Solution Value Chain

A project manager plays an active role in identifying and mapping various digital capabilities needed during the entire journey of a digital user.

We can identify the user journey at the overall digital solution level and identify various customer touch points and map them to their corresponding digital capabilities. This exercise is normally done at the project level during requirements elaboration to determine various solution capabilities. Business analysts, solution architects, and project managers participate in this activity.

Digital project managers can use their project management experience and contribute to this exercise. They can bring in their experience of various digital products and capabilities that worked best in their earlier engagements and then refine the digital capability mapping. Figure 1-1 shows a sample digital capability mapping for a digital commerce user journey. The touch points referred to in Figure 1-1 are the user functionalities through which the user interacts with the system. Digital capabilities refer to various features and functionalities harnessed from digital technologies and products. For instance, during the marketing and sales phase of the e-commerce solution, the end user normally learns about the solution through a web search. To target the right customer in the right context, we could use digital capabilities such as Search Engine Optimization (SEO), Search Engine Marketing (SEM), promotions, and so on.

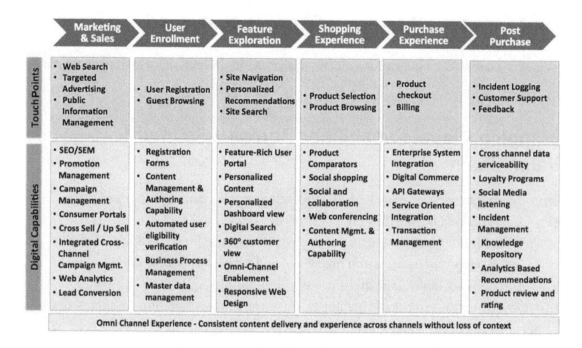

Figure 1-1. *Digital capability mapping for an e-commerce solution*

This mapping exercise can help project managers identify necessary digital technologies and products and then staff the appropriate resources.

Digital Project Phases

There are typically three phases in digital projects:

- *Planning phase*: During this phase, project initiation activities are performed. We define the scope and determine the functional/non-functional requirements. The project manager performs activities such as scope planning, schedule planning, cost and effort planning, resource planning, communication planning, and risk planning.

- *Execution phase*: Code development and testing are the main activities of this phase. The project manager carries out various quality control measures and performs risk management activities during this phase.

- *Maintenance phase*: During this phase, we maintain the solution and add incremental enhancements. Post-production deployment, the project enters into steady state operations mode. The project manager is involved in release management, change management, defect management, SLA monitoring, and other production-related operations.

Table 1-2 provides phase-wise milestones, activities, and deliverables for digital projects. The project lifecycle stages Requirements Elaboration and Architecture and Design are part of project planning phase. The Build and Test activities are part of the project execution phase and the Support and Maintenance step is part of the project maintenance phase.

Table 1-2. *Stage-Wise Activities and Deliverables for Digital Projects*

Digital Project Lifecycle Stage	Key Milestones	Activities	Deliverables
Requirements Elaboration	• Baselined requirements • Detailed implementation plan • Testing strategies and acceptance criteria • Project Governance definition and project execution structure	• Prioritization of requirements with business and IT stakeholders • Define scope and project plan • Understand key constraints and establish dependency/issues tracking • Establish processes, templates and tools for development • Identify and establish Project Management Office (PMO) for governance and change management • Define Non Functional Requirements (NFR) and establish benchmarks for system requirements • Establish necessary infrastructure for development/SIT/UAT environment • User profiling to validate UI requirements and determine ease of navigation • Map all the requirements to use case and identify any missing links • Understand business processes • Interaction with stakeholders and business end users to understand end user requirements, user journeys, navigation model, interaction model, and layout plan • Develop a requirements traceability matrix; requirements traceability matrix is a cross reference table linking every stage of the application lifecycle with the previous and next stages • Identify interface requirements and, based on that, prepare integration requirements • Review requirements specification and acceptance criteria documents by business stakeholders • Identify development resource requirements (software, hardware, and infrastructure to be used during project execution)	• Project plan • Validated system requirements specification • Validated UI standards and specifications • [Optional] Migration requirements document

Architecture and Design	• Define standards for the design and development activities	• Sequence diagrams and business process diagrams
• Technical architecture document definition	• Choose templates and checklists for key project deliverables	• Detailed development plan
• Detailed design definition	• Prepare functional design specifications document	• High-level test plan
• Wireframe creation	• Prepare integration and system test plans	• Detailed test plan
• Visual design	• Update traceability matrix to ensure complete and accurate coverage of all requirements	• Software architecture document
	• Design review session will be conducted to capture any missing requirements and analyze any process gaps	• Detailed design document
	• Review and stakeholder sign-off of key design deliverables	• Information architecture
	• UI design – information architecture, layouts, navigation flows, etc.	• Wireframes and visual design and visual style guide
	• Review project specifications	• Content strategy definition
	• Plan unit testing	
	• Review unit test plan	
	• Plan for using reusable components	
	• Update traceability matrix with details like the functionality being addressed	
	• Identification of critical scenarios for uses cases and prototyping	
	• Medium fidelity wireframes for typical use cases	
	• One to two concept designs for key pages	
	• Obtain Stakeholder buy-ins	
	• Creation of visual design style guide and graphic assets	
	• Design validation proof-of-concept (PoC)	

(continued)

Table 1-2. (*continued*)

Digital Project Lifecycle Stage	Key Milestones	Activities	Deliverables
Build and Test	• Source code development • Unit, functional, integration, and system testing • Code review sign-off • Testing sign-off • Production go live	• Develop code • Conduct code review • Unit testing of code modules • Incorporate feedback from interim functional checkpoints • Explore the possibility of making reusable components • Update traceability matrix • Defect prevention activities to identify causes of defects, thereby taking action to prevent recurrence • Continuous integration and testing • Release management and deployment	• Code artifacts • Detailed test cases
Support and Maintenance	• Iterative releases • Patching • Product upgrades	• Production incident management and defect fixes • Implementing enhancements • SLA monitoring in production environment	• SLA reports • Production incident report

Content Project Activities

This section looks at high-level project management activities across various phases (see Table 1-3). It will use a content management project to look at various activities in project management phases.

Table 1-3. *Content Project Management Activities*

Activity Category	Activities	Deliverable
Project Planning Phase		
Requirements elaboration	• Understand project scope, content requirements • Understand business processes related to content activities • Understand content flows and content migration requirements if any	• Functional and non-functional requirements • Business process models • Project plan • Communication plan • [Optional] Content migration requirements
Content architecture and design	• Evaluate and select Content Management System (CMS) and other tools and frameworks • Define content strategy • Create high-level content architecture • Define content metadata • Design content components (templates, workflows, services, CMS components, libraries) • Proof-of-concepts to validate core design • Design content interfaces (service-based, API-based) • Create test plans for testing content components • Infrastructure plan and business continuity plan • Disaster recovery design • [Optional] Develop content migration plan and approach	• Content interface design document • Content strategy document • Content solution architecture • Content design document • UX creatives (visual design, wireframes, mockups) • Information architecture definition • Content test plans • CMS infrastructure architecture • Content metadata design • Content security design • Content governance plan • [Optional] Content migration plan and tools

(continued)

Table 1-3. (*continued*)

Activity Category	Activities	Deliverable
Project Execution Phase		
Content development and testing	• Develop content components (templates, workflows, CMS components, sites, layouts, connectors, libraries, pages, scripts, etc.) • Integrate with other systems (for translation, digital assets, and such) • Author content as per requirements	• Delivery of content components (templates, interfaces, services, workflows, and libraries) • Delivery of Web content fragments • Delivery of Pages
[Optional] Content migration	• Evaluate tools for migration automation • Perform content migration • Migration validation	• Migrated content
Project Maintenance Phase		
Content production deployment	• Perform multi-site content deployment	
Support and maintenance	• Handle production incidents • Update CMS with periodic patches • Change management • Content backup and synchronization • Content enhancements	• Incident handling • Patch deployment • Platform upgrades • Fix deployment • Release deployment • Production monitoring

Project Governance

Project governance is a framework with a well-defined accountability structure that can be used to realize and sustain the business strategy. Project governance assigns well-defined roles and responsibilities and decision-making structure to drive the project to achieve its intended objective.

A robust governance model is needed to oversee and control the project execution and delivery quality. The coming sections look at a sample governance structure for digital projects. We have elaborated robust digital governance model in chapter 8.

Governance of Digital Projects

This scenario takes a CMS project as an example to define governance. A sample project governance structure, activities, and communication frequency are depicted in Figure 1-2.

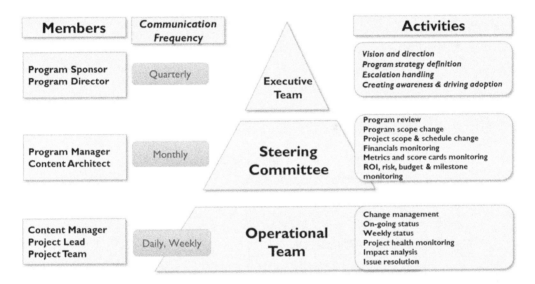

Figure 1-2. *Sample governance model for digital content projects*

At a project level, the content governance involves a project management office (PMO) to manage project-level activities. The main roles and responsibilities in the PMO are listed in Table 1-4.

Table 1-4. *PMO Roles and Responsibilities*

PMO Roles	Responsibilities
Project Sponsor	<ul><li>Provides executive sponsorship</li><li>Single point of contact for executive leadership and CXO communications, concerns, or issues</li><li>Set/clarify strategic direction and vision to assist project progress and success</li><li>Provide guidance on priorities and resolution of core project issues</li><li>Participate in steering workshops and meetings as required</li><li>Drive innovation and continuous improvement opportunities</li></ul>
Project Director	<ul><li>Responsible for successful execution of the project</li><li>Foster knowledge management environments, introduce new capabilities through tools introduction and process optimizations</li><li>Establish risk management framework</li><li>Handle escalation</li></ul>
Project Manager	<ul><li>Act as Single Point of Contact (SPOC) for project reviews</li><li>Manage project scope and schedule</li><li>Monitor project scorecard and critical metrics</li><li>Monitor ROI, budget, and project milestones</li><li>Manage and coordinate stakeholders</li><li>Provide the overall leadership and guidance for the delivery</li><li>Define project governance model, change control process (to handle business changes, schedule changes, design changes and contract changes), and project rollout strategy and plans</li></ul>

(*continued*)

Table 1-4. (*continued*)

PMO Roles	Responsibilities
Content Architect	• Bring deep content experience and understanding of ways of working with creative agencies • Define content standards, content strategy, content architecture, content design, and content integration methodologies • Review and understand the current architecture of the solution completely • Translate business flows into content workflows • Provide any suggestions for improvements/optimization to the current architecture that would be beneficial • Interface with business stakeholders to understand the asset requirements and prioritize them • Identify key business value drivers and use them as input to structure the projects • Drive a deeper understanding of the processes to help project director drive optimization
Content Manager	• Track completion of deliverables against defined milestones • Drive adherence to SLAs • Manage open issues across teams/BUs for resolution • Enable SLA and KPIs driven end-to-end content template assembly for all kinds of assets • Create weekly status reports and communications as needed • Proactively manage stakeholder expectations, resources, resource concerns, and deliverables • Manage, build, test, and hand over content deliverables • Drive delivery optimization over time by automating the build as well as test the steps • Manage the delivery team and quality assurance teams • Proactively identify and mitigate project risks • Ensure proper use of project delivery methodology, standards, tools, processes, and procedures • Analyze risks, establish contingency plans, and identify and execute mitigating actions • Monitor the quality plan in order to adhere to specified deliverables • Proactively identify scope changes and ensure appropriate planning measures are taken with stakeholders to reassess and amend the scope, budget, and timeline

Digital Project Execution Models

This section covers various execution and delivery aspects of digital projects. It closely looks at various execution models and discusses iterative and Agile models in detail. We start by looking at common challenges found in digital projects.

Challenges in Digital Project Execution

The most common list of challenges we will face during digital project execution are listed here.

- *Niche technologies*: The digital technology ecosystem is under constant evolution. New technologies and tools are added on a frequent basis. Hence, it is critical to evaluate the right set of tools and frameworks for the solution domain. It is equally important to select the right team and execution methodology. In order to fully understand the solution "fit" (suitability/applicability of a technology solution for a given set of requirements) and feasibility of the tool/framework, we need to evaluate the tools/technology/ framework through a proof-of-concept (PoC). PoC should be carried out for the prominent use cases for the solution domain. This should be followed by a robust product/technology evaluation (with PoC outcome as one of the evaluation factors) to select the most appropriate technology/product.

- *Availability of the right skillset*: A quality delivery needs a team with the right skillset. We need to build the right team through recruitment, trainings, and workshops and through hands-on exercises.

- *Selection of appropriate execution methodology*: Using the correct project execution methodology is one of the most important factors for the project's overall success and long-term adoption. In addition to the traditional waterfall model, you can use the iterative delivery model or an Agile model. The project manager needs to select the appropriate one for the solution. Most modern digital projects adopt an iterative or Agile methodology for quicker time to market.

- *Incomplete and ambiguous requirements*: An incomplete requirements set impacts other project phases. It is important to have a comprehensive requirements document (or business requirements document or functionality specification document) reviewed and signed off on by all stakeholders. The requirements document should fully capture all functional and non-functional requirements along with all associated business rules and flows.

- *Cross-team collaboration*: Digital projects involve various technology teams, operations teams, product vendors, support team, infrastructure teams, Subject Matter Experts (SMEs), and independent consultants across distributed locations. We need to establish clear channels of communication and collaboration across all teams to build a "one global team" approach. Various tools such as video conferencing tools, continuous integration tools, and centralized knowledge repository play a key role in building one global team.

- *Time to market and time consuming integration/build processes*: As the software becomes complex with many integrations, the build and release management processes become time consuming. The release management pipeline includes build, integration testing, performance testing, security testing, packaging, and deploying. In complex scenarios, all these steps will delay the overall release process and ultimately impact the time to market. Deploying a small fix will tend to become a time-consuming process. Agile and iterative delivery models address this problem from a release dimension by releasing code bases in smaller iterations instead of a big bang release. You can also use a continuous integration methodology (discussed later) to address this challenge.

Characterization of Execution Methodologies

A brief set of characteristics of execution methodologies, namely the waterfall, iterative, and Agile models, are depicted in Figure 1-3.

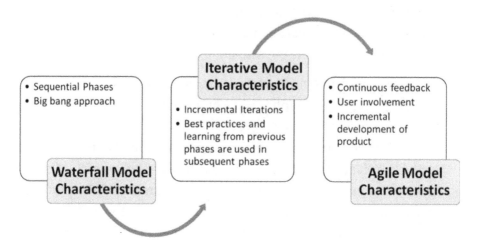

Figure 1-3. *Characteristics of execution methodologies*

Digital projects mainly cater to the Internet audience and hence time to market, agility, and tolerance to changes become crucial requirements. Hence, in the vast majority of digital projects, Agile execution is the preferred execution methodology, followed by the iterative model.

The coming sections cover these two execution methodologies in detail.

The Iterative Model

With an iterative model, an application is developed incrementally in repeated iterations, as depicted in Figure 1-4. In this model, each iteration adds required capabilities. As the application is developed in iterations, businesses and end users can realize the value sooner than with traditional execution methodologies.

Figure 1-4. *Iterative model*

The iterative model elegantly handles evolving requirements and associated risks that are found in most complex digital projects. We can manage changes more efficiently through iterative delivery. Hence, digital projects, which are complex with ambiguous requirements, are best suited to the iterative model.

Advantages of the Iterative Model

The design and integrate phases are iterative in nature. This approach has the following advantages:

- *Quick wins*: The proposed schedule ensures that business functionality is added incrementally. This enables the project teams to achieve quick wins in delivering the solution to the business. The business has an early realization of the solution benefits.

- *Quicker time to market*: We can plan the iterations based on prioritized business capabilities. We can deliver initial iterations quickly, thereby providing early view of the new capability to business and end users. Detecting and fixing issues earlier improves overall delivery quality and reduces rework efforts. As a result, the business can realize the value and get early end-user feedback (which can be addressed in subsequent releases).

- *Serviceability*: Customers are provided incrementally with new chunks of features, thus keeping in mind the time to market and necessary course corrections can be made well in advance.

- *Predictability*: When there are multiple niche technologies, a phased approach ensures a period of application stability before a change is introduced into the production environment. This assists in ensuring predictable results and mitigating risk.

- *Simplicity*: A staggered capability approach that's mindful of out of the box capabilities and external integrations keeps the solution simple and the overall goals achievable. Training and transition of business users and IT teams can also be performed in iterations.

- *Minimized risk*: We can greatly reduce the risk of a big-bang release. Early validation, faster time to market, and end user feedback greatly minimizes the risks related to quality, expectation mismatch, and so on.

Iterative Model for Digital Projects

This section looks at a sample iterative delivery model for a digital project. Figure 1-5 shows the evolution of Enterprise Information Portal (EIP) digital platform that uses an iterative release model. EIP solutions are mainly used as personalized presentation and experience platforms and they aggregate information from multiple sources. They are widely used for B2C scenarios.

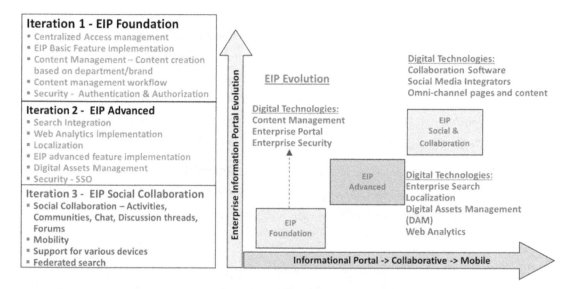

Figure 1-5. *Evolution of digital platform based on portals*

Figure 1-5 depicts the evolution of a portal based digital platform. The evolution can be implemented in three iterations, with each iteration adding the needed capabilities for the evolution phase. EIP foundation iteration, which is the initial iteration, builds the basic platform with core capabilities. We can use CMS, portal, and enterprise security technologies to enable capabilities such as content management, content workflows, and security. We can also develop the quick wins and prioritized requirements (such as EIP home page, security integrations, visually redesigned user experiences, and optimized content publishing processes).

EIP advanced iteration enables advanced features such as content search, site search, localization, Digital Asset Management (DAM), and single-sign-on. In this iteration, you can leverage Enterprise search, DAM, and web analytics technologies.

In the final iteration, we can enable social media integration and collaboration (such as chat, activities, communities, threads, and forums) features. We can also make the EIP pages omni-channel enabled through RWD and adaptive techniques. Based on the complexity, each iteration can be executed in 2-3 months.

The Agile Model

The Agile model is a collection of best practices used to develop a system in smaller increments continuously. The main philosophy of the Agile model revolves around users' active involvement (to involve users in all phases to solicit feedback), automated testing (to provide continuous testing for complete code coverage), iterative development (to deliver in phases), and continuous integration (to create automated and continuous builds, integration, and testing). The Agile model is more tolerant to dynamic requirements (by absorbing changes in subsequent iterations) and focuses on end users.

The Agile model can be used mainly for projects with niche technologies, evolving requirements, with short delivery times and needs close collaboration with customers and other stakeholders.

Ideal Scenarios for the Agile Model

Key scenarios that are best suited for Agile include the following:

- When requirements are not clear or changing or evolving then you can use Agile to incrementally build the product.

- When the product requires a lot of interaction with the end user, adopt the Agile model to involve customer during the development phases and get early feedback about the deliverables.

- Complex requirements using niche technologies can be best executed through the Agile model.

Advantages of the Agile Approach

Key advantages of the Agile model include:

- Promotes self-organizing teams to create a collaboration model for efficient delivery.

- Provides quicker time to market and end user feedback.

- Incorporates many best practices such as test driven development, continuous integration, automated testing, and requirements prioritization, which bring more efficiency to execution.

The Scrum Methodology

The Scrum methodology is one of the popular Agile models that is widely adopted for digital projects. In this methodology, a product is incrementally developed in multiple sprints (iterations), as depicted in Figure 1-6. Each sprint is time-boxed with a specific set of goals. Normally each sprint lasts about 6-8 weeks.

The main Scrum roles include the product owner, who owns product backlog and prioritizes requirements, the Scrum master, who resolves conflicts and dependencies and works with team members, and self-organized teams, which estimate and work on user stories.

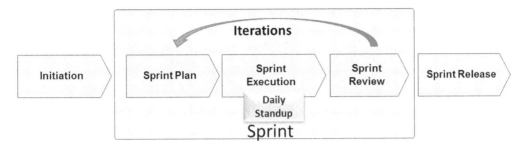

Figure 1-6. *The Scrum methodology*

Key practices of the Scrum methodology include the following:

- *Sprint planning*: Product owner creates the product backlog (compilation of tasks or user stores) and discusses it with the team. The team decides on the required sprints, sprint goals, and the delivery schedule. All identified features (user stories) go into the Sprint backlog.

- *Sprint*: Each Sprint is time-boxed for a fixed time (usually 3-6 weeks based on the deliverables and project complexity) and uses a sprint backlog for execution. Sprint activities are monitored through standup meetings and through burndown charts.

- *Daily standup calls*: The product owner, Scrum master, and team members participate in short daily meetings to discuss the previous day's work and the current day's planned work along with any challenges/roadblocks. These meetings contribute to the overall health of the sprint and enable self-organizing teams.

- *Sprint review*: At the end of each sprint, the team reviews the sprint accomplishments and lessons and discusses the plan for the next sprint. During the process, the team also identifies the scope for reusability and tools/frameworks. The team also provides a product demo to stakeholders.

- *Sprint artifacts*: The main Sprint artifacts are as follows:

    - *User story*: The basic work unit of a sprint. It describes the who, what, and why of the requirements. User stories provide an effective mechanism to break the work down into independent, testable, and deployable units. User stories can be classified as functional and non-functional.

    - *Product backlog*: A list of user stories managed by the product owner. It forms the repository of user stories for the sprint backlog.

    - *Sprint backlog*: Consists of all tasks/features that are part of a given sprint. The team uses a product backlog to create tasks of sprint backlog based on priority and complexity.

Agile Case Study: B2B CMS Portal Execution

This section looks at a simple case study using the Agile model. A business to business (B2B) portal was developed using a Content Management System (CMS). The development team had to extend the built-in security model of the CMS portal for authentication. The CMS portal was also integrated with many internal systems that needed high-level commitment and coordination with multiple teams and SMEs. Traditional execution models, such as waterfall, result in increased delivery times and a high defect rate. The main drivers for adopting the Agile model are as follows:

- *Creates self-organized teams*: One of the primary goals for moving towards an Agile model is to create efficient teams.

- *Reduces siloes*: Minimize silos across various teams through constant interactions and daily standup meetings.

- *Encourages effective collaboration*: Increase collaboration within a team and across different teams for efficient integration and testing.

- *Invites change tolerance*: Absorb changing user stories based on customer feedback in subsequent sprints.

- *Reduces time to market*: Leverage sprint-based iterations to reduce release time.

Sprint-based releases were adopted for the project and the delivery model with the following features:

- Requirements and features were developed as user stories and were prioritized.

- User stories were selected based on their business criticality and end user importance.

- One-month sprints were planned. Each sprint had a product demo sent to business stakeholders and end users to obtain their feedback. Feedback was incorporated into subsequent sprints based on importance.

- Teams used a central source control system which used various techniques such as continuous integration, automated code analysis, and automated testing for increased productivity.

- Sprint-based execution increased collaboration across teams and created cross-functional self-organized teams that were aligned with sprint goals.

- Backlog prioritization improved team utilization and productivity.

- Continuous integration and configuration management improved the overall sprint delivery quality.

Risk Management

Risk management involves early identification, prioritization, and impact quantification of all risks. For each of the identified risks, the project manager defines a mitigation plan and communicates the risk management plan to the PMO. A well-defined risk management process helps in anticipating risks and proactively minimizing their impact as opposed to ineffective, post-facto "fire-fighting," which only leads to costly slippage in terms of effort, time, quality, and cost. Therefore, proactive management and containment of risks is crucial to the success of the project. The essential phases of the risk management process are depicted in Figure 1-7.

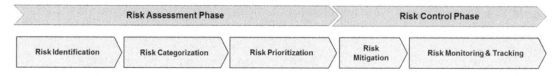

Figure 1-7. *Risk management phases*

In content projects, a proactive risk mitigation approach needs to be adopted to ensure high-quality content. A sample risk mitigation matrix is shown in Table 1-5. The risk mitigation measures are not listed in any particular order. Project managers can use this list as a reference.

Table 1-5. *Risk Mitigation Approach*

Risk	Risk Mitigation Approach
Organizational resistance to process standardization and content changes	• Iterative prototyping approach to ensure fit for purpose • Early engagement of all relevant business stakeholders • Executive alignment and expectation-setting with all concerned stakeholders • Strong standards for allowable customization
Content migration risk	• Completely defined migration user stories covering all migration scenarios and non-functional requirements (such as performance and scalability) • Evaluate migration approach and tools through design validation proof-of-concepts (PoCs) • Develop robust test cases to ensure completeness and accuracy of content migration • Employ content transformation and migration tools to automate migration and achieve improved productivity

(continued)

Table 1-5. (*continued*)

Risk	Risk Mitigation Approach
Scope creep risk due to unclear and incomplete content requirements	• A strong requirement change management process to be defined • Requirement changes to be approved only after assessing the criticality and need for the change and its impact on schedule and cost • Ensure that appropriate steering and core teams are set up and identified at the start of engagement and define roles and responsibilities thereafter • Understand and clearly define the scope during requirements elaboration phase and validate it through requirements elaboration sessions, joint workshops, early prototypes and such
Content quality risk due to insufficient testing	• All content extraction, cleansing, and transformations to be planned with sufficient details • Test cases to cover all content and data scenarios such as completeness of the content, content migration, content integrity, and such • Content extraction and cleanup to be planned in the early stages of the project • User acceptance testing to include all major data combination scenarios • Testing stages to have actual past data to the maximum extent possible • Ensure good code coverage for test cases
Content testing risk	• Design a comprehensive testing plan to cover all real-world scenarios • Adopt continuous integration and testing methodology • Define and use an end-to-end traceability matrix that maps the requirements to user stories to code artifacts to test cases
Functional silos risk	• Cross track/functional design review sessions for process integration with end-to end scenarios

Best practices in risk management include the following:

- Quantify the risk through a risk scoring model. The model could be effectively used to measure the exposure of risks with respect to probability, impact, and cost of mitigation. Risk scoring also helps escalate high risks to PMO to secure required resources for addressing the risk. In a risk scoring model, each risk is assessed for its likelihood of occurrence (LO) and impact of risk (IR). Overall risk value of the issue is a multiplication factor of LO and IR. Overall risk = LO x IR.

- Identified risks are tracked regularly (weekly/bi-weekly) and mitigation plans are developed. Risks are also retired as appropriate and new risks are added to the list as they are discovered.

- Identify risk triggers to take action on potential risks by using historical data.

- Include risk status communication as part of the communication strategy. All concerned stakeholders should receive regular communicated about risk status and risk mitigation progress.

Change Management

Handling scope changes and requirement changes is a crucial activity in digital projects. We need a fine balance of project effort/schedule/cost with user satisfaction, adoption, and success. A solid change management process is needed to efficiently handle the changes.

The entire change management process is managed and controlled by a consultative body called Change Advisory Board (CAB) (also referred to as Change Management Board or the Configuration Control Board). It's comprised of key stakeholders from all concerned departments and meets regularly to assess, prioritize, plan, approve, and implement changes. The primary functions of CAB include the following:

- All change requests (CR) raised are maintained in a change request log.

- Evaluation of change on impact, cost, benefits, criticality, and prioritization. Go/no-go calls are made by the board.

- Change communication to all stakeholders.

- Change release planning.

Change Management Process

The following are the salient characteristics of the change management process:

- Threshold limits to invoke the change management process are mutually agreed upon at the start of the engagement. The stakeholders agree on the thresholds limits for variance in effort/cost/schedule needed to implement a change. For instance, stakeholders might decide that any change that requires more than 1 person's day of implementation effort qualifies as a change request.

- Change management process covers:

  - New requirements

  - Changes to validated requirements

  - Changes to work-in-progress

  - Changes to schedule

  - Change to test cycles

  - Changes to signed-off deliverables

- The typical scenarios that fall under the change management process purview are:

  - Business-driven changes to requirements that trigger addition or modification of test cases and reports

  - Changes to deliverables after they have been accepted and signed off

The various phases of change management are depicted in Figure 1-8.

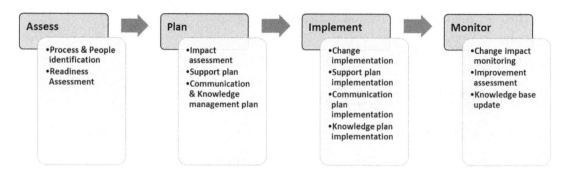

Figure 1-8. *Change management phases*

The change management process is initiated when you get a change request (CR). The process consists of four phases: assess, plan, implement, and monitor. During the Assess phase, you identify the impacted processes and people. Normally a small and focused development team will analyze the effort needed to implement the change, cost, and schedule impacts. During the Plan phase, you do a detailed impact analysis and develop an impact communication, support plan, and knowledge management plan. Wherever required, you need to adjust project plans and scope and provide directions to development team to incorporate approved changes. During the Implement phase, the change request is implemented along with implementation of the support plan and knowledge management plan. Implemented changes are monitored during the Monitor phase. The established KPIs and SLA metrics are tracked during the monitor phase after implementing the change. When best approaches are followed, known troubleshooting tips are updated in the knowledge base.

Release Management

The release management team is responsible for managing ongoing releases across all environments. The release management team takes a holistic view of a change to IT services and ensures that all aspects of a build, both technical and non-technical, are considered together in order to meet the goals of successful infrastructure/application rollouts using controlling processes and efficient procedures.

The release management operations consist of following activities:

Policy & Build Planning

- Agreeing to the phasing over time and by geographical location and business units

- Assigning roles and responsibilities

- Work with the capacity planning team (infrastructure team), procurement team, and suppliers for new hardware/ software for the environment wherever needed

- Setting up a continuous integration (CI) infrastructure with all tools and CI processes (we discuss CI in detail in the coming sections)

- Obtain acceptance by all stakeholders for the plan and schedule.

Designing, Building, and Configuring a Build

- Setting up the environment and configure builds for release deployments

- Writing automated installation routines for Infrastructure specific distribution, to ensure accurate rollout of builds (including executables, configuration files, libraries and such) wherever possible

- Schedule builds wherever applicable

Build/Release Acceptance

- Perform build and backout tests (to roll back changes)

- Get sign off from stakeholders (testing team) after post build/release review

Rollout Planning

- Produce exact detailed timetable of the events and resource plan

- List change requests to be implemented and decommissioned

- Plan and coordinate activities/communication with a testing team

- Acquire hardware and software required for the build

Communications, Preparation, and Training

- Establish a communication plan with project team and stakeholders

- In the case of major releases or complex deployments, organize meetings with all parties to inform the problems and changes that need to be made during the build. Communicate the constraints or impact on test cycles, if any, to the testing team appropriately

Distribution and Installation

- Ensure build software/hardware is delivered safely at all expected sites; for cloud-based solutions, the final release can be deployed to the cloud environment

- Installation procedure has to be carried out as per rollout plan

- Final acceptance test to be performed by the testing team remotely

A sample release plan for a digital project is depicted in Figure 1-9.

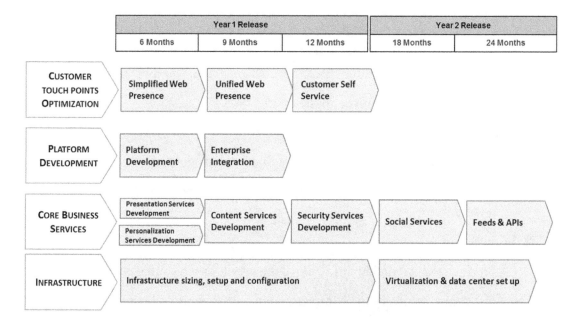

Figure 1-9. *Sample release plan for a typical digital project*

The two-year release plan depicts various capabilities enabled in iterations. In each of these iterations, you carry out the release operations such as build planning, rollout planning, build configuration, communications, training, distribution, and installation.

Summary

This chapter discussed various aspects of digital project management:

- The three phases of digital projects are planning, execution, and maintenance. The planning phase includes requirements elaboration and architecture/design activities; the execution phase involves development and testing; and the maintenance phase involves on-going operations, support, upgrade, and other such activities.

- Project governance provides a control and command structure for structured content execution. It provides accountability and role-responsibility to execute the business strategy.

- The governance model consists of an operations team (to look after day-to-day operations), a steering committee for project review and scope/schedule management, and an executive team to set the project direction and provide a vision.

- Common challenges in digital project execution are niche technologies, availability of the right skillset, selection of the appropriate execution methodology, incomplete and ambiguous requirements, cross-team collaboration, time to market, and time consuming integration/build processes.

- Main execution models are the waterfall model, iterative model, and the Agile model.

- In the iterative model, the application is incrementally developed in repeated iterations. Each iteration adds capabilities. Key advantages of the iterative model are quick wins, quicker time to market, serviceability, predictability, simplicity, and minimized risk.

- The Agile model is a collection of best practices to develop the system in smaller increments continuously.

- If the project has changing or ambiguous requirements with niche technologies, it is better to adopt an Agile model.

- The Scrum methodology is an Agile model wherein the product is incrementally developed in multiple sprints/iterations.

- The Scrum methodology consists of sprint planning, daily standup calls, sprint review, and sprint release.

- The key sprint artifacts are the user story, product backlog, and sprint backlog.

- Project risk management consists of risk identification, risk categorization, risk categorization, risk mitigation, and risk monitoring.

- Change management consists of the change assessment phase, the change planning phase, change implementation, and change improvement.

- Release management consists of activities such as policy and build planning, designing, building and configuring a build, build/release acceptance, rollout planning, communications, preparation and training, and distribution and installation.

- Project management best practices are continuous integration, knowledge management, center of excellence, continuous improvement, stakeholder management, quality assurance process, communication process, project metrics, and automation tools.

- CI is a release management activity wherein you build and integrate the code on a frequent basis. CI automates build and release activities, improves productivity, enhances delivery quality, and efficiently integrates the code base.

CHAPTER 2

Consulting and Presales in Digital Projects

Organizations that embark on the digital transformation journey identify the main digitization opportunities and business values. Business teams within the organization come up with the key requirements for their future digital platform. Digital consultants and strategists (from within the organization or from external agencies) then analyze the requirements through a consulting exercise. Digital consulting is the key exercise that is designed to determine the digital program vision, create a digital strategy for the program, evaluate candidate digital products and technologies, and define a capability roadmap for the entire digital program. The digital consulting engagement lays the groundwork for future phases of the digital program. A presales engagement is mainly an exercise to showcase the suitability of products and technologies through demos, PoCs, and workshops and define the win themes of the engagement. Digital consultants, product vendors, technology partners, and system integrators (SI) are involved in the presales stage of the engagement. Various solution approaches, along with their pros and cons, are discussed the during presales engagement. The activities of digital consulting and presales overlap in some stages. An effective combination of consulting and presales is needed to define a robust digital strategy and implementation plan.

This chapter discusses various aspects of digital consulting and key points of presales engagements. It also includes a consulting case study at the end of this chapter.

Digital consultants, pre-sales consultants, digital program managers, and digital strategists will find the content in this chapter useful.

© Shailesh Kumar Shivakumar 2018
S. K. Shivakumar, *Complete Guide to Digital Project Management*,
https://doi.org/10.1007/978-1-4842-3417-4_2

Digital Consulting Framework

Consulting engagement is carried out to sharpen the digital strategy and identify the key digital capabilities, digital building blocks, and roadmap along with an implementation plan. Digital consultants gather insights through stakeholder interviews and workshops to arrive at the right set of digital products and technologies. The digital consulting framework is depicted in Figure 2-1.

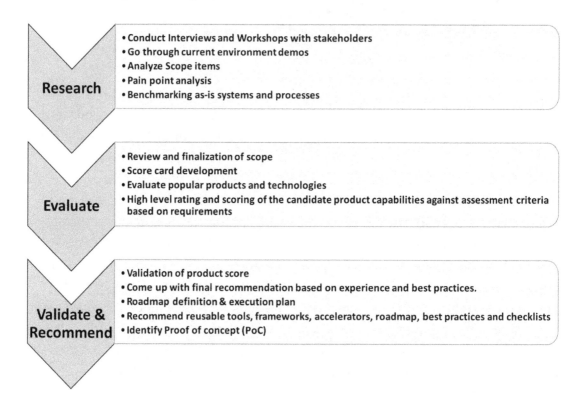

Research
- Conduct Interviews and Workshops with stakeholders
- Go through current environment demos
- Analyze Scope items
- Pain point analysis
- Benchmarking as-is systems and processes

Evaluate
- Review and finalization of scope
- Score card development
- Evaluate popular products and technologies
- High level rating and scoring of the candidate product capabilities against assessment criteria based on requirements

Validate & Recommend
- Validation of product score
- Come up with final recommendation based on experience and best practices.
- Roadmap definition & execution plan
- Recommend reusable tools, frameworks, accelerators, roadmap, best practices and checklists
- Identify Proof of concept (PoC)

Figure 2-1. *Digital consulting framework*

The consulting framework consists of three main phases: the Research phase, the Evaluate phase, and the Validate & Recommend phase. This section discusses various activities in each of these phases. The digital consulting case study in this chapter explains these concepts in more detail as well.

The Research Phase

Digital consultants gather understanding of the existing systems during the Research phase. The main activities in this phase are related to requirements gathering, as-is system analysis, and research about the applicable products, technologies, best practices, and trends.

The key activities during the Research phase are as follows:

- Identify/secure key stakeholders who have an interest in the digital program.

- Identify key business users/SMEs who are part of the digital program.

- Block business users/SMEs calendars for requirement interviews and workshops.

- Identify the success metrics for the digital program.

- Review current state documentation of the existing technology and business ecosystem.

- Get scope items and gather requirements related to functional and non-functional items (performance, scalability, modularity, etc.).

- Review documentation to understand the current state and the current application portfolio.

- Conduct requirements elaboration workshops with the stakeholders and prioritize the requirements.

- Conduct technology research to understand trends and standards that can be used in the program.

- Analyze painpoints of the current systems and business processes.

- Identify gaps in existing processes and systems.

- Understand the challenges faced by current users in executing a business process.

- Understand the wish list and preferences from stakeholders and users. If there are any conflicting requirements, clarify the requirements at an all-hands meeting and prioritize the requirements for implementation.

- Have the demo of existing systems, and business processes.

- Benchmark existing processes and systems against industry standards.

- Finalize the scope document.

- Prioritize requirements through a requirements workshop.

- Have the stakeholders validate the scope document and secure sign-off.

During the Research phase, the key activities are technology research, requirements workshop, persona definition, and competitive benchmarking. They are discussed more in the following sections.

Technology Research

Technology research is undertaken to explore the emerging trends and innovative digital technologies that can be used in the program. Broadly, this exercise consists of the following activities:

- Identify market leading digital products and technologies that can be used in the digital program. Keep a watch on emerging digital technologies and leverage them for the digital project wherever applicable.

- Identify any reusability of tools, frameworks and technologies within the existing ecosystem.

- Identity and analyze emerging trends and industry standards.

- Identify growth opportunities for the business domain.

At the end of the technology research exercise, digital consultants create an inventory of reusable tools and frameworks and arrive at the list of standards for the digital program.

Requirements Workshops

Workshops are conducted to have focused discussions about requirements, brainstorm user experience design options, and conduct the demos. Workshops are primarily aimed at understanding the scenarios and defining the challenges and problem statement. Once the problem is defined, future demos aim at solving the problems by brainstorming ideas and prototype demos. Joint workshops include user experience workshops, business process workshops, and demo workshops. User experience workshops discuss the visual design, wireframes, navigation model, and information architecture; business process workshops mainly focus on the business process models and discuss business rules; demo workshops are conducted to demo the solutions, products, and intermediate deliverables.

Digital consultants conduct the requirements workshop with concerned stakeholders to define and prioritize the critical business requirements. When prioritizing requirements, digital consultants use a matrix approach to map the requirements along the "business value" and "implementation complexity" dimensions, as shown in Figure 2-2.

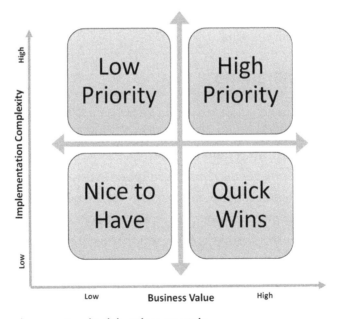

Figure 2-2. *Requirement prioritization matrix*

The requirements that deliver a high business value and that can be implemented with little effort are categorized as "quick wins". They are low hanging fruits that will be incorporated into initial releases. The requirements that have a high business value but have a higher implementation complexity need detailed requirements elaboration workshops and proof of concepts (PoCs) and they will be accordingly incorporated into subsequent iterations. Low business value items with a high implementation complexity are given a low priority for implementation. Low business value items with a low implementation complexity will be categorized as "nice to have" and will be incorporated only on demand. Before the actual implementation, the dependent components should be developed.

Persona Analysis and Definition

Defining the persona is one of the main activities of designing the user experience. During the Research phase, we understand users, usage patterns, context, and user needs. Based on these insights, we identify and categorize users into logical groups called "persona". The representative characteristics of the group define the persona of that group. The needs and expectations of each persona are identified to provide the essential elements of the user journey. Personalization and information placement are modeled based on the user persona.

Competitive Benchmarking

Competitive benchmarking compares existing systems and processes against competitors, existing trends, and industry standards. Digital consultants define the key comparison parameters and compare them against the industry leading solutions and competitors. Competitive benchmarking helps us to understand the gaps and areas of improvement. Digital consultants also provide the needed improvements and recommendations as part of the competitive analysis report. Normally Four categories of ratings are used in the competitive analysis report: lagging, mainstream, leading, and pioneer. Lagging indicates that existing systems are behind the competitors and industry standards on evaluation parameters; mainstream indicates that existing systems are on par with latest industry trends and technologies; leading indicates that existing systems are ahead of competitors; pioneer indicates that existing systems have introduced the relevant technology to the industry. A sample benchmarking report is shown in Table 2-1.

Table 2-1. *Sample Competitive Benchmarking Report*

Category	Rating	Observations	Recommendations
Overall user experience	Lagging	• Has traditional look and feel • Scope for introducing immersive (design that offers visually rich and collaborative), interactive (design that provides actions and responses), and responsive experience • Scope for better branding and visual appeal	Enhance brand value and visual appeal through the following improvements: • Provide immersive, interactive, and responsive user interface • Create a clear visual information architecture and provide greater priority (color/size/position) to the most frequently accessed tools/features/content. Provide visual cues (such as contextual help, tips, and examples) for ease of use and to augment visual hierarchy to help novice users • Provide personalized/context-based information wherever possible • Provide simple and consistent page layouts • Provide seamless multi-device user experience
Information architecture	Lagging	• Traditional navigation features Challenges in locating the right information quickly (typically less than a second) • Lacks intuitive information grouping and navigation aids like breadcrumbs (a navigation aid that shows the current location of the user on the website); main menu is primary source of navigation	• Improve search effectiveness • Add multiple navigation aids like drop-down menus, expanded menus, etc. • Provide consistent page layout with reduced information clutter • Develop an intuitive and logical information architecture to help users understand how things relate. Group related objects/tasks • Enable content metadata based information discovery • Provide consistent navigation and site hierarchy structure • Provide simple menu structure

(*continued*)

Table 2-1. (*continued*)

Category	Rating	Observations	Recommendations
Social features	Lagging	• Minimal social and collaboration support in landing page (first page after login) • Can explore opportunities to engage customers and partners in a more active fashion • Can provide personalized experience through multiple channels	Leverage social media to promote their products and brands. Provide integration with popular social media platforms. Provide collaboration features such as wikis, blogs, communities, etc.
Information discovery	Leading	• Search is the primary tool for discovering information	• Can complement search with other accessibility aids like sub-menus, expanded footer links, etc. • Add sorting and filtering search results • Use machine learning and AI (Artificial Intelligence) to complement search and recommendations

(*continued*)

Table 2-1. (*continued*)

Category	Rating	Observations	Recommendations
Content effectiveness	Lagging	Traditional text-based content; website content does not work on mobile devices	• Provide customized and personalized content • Provide easy to understand error messages and FAQs • Provide contextual content such as recommendation, help, policies, etc. wherever possible • Provide rich content: provide dynamic, layered content complemented by media and digital assets (images, video, animation) • Provide functional content: provide consistent content structure that clearly communicates hierarchy and enhances content readability • Provide content that communicates a consistent brand story • Improved content strategy and freshness • Enhance the decision making of the user through product comparison content, testimonials, product reviews
Navigation	Lagging	Inconsistent navigation structure Lacks robust information architecture	• Provide consistent navigation objects (breadcrumb, context menu matching breadcrumb) • Avoid multiple navigation items such as multi-level breadcrumbs
Self service	Lagging	Missing self-service and decision-supporting tools	• Provide collaboration tools such as chat, blog, wiki, communities, forums, etc. • Provide decision making and persuasion tools such as calculators, reviews, rating, comparison tools, recommendation, etc.

Deliverables

The key deliverables of the Research phase are the requirements and scope document (the document that details in-scope and out-of-scope items), the use cases document (the document that details requirements through use cases), the painpoint analysis document, and the competitive analysis and benchmark report. On the user experience track, the key deliverables of this phase are user journey models and user design requirements.

Evaluate Phase

During the Evaluate phase, consultants evaluate various products and technologies suitable to implement the digital vision. The main activities in this phase are as follows:

- Develop product and technology evaluation scorecard.

- Develop high-level digital product and technology evaluation scorecard.

- Include factors such as functionality suitability, architecture suitability, and platform suitability as key categories.

- Discuss the importance of each evaluation parameter with business stakeholders and accordingly assign suitable weights.

- Identify candidate digital products and technologies.

- Short list candidate products and technologies that are best suited to the given set of requirements.

- Finalize user personas in the user experience track.

- Start scoring the identified products and technologies jointly with the stakeholders.

- Use weighted scoring of products and technologies to arrive at a final ranking.

Defining product and technology evaluation scorecards are some of the key activities in this phase, and are described in the following section.

Scorecard Definition and Evaluation

Scorecards essentially list all the requirements and capabilities and evaluate the various candidate products and technologies against those capabilities. The capabilities and requirements are grouped under main logical categories such as technical capabilities, functional capabilities, architecture capabilities, etc.

Based on the business importance of each requirement, weights are assigned to them. Digital consultants score the products on a numerical scale. A weighted score is taken for each requirement. The final score will be calculated based on the sum of the weighted scores for all requirements.

Appendix E provides a sample scorecard for evaluating a content management system (CMS).

Deliverable

The main deliverables in this phase are the product/technology evaluation scorecards and identification of candidate digital products and technologies.

Validate and Recommend Phase

During the Validate and Recommend phase, consultants recommend the final set of technologies and products along with an implementation roadmap. The key activities of this phase are as follows:

- Prepare a product assessment report after these validations:

  - Validate the product rating.

  - Recommend the final product and technology to the stakeholders.

- Develop a high-level architecture and a content strategy.

  - Develop the reference architecture and the high-level technical solution architecture.

  - Develop a high-level solution architecture based on the selected product and technology.

- Define a roadmap consisting of the following:

    - High-level capabilities to implement the digital strategy

    - Define the user experience (UX) strategy (the plan for user interface design, navigation design, information architecture, and such) and roadmap

    - High-level execution plan with schedule and budget

- Provide other relevant recommendations such as the following:

    - Frameworks and open source libraries

    - Reusable tools and frameworks

    - Emerging trends/disruptions in digital space that could potentially impact the digital program

    - Applicable industry best practices

    - Applicable industry standards

Defining content strategy is one of the main activities of the Validate and Recommendation phase. The details are discussed in the following section.

Content Strategy

The content strategy exercise is carried out to evaluate and recommend the best content plan for building the digital solution. The content strategy mainly consists of the following elements:

- *Content planning and analysis*: Audit the existing content inventory and evaluate its reusability. Mark the redundant and duplicate content for replacement.

- *Content architecture*: Define the content granularity (such as page level content and content chunks). Come up a with reusability plan to make the content effective. Define the content templates for enhanced reusability and extension.

- *Content governance*: Define the content workflow processes, content maintenance processes, and metadata tagging processes.

Content strategy aims at enhancing the usability of content (by making it simple and easy to understand) and the effectiveness of the content (by providing relevant content through enhanced information discovery).

Deliverables

The main deliverables of this phase are the product assessment report, the solution architecture, and the roadmap. On the user experience front, the key deliverables of this phase are the visual style guide, the information architecture, HTML prototypes, a visual design, and wireframes.

Risk and Mitigation

Like any other project phase, the consulting phase carries its own set of risks. Table 2-2 summarizes the main risk items and the mitigation plans during the assessment phase.

Table 2-2. *Risk and Mitigation Plan for the Digital Consulting Exercise*

Risk	Mitigation Plan
Requirements not fully captured during Research phase	Capture functional and non-functional requirements from all concerned stakeholders. Prioritize the requirements from all stakeholders. Create a traceability matrix for requirements that will be later mapped to code artifacts and test cases.
Challenges in availability of stakeholders for requirement workshops and interviews	Identify all the SMEs and stakeholders needed for the plan and publish a detailed plan for the Research phase. Schedule meetings upfront to ensure availability of stakeholders.
Redefining existing processes	Secure the availability of process SMEs to redefine and agree on the To-Be process models during the early stage of the research phase.
Lack of third-party licenses (if any) for evaluation purposes	Decision to be made on leveraging trial licenses as appropriate and as per the organization's software governance policies Support from the organization to expedite procurement of trial licenses from identified vendors as required Early identification of third-party tools and availability of evaluation licenses to initiate discussions with the respective vendors

Presales Engagement

Presales engagement is typically carried out by product vendors, system integrators (SI), or digital consultants to showcase various capabilities and offerings. Presales are embedded as part of the consulting exercise and are typically part of the Validate and Recommend phase, wherein product demos, solution discussions, and recommendations happen. This section covers the key activities of the presales engagement and discusses the proof of concept, articulation of win themes, and value propositions.

Proof of Concept (PoC)

A proof of concept is an exercise to validate and define the feasibility of a solution. PoC can be carried out to determine the product and technology fitment for a given solution and to understand gaps in the products and technologies, risk and feasibility, time and effort, and implementation complexity. When there are complex scenarios or unknowns in the requirements or when we are using niche/unproven technologies, digital consultants propose a PoC to minimize risks.

Prerequisites for the PoC

The generic prerequisites for the PoC are as follows:

- The functional requirements and non-functional requirements that need to be evaluated.

- List of scenarios that need to be evaluated. Normally scenarios chosen for PoC are complex and unproven in nature. For instance, scenarios such as custom authentication, complex workflow modeling, complex integration, and single-sign-on (SSO) use cases are used for validation.

- Define a list of products and technologies that need to be evaluated.

- Define the objectives and success criteria for the PoC. For product evaluation PoC, the main success criteria are ease of use, out of the box solutions, and the amount of customization needed to implement the requirement.

- Secure all needed software and hardware and the approvals to use them.

Execution of the PoC

To execute the PoC, you use these main steps:

- Identify the PoC execution team and plan the sprints for the PoC execution.

- Develop the product and technology evaluation scorecard if the main objective of the PoC is to evaluate the product. Rate the products and technologies based on performance in the PoC. Rate the products and technologies against the predefined objectives and success criteria.

- Demo the scenarios to concerned stakeholders.

- Engage the stakeholders who have an interest in the PoC for the evaluation. Stakeholders can rate based on the scenario demo.

Results of the PoC

The results of the PoCs are explained in a formal meeting with all stakeholders. The ratings and rankings are discussed in the meeting, along with recommendations. During the same meeting, the digital consultants lay out the recommended implementation and governance plan to the stakeholders.

Articulating Win Themes and Business Value Propositions in the Solution

The win themes provide value differentiators of the proposed approach and solution. Salient points of win themes are listed here:

- Win themes should be aligned with the stated program vision and objectives. Win themes should clearly articulate the value additions of the proposed solution and approach.

- Win themes should convey deep understanding of the solution requirements.

- Value differentiators in quality, governance, cost, and schedule should be part of the win themes. For instance, solution accelerators, intellectual property (IP), and innovative costing model act as value differentiators.

The next section covers the various elements needed to craft effective win themes and business value proposition in the solution presentation.

Understanding Key Business Drivers and the Digital Program Vision

Digital consultants need to understand the main business drivers for the digital transformation journey. The common business drivers are listed here:

- Enhance customer engagement through various channels and devices by leveraging digital technologies.

- Use digital technologies to simplify processes and business models and enhance productivity.

- Increase automation and operation efficiency.

- Develop scalable and flexible platforms.

- Adopt advanced analytics to drive insights-driven personalization (contextualize content and functionality based on user's preferences and past behavior).

- Provide enhanced, personalized, and responsive user experience.

- Develop self-service model for end users, business users, and administrators.

Understanding Existing Challenges and Defining the Future State

Digital consultants analyze existing painpoints to arrive at the desired end state. The desired end state not only addresses the painpoints, but it also acts as a value differentiator for the win themes. A sample painpoint analysis is shown in the Table 2-3.

Table 2-3. *Sample Painpoint Analysis*

Category	Challenges	Desired State
Information discovery	Difficult to find right information quickly	Personalized, contextual information delivery to get right information at right place at right time Enhanced self-service through collaboration (among end users, partners, site administrators) and knowledge base
User experience	Incompatible content on mobile devices Challenges with accessibility and non-standard HTML content	Optimized user experience on mobile and hand-held devices Compliance to HTML standards And Web Content Accessibility Guidelines (WCAG) standards for accessibility Seamless user experience at all touch points
Incident management	Multiple process steps and long resolution times	Optimized incident management processes, first time resolution, personalized interaction
Search experience	Too many irrelevant results	Personalized search, concept search, relevant content recommendations
Administrator experience	Absence of self-service controls	Analytics driven insights, configuration driven workflows, campaign management (for managing marketing campaigns), unified view of all customer interactions; intuitive reports related site traffic, abandonment analysis (analyzing the website exits from end users), etc.

Articulating the Digital Transition Themes

The digital transition themes clearly call out the key solution tenets and main dimensions of the transition to the proposed solution. Table 2-4 provides common transition themes for the next generation digital solution.

Table 2-4. *Common Digital Transition Themes*

Category	Existing State	Digital Enterprise Transition Theme
Technology ecosystem	Multiple products and technologies Integration needed to realize all the needed capabilities	Unified platform providing out of the box capabilities, pre-integrated technology stack, vertical solutions, lean stack, service oriented design, unified content management, and integrated marketing
End user relationship	Transaction-oriented, reactive customer service	Relationship oriented, rewarding loyalties, seamless cross-channel optimization, proactive self-service model, personalized and targeted content delivery, continuous engagement at all touch points
Business productivity	High dependency on IT teams	Business self-service, configuration driven, business self-service through intuitive admin screens, workflow/rule management, customizable UI; customizable forms and reports
Analytics	Minimal or no analytics	Insights about customer behavior, content recommendation based on past behavior, analytics driven targeted content delivery, real-time reports, continuous monitoring
Social engagement	Minimal or no social features	Social integration, collaborative features (blog, wiki, community), social analytics, social marketing, increased brand reach
User experience	Mainly desktop oriented, separate channels for mobile devices	User-centric design, mobile enabled content, mobile web and mobile apps, unified 360 degree view, mobile-first strategy

(continued)

Table 2-4. (*continued*)

Category	Existing State	Digital Enterprise Transition Theme
Security	Traditional security model	Granular layered security model
Content management	Traditional content management systems (CMS), absence of metadata strategy	Adaptive content, metadata tagging, fine grained content model, reusable content, intuitive information architecture
Release management and deployment model	Long deployment cycles, in-house/on-premise deployment	Agile delivery, iterative releases, faster time to market, cloud-based deployment, remote deployment

Articulating Solution Tenets

Building a future-ready next generation digital solution requires design principles and solution tenets that define the solution. The main solution tenets of a next generation digital solution are defined here:

- *Integrated and optimized business processes:* Develop configurable processes to enable business self-service. Automate and minimize process steps for an enhanced user experience.

- *Lean platform:* The digital platform should be built on lean principles such as lightweight presentation components and lightweight integration models (such as micro services and REST-based integration).

- *Reusability and extensibility:* Design and build modular platform components that can be easily reused and extended for future needs. Wherever possible, leverage proven open source technologies to augment the solution.

- *Continuous quality:* Leverage continuous integration tools to ensure iterative code analysis, testing, and deployment for enhanced delivery quality.

- *User centricity:* Develop all aspects of the digital platform around the user. This includes user-centric design, personalized content, analytics based insights gathering, and self-service models.

Articulating Value Proposition

The solution recommendation document should clearly articulate the value differentiators. The main qualities of an effective value proposition document are as follows:

- Provide tangible improvements such as quantifiable improvements to revenue, site traffic, and so on.

- Quantify the effort and cost savings by using proprietary solutions and accelerators.

- Quantify the quality improvements (average reduction in defect count and average improvement in turnaround times) by adoption of quality practices.

Digital Consulting Case Study

This section describes a case study for a digital consulting engagement. It details various activities and deliverables from each of the consulting phases.

Case Study Background

An enterprise is currently maintaining online channels through a legacy website. The legacy website is primarily an information portal providing information about various products and services to Internet users. The main business drivers for this technology transformation are as follows:

- Develop a responsive next generation digital platform providing user engagement, search, and collaboration features. The platform should be extensible and scalable to cater to future growth and innovation needs.

- Provide an intuitive omni-channel user experience.

- Develop a self-service platform to enhance the end user experience.

- Provide personalized and context sensitive information to the user based on user preferences and past behavior.

- Provide seamless web content management and secured access to information.

- Leverage the latest digital technologies such as artificial intelligence and machine learning to provide highly effective content recommendations.

The key painpoints of the current website are as follows:

- The website is built on legacy technologies and hence does not provide the responsiveness and interactiveness that modern digital consumers expect.

- The website has poor user experience without any structured information architecture.

- The website lacks a responsive web design and hence does not work easily on mobile devices.

- The website lacks all the self-service tools and seamless navigation features.

The organization embarked on a five-week digital consultation engagement to come up with a digital strategy and implementation plan to develop a next generation digital platform. This section highlights the key activities of each phase: the Research phase, Evaluation phase, and Validate and Recommend phase. As the redesign of user experience (UX) is one of the main drivers for the engagement, the activities related to the UX redesign are listed in each of the phases.

The various activities of the six-week consulting engagement are detailed in Figure 2-3.

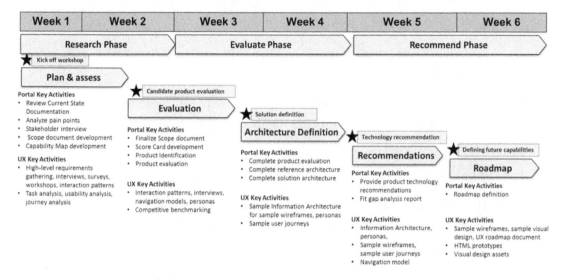

Figure 2-3. *Six-week consulting plan*

Activities During the Research Phase

During the Research phase, the digital consultants held various requirements elaboration workshops with stakeholders to get insights into the current website, desired end state, and program objectives. A sample set of requirements and capabilities are categorized into broad areas, as shown in the Figure 2-4.

Multi Channel / Device	Integrated Dashboard View	Client View	User Management
The portal to be developed with support for multi channel / devices providing a rich responsive user interface. Ability to manage devices seamlessly	Unified view for users across all clients	Secured view of client specific content through authorized services	Admin view for user management and client services management

Content Distribution	Flexible Content Authoring	Extensible Provide	Surveys On	Search
Efficient & secured distribution of client content	Ability to perform content authoring for digital channels	framework to extend solution features seamlessly with minimal disruptions	demand surveys	Ability to search relevant content

Data Loss Prevention	Data Isolation at Rest	Artificial Intelligence and Machine Learning
Identify, protect and prevent accidental disclosure of sensitive information across clients. Restrict and prevent download, email forwarding, printing, etc. of secured content	Provides data isolation at rest to maintain client specific data separately and provided high data security and access control to prevent data leak across users	Data analytics of historical data and implement potential use cases for business development

Document Generation	Integration Services	Workflow Services	
Generate documents online by filling in questionnaires	Availability of services to integrate with underlying source systems	Workflow jobs and automation process for implementing business flow	

Video Meetings	Collaboration	Personalization	Document Sharing
Integration for video meetings / conference	Seamless collaboration within portal members to share ideas, questions, updates, etc.	Capability to personalize content by end users	Secured bidirectional document sharing

Security
Enhanced authentication & authorization feature to cater to individuals and partner organizations through B2B federation, OpenID, oAuth

Figure 2-4. *Key capabilities of the digital program*

Digital Capability Map

Based on the requirements workshop results, the digital consultants defined a digital capability map listing all the key capabilities under three broad categories. The key capabilities needed for the digital application are listed on the digital capability map. The capabilities will be later used for product and technology evaluation. The capability map is depicted in Figure 2-5.

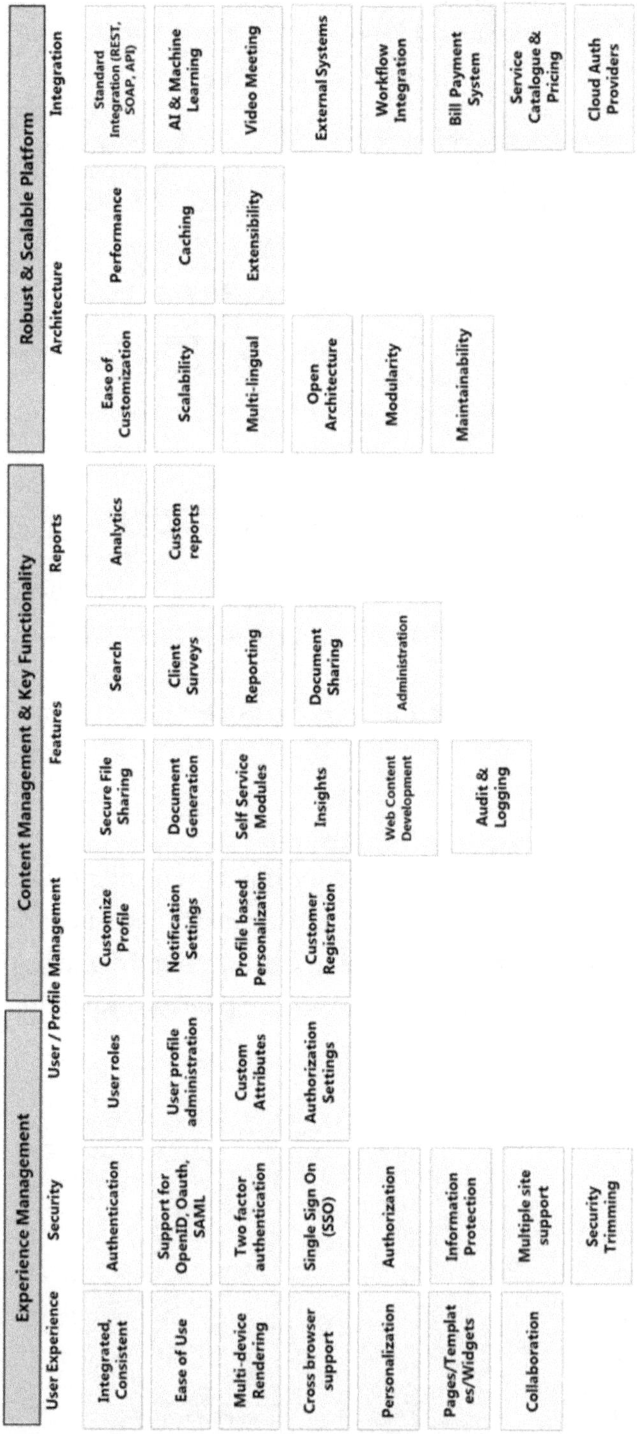

Figure 2-5. *Digital capability map*

The digital capability map provides guidance about the needed features. Each capability will be used as evaluation criteria during product and technology scorecard development and evaluation.

User Experience Related Activities

As one of the main objectives of the digital program is to improve the user experience, a design architect and consultant were engaged during the consulting phase. The main methods and activities related to user experience are detailed in Table 2-5.

Table 2-5. *User Experience Related Activities*

Methods Adopted	Activities
<ul><li>User surveys</li><li>Stakeholder interviews</li><li>Requirements workshops</li><li>Task analysis</li><li>Journey analysis</li><li>Usability analysis</li><li>Heuristic analysis (evaluate content, layout, and web application characteristics and report issues categorized as showstopper, major, and minor with heuristics)</li><li>Content auditing (analyzing content for reusability, retiring, or repurposing)</li></ul>	<ul><li>Interaction with business SMEs, business, and users for user surveys and stakeholder interviews</li><li>Understand the existing technologies and ecosystems through requirement workshops</li><li>Conduct workshops to understand goals</li><li>Understand user expectations, user tasks, and user needs and motivations as part of task analysis and journey analysis</li><li>Define a UX revamp approach through usability analysis and heuristic analysis</li><li>Freeze user requirements through user workshops</li><li>Analyze existing painpoints</li></ul>

Activities During the Evaluation Phase

During the Evaluation phase, digital consultants developed the product scorecard and finalized the scope document. Digital consultants shortlisted the potential products and technologies based on the capabilities gathered during the Research phase.

Product Evaluation Scorecard

During the Evaluation phase, digital consultants developed the scorecard with weights to evaluate the products and technologies. They used the key capabilities and their business importance to develop the scorecard. A sample scorecard based on the capability map is shown in Table 2-6. It splits the capabilities into two main categories—business capabilities and technical capabilities—with weights of 58% and 42%, respectively. Within each category, the key requirements and their weights are listed.

Table 2-6. *Sample Scorecard*

Business Capability	Weight	Product 1	Product 2	Technical Capability	Weight	Product 1	Product 2
Security	10%			Architecture	8%		
Personalization	5%			Integration	6%		
Self-service	10%			Search	6%		
User experience	8%			Workflow	2%		
Ease of use	8%			Future readiness	4%		
Extensible, scalable platform	5%			Flexibility	4%		
Information management	5%			Accelerator and plugins	3%		
Web content management	4%			Service-oriented design	5%		
Reports	1%			Collaboration	2%		
Cloud deployment support	2%			Multi-lingual capability	2%		
Total	58%			Total	42%		

User Experience Related Activities

The main UX activities of the Evaluation phase are detailed in Table 2-7.

Table 2-7. *Evaluation Phase UX Activities*

Methods Adopted	Activities
• User feedback analysis • Evaluate style guides • Evaluate information architecture • Evaluate user Personas • Competitive benchmarking	• Record user feedback on sample wireframes (represents a page blueprint and layout) during user feedback analysis • Create a style guide for sample wireframes and visual design as part of style guide evaluation • Develop low-fidelity wireframes (low-fidelity sketches, wireframes without graphics, branding and visual style guide) • Asset design during style guide evaluation • Navigation model development as part of information architecture evaluation • User personal definition as part of persona analysis

Activities During the Validate and Recommend Phase

During the Validate and Recommend phase, the digital consultants finalized the product and technology ratings and provided the reference architecture.

Reference Architecture

The reference architecture depicts the key capabilities that need to be present in the digital platform to build the solution.

The reference architecture for the digital platform is depicted in Figure 2-6. It depicts sample layers and components.

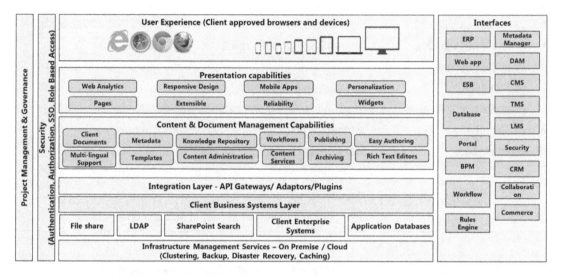

Figure 2-6. *Sample reference architecture for the next generation digital platform*

The following guiding principles are defined for the next generation digital platform architecture:

- Highly responsive next generation portal platform based on lean principles that provides a personalized experience

- Platform capable of providing self-service capabilities

- Platform using open standards providing optimal performance to users

- Secured content delivery with seamless collaboration

- Service-oriented design with lightweight integration approach

- Technology stack selection to speed up development time

- Long-term scalability and maintainability of solution

Activities for User Experience (UX) Design During the Validate and Recommend Phase

The key UX activities are defined in Table 2-8.

Table 2-8. *UX Activities During the Validate and Recommend Phase*

Methods Adopted	Activities
• Elicitation Templates • UX strategy and roadmap • Sample wireframes and visual design • A/B testing	• Deliver sample user journeys as part of UX strategy and roadmap • Deliver personas and sample high-fidelity wireframes (wireframes with visual design elements and branding elements) • Visual design (visual design for elements such as tabs, buttons, background layouts, headers, step-based flows, navigation, banners, posters, logos, graphics, charts, and graphs) • Brand elements as part of visual design • Create style guide (documenting presentation styles, font details, color details, element details) • Deliver HTML prototype as part of visual design • Deliver UX strategy and roadmap as part of UX strategy and roadmap • Define UX roadmap as part of UX strategy and roadmap

We should follow a rapid prototyping model to create the high-fidelity wireframes and mockups through brainstorming sessions and workshops. This helps quickly communicate ideas to various stakeholders.

Roadmap Definition and Implementation Plan

Digital consultants and strategists also define the roadmap for the implementation of the digital program. The roadmap document consists of phase-wise capabilities along with schedule details. Optionally, the operating model and governance structure for the digital program are also defined.

Summary

In this chapter we discussed various aspects of consulting and presales:

- The consulting framework consists of three main phases: the Research phase, Evaluate phase, and Validate and Recommend phase.

- Digital consultants gather understanding of the existing systems during the Research phase. The key activities in this phase are: identify/secure key stakeholders who have an interest in the digital program, review the current state of the documentation of the existing technology and business ecosystem, analyze painpoints of the current systems and business processes, and finalize the scope document.

- Technology research is undertaken to explore the emerging trends and innovative digital technologies that can be used in the program.

- During the Research phase, digital consultants create an inventory of reusable tools and frameworks and arrive at the list of standards for the digital program.

- Workshops are conducted with focused discussions about requirements and user experience design options and to conduct demos.

- User experience workshops discuss the visual design, wireframes, navigation model, and information architecture; business process workshops mainly focus on the business process steps and business rules; demo workshops are conducted to demo the solutions, products, and intermediate deliverables.

- Competitive benchmarking compares existing systems and processes to competitors and industry standards.

- During the Evaluate phase, consultants evaluate various products and technologies suitable to implement the digital vision.

- Key activities of the Evaluate phase are scorecard development, identification of candidate products and technologies, and scoring of products.

- During the Validate and Recommend phase, consultants recommend the final set of technologies and products along with an implementation roadmap. The main activities during this phase are to prepare a product assessment report, develop a high-level architecture, roadmap definition, and other recommendations.

- The content strategy exercise is carried out to evaluate and recommend the best content plan for building the digital solution.

- Presales engagement is typically carried out by product vendors, system integrators (SI), or digital consultants to showcase various capabilities and offerings.

- A proof of concept is an exercise to validate and understand the feasibility of a solution.

- Win themes provide value differentiators of the proposed approach and solution.

CHAPTER 3

Digital Project Planning

Project planning takes place during the initial stage of the project lifecycle. The planning exercises lay the groundwork for future phases. The project manager defines various processes and governance structures for the future phases as part of the project planning process. The project manager has to work on various planning activities related to quality management, staffing plans, training plans, stakeholder communication plans, and risk management plans.

The key activities of the digital project planning process are depicted in Figure 3-1.

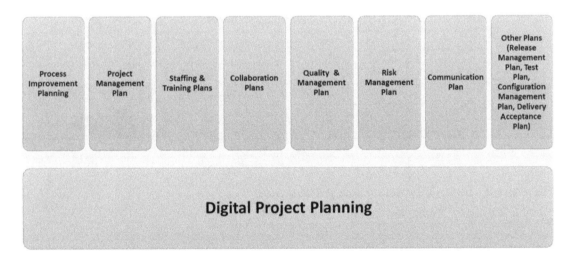

Figure 3-1. Project planning activities

This chapter elaborates on the various activities and success criteria of each planning exercise. It also discusses the high-level details of the test, release management, configuration management, and delivery acceptance plans.

This chapter covers various aspects of the project planning activities. Project managers, program managers, and account managers will find this chapter useful.

© Shailesh Kumar Shivakumar 2018
S. K. Shivakumar, *Complete Guide to Digital Project Management*,
https://doi.org/10.1007/978-1-4842-3417-4_3

The Project Management Plan

The project management plan is the main activity of the project planning exercise. The project management plan details all the tasks, task dependencies, ownership, and timelines. A detailed project plan helps the project manager track and monitor the project activities. A detailed project management plan acts as a guide to help the project manager design, implement, and execute the project. A sample project management plan for a digital portal project is shown in Figures 3-2 and 3-3.

Dependencies	Project Lifecycle Stage	Requirements Elaboration + PoC + Design					Architecture + Design			BUILD+Testing									
	Week	W1	W2	W3	W4	W5	W6	W7	W8	W9	W10	W11	W12	W13	W14	W15	W16	W17	W18
	Requirements Elaboration																		
	Functional Requirements																		
1	PoC (integration, taxonomy usage)																		
	Functional Requirements																		
	Non Functional requirements																		
	Technical Design																		
	Detailed technical design																		
	Design review																		
	Design sign-off																		
	Development																		
2	Page development																		
	Portlet development(Email portlet, Product selector widget, product details portlet, related details portlet, Solution portlet, rating widget)																		
3	Services integration																		
	Personalization																		
	Search Functionalities																		
	Solution functionalities																		
	Email related functionalities																		

Dependencies — 1 Need UI build kit from UX team along with HTML, CSS, JS for English, German & Simplified Chinese — 2 Infrastructure dependency including readiness of development systems, servers, software and security (SSO) — 3 Availability of services (Solution, Subscription, product etc.) for integration.

Figure 3-2. *Sample project management plan*

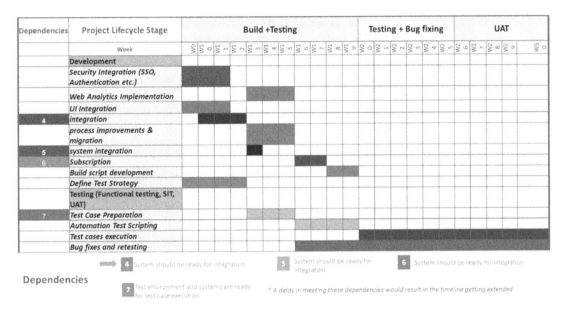

Figure 3-3. *Sample project management plan (cont.)*

Figures 3-2 and 3-3 depict sample project activities that take place during the requirements elaboration, design, development, and testing phases. These dependencies and timelines are defined for each activity. The project management plan can be further used to develop a staffing plan and for resource costing purposes.

Key Points of the Plan

The project management plan should cover these key items:

- A detailed list of deliverables at the end of each milestone. This helps track milestones easier.

- A link to the risk management plan to depict high-level risks, assumptions, and constraints.

- The project manager has to determine the review authorities for various deliverables and set the expectations of all concerned groups and stakeholders. A sample review plan involving all the boards across the project's stages is shown in Figure 3-4. Figure 3-4 depicts various review boards needed for a large project consisting of several stakeholders. Based on the project's complexity, the reviewer group could change. For instance, a single board might perform the architecture review and the technical review if the project is not very technically complex.

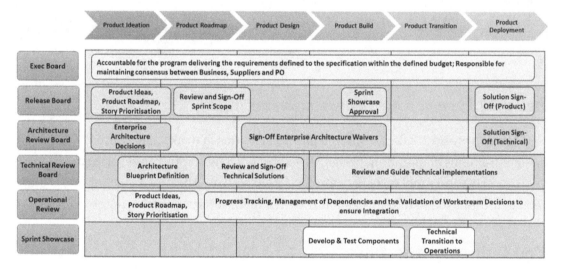

Figure 3-4. *Sample review plan across all project stages*

- A detailed list of activities and sub-activities assigned to resources and timelines. The milestones should be marked for easier understanding. The project management plan should also list various activities and deliverables during each project stage. A sample plan depicting the deliverables and activities for each project stage is shown in Figure 3-5. The project stages in Figure 3-6 depict various stages. In a typical three-phase project model, plan and analyze are part of the "project planning" phase, elaborate, construct, and user acceptance testing are part of the "development" phase, and deployment and transition are part of the "project maintenance" phase.

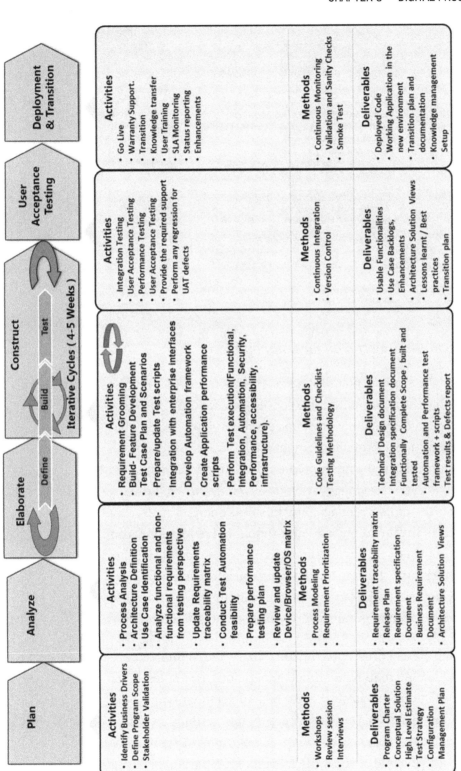

Figure 3-5. *Project plan with activities and deliverables*

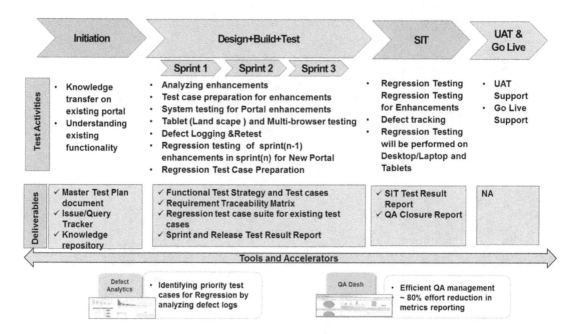

Figure 3-6. *Sample project plan for testing project*

During the project planning stage, the main activities involve defining the requirements to identify the scope and business drivers. Requirement workshops and interviews are popular methods to perform requirement analysis. At the end of the planning phase, the finalized project charter document, high-level estimate, and test strategy will be delivered. During the analyze phase, the project manager and business analysts analyze and detail all key functional and non-functional requirements and other business processes. Business process modeling will be done to understand the detailed flows and business rules. The key deliverables at this stage are the traceability matrix, the release plan's detailed requirements document, and the solution views.

During the elaborate and construct stages, the solution is developed iteratively. All requirements and integrations are implemented and tested. During this stage, the test-related documents and executable code are delivered. During user acceptance testing (UAT), the code undergoes various kinds of testing. Continuous integration tools such as Jenkins are used during this stage. At the end of this stage, the overall test reports are generated.

During the "deployment and transition" stage, various post-production activities—such as monitoring, knowledge transfer, SLA reporting, and enhancement—are conducted. As a part of the deliverables, you can include the transition plan, knowledge management setup, and other post-production activities.

- The project activities and deliverables are dependent on the nature of the digital project (such as development, testing, maintenance, support, etc.). A development project's activities are different from a support project's activities. A sample project plan for a testing project is shown in Figure 3-6.

As you can see in Figure 3-6, the activities of a testing project are mainly related to knowledge transfer, defect testing, and other various testing activities. Whereas in a development project (Figure 3-5), the activities are mainly about requirements understanding and feature development.

Drivers for the Project Management Plan

The main drivers of a project management plan are given here:

- It should detail all activities with timelines and dependencies. A detailed plan enables the project manager to get better control of the project.

- It can be used to communicate the status of the project to various stakeholders.

- It should act as a control tool and provide a baseline for status measurement.

- It should aid information-driven decision making for impact analysis, change request handling, scope management, schedule management, and release planning.

Key Success Factors

The main success factors of an efficient project management plan are as follows:

- The activities should be highly detailed so that they can be directly translated into a work breakdown structure (WBS) that can be easily assigned and monitored.

- The project management plan should be reviewed and signed off on by all stakeholders.

Collaboration Plan

Due to the diverse nature of globally distributed teams and the diverse nature of skillsets and technologies needed for digital projects, it is imperative that a digital project manager establish a collaboration plan at the beginning of the project. The collaboration plan defines the collaboration methods, tools, and metrics used for team collaboration.

Key Points of the Plan

The collaboration plan should cover these salient points:

- The digital project manager has to identify the key collaboration tools such as wikis, forums, communities, shared calendars, centralized knowledge bases, chats, and such.

- The project manager has to define the knowledge creation and sharing process and communicate them to the team. Artifacts such as best practices, lessons, how-to articles, tutorials, induction kits, certification content, and documentation can be best shared using these communication tools.

- The project manager has to closely track the use of the collaboration tools using metrics such as articles read, documents downloaded, blogs shared, etc.

- The project manager has to create rewards, recognition, and incentives to increase the adoption and usage of the collaboration systems. The incentives include rewarding frequent contributors with loyalty points.

Drivers of the Collaboration Plan

The main drivers of the collaboration plan are as follows:

- Enable the team to coordinate and enhance team productivity.

- Harness the collective intelligence of all subject matter experts and reduce turnaround time.

- Enable faster exchange and information sharing among team members.

- Leverage collaboration channels for combined problem solving.

- Create a common place of reference for best practices, documents, lessons, and reusable artifacts.

Key Success Factors

The key success factors for the collaboration plan are:

- Active participation of all team members in using the collaboration tools for information sharing and collaborative problem solving. Encouraging active participation through incentives will increase contribution.

- Efficient tracking of collaboration usage metrics.

- Involvement of all stakeholders in developing the collaboration plan.

Quality Management Plan

A quality management plan outlines the main quality and governance processes for the project. The quality management plan also defines the quality goals and associated metrics that can be used to measure overall project quality. We briefly discussed the key aspects of the plan in this section; Chapter 7 discusses the detailed aspects of the quality strategy and framework.

Key Points of the Plan

The quality management plan should cover these salient points:

- Map the quality goals to the overall digital program vision and objectives. Based on the nature of the digital program, the objectives and hence the quality goals will be different. A digital transformation project has a different set of quality goals when compared to a maintenance project.

- For each quality goal, identify the associated quality metrics. The metrics should be used to quantify changes and improvements.

Drivers of the Quality Management Plan

The main drivers of the quality management plan are as follows:

- Define and track the key quality goals.

- Adhere to the specified SLAs.

- Quantify the quality improvements.

Key Success Factors

The key success factors of the quality management plan are:

- The project manager has to set up the tracking and monitoring infrastructure to track the defined quality metrics.

- For strict SLAs (such as performance and scalability), the project manager has to track the SLAs in real time to monitor the related quality metrics.

- The project manager has to set up the notification and reporting infrastructure to communicate the quality metrics to the stakeholders.

Staffing Plan and Training Plan

The staffing plan mainly provides details about human resources for the duration of the project. Staffing plan is used for resource on-board planning, resource cost estimation, and project schedule planning.

Key Points of the Staffing Plan

The staffing plan should cover these salient points:

- Clearly explain the distribution of resources across various project phases.

- Provide the exact timeline allocated for resources.

- Cover the leave plans for various resources and transition planning.

- Provide resource details at each project stage.

A sample staffing plan is shown in Figure 3-7.

Phase	W1	W2	W3	W4	W5	W6	W7	W8	W9	W10	W11	W12	W13	W14	W15	W16	W17	W18	W19	W20	W21	W22	W23	W24	W25	W26	W27	W28
Requirements/Discovery Phase																												
Architecture/Detailed Design																												
Development +Unit Testing																												
ST+System Integration Testing+PT																												
User Acceptance Testing Support																												
Deployment and Go-Live Support																												
Post Prod Support																												

Role	W1	W2	W3	W4	W5	W6	W7	W8	W9	W10	W11	W12	W13	W14	W15	W16	W17	W18	W19	W20	W21	W22	W23	W24	W25	W26	W27	W28
Program Manager	1	1	1	1	1	1	1	1	1	1	1	1	1	1	1	1	1	1	1	1	1	1	1	0	0	0	0	
Architect	1	1	1	1	1	1	1	1	1	1	1	1	1	1	1	1	1	1	1	1								
Software Developer						6	6	6	6	6	6	6	6	6	3	3	3	2	2	1	1	1	1	1	1	1	1	1
UX Architect	1	1	1	1	1	1	1	1	1	1	0	0																
Database Architect		1	1	1	1	1	1	1	1	1	1	1	1	1	1	1	1	1	1	1	1							
Integration Architect	1	1	1	1	1	1	1	1	1	1	1	1	1	1	1	1	1	1	1	1	1							
Software Lead							1	2	2	2	2	2	2	2	1	1	1	1	1	1	1	1	1	1	1	1	1	1
Software Tester	1	1	1	2	2	2	3	3	3	3	3	3	3	3	2	2	2	2	2									
Functional Lead				1	1	1	1	1	1	1	1	1	1	1	1	1	1	1	1	1	1	1	0	0				
Business Analyst	1	1	1	1	1	1	1	1	1	1	1	1	1	1	1	1	1	1	1	1	1							
Project Manager	1	1	1	1	1	1	1	1	1	1	1	1	1	1	1	1	1	1	1	1	1	1	1	1	1	1	1	1

Figure 3-7. *Sample staffing plan*

Drivers of the Staffing Plan

The key drivers of the staffing plan are:

- Helps the project manager provide accurate cost analysis for the project.

- Helps the project manager accurately plan the schedule.

- Helps the project manager create the induction and training plans based on the staffing plan.

Key Success Factors of the Staffing Plan

The key success factors of the staffing plan are as follows:

- The staffing plan should match the estimation done during the estimation exercise. The total days of effort should match the overall staffing plan.

- The project manager has to staff resources mainly based on the lifecycle stage. For instance, more architects and business analysts are needed during the requirements elaboration phase and more software developers and software testers are needed during the development and testing phases.

- The staffing plan should have the right mix of roles. Typically the project team consists of various delivery modules working in parallel. Each delivery module is led by a senior software developer and a module team consisting of about three software developers, depending on the complexity of the module. The staffing plan should accurately reflect this role ratio.

The Training Plan

The training plan must focus on the group's training needs, especially in the technology and functional domains.

Key Points of the Training Plan

The training plan should cover these salient points:

- The project manager has to assess the skill levels of the team members and plan for training to upgrade their skillset. Based on the individual and project needs, the project manager can also plan for behavioral training, soft skills training, cross-culture sensitivity training, and more.

- The project manager can discuss and develop the training plan during performance appraisal discussions with each team member. This helps the team fill in skill gaps and reach its full potential.

- Due to rapid and frequent changes in digital technologies, the project manager has to provide the team members with self-learning materials and e-learning courses, which the team members can use to learn on their own.

- The project manager also has to plan for internal and external technical certifications for the team. Technical certification courses ensure that team members understand the core concepts, best practices, and proven methods for a given technology.

- The project manager can add all the training resources to the centralized knowledge base, which the team can then access.

- The project manager can get external trainers for the technical staff if the budget permits. Alternatively, senior members or technical SMEs can conduct internal training sessions.

Drivers of the Training Plan

The key drivers of the training plan are:

- Enable the team members to gain the technical competency needed for the role.

- Fill in the skill gap among team members.

- Ensure compliance levels needed for quality standards are met.

Key Success Factors

The key success factors of the training plan are:

- Training materials should be available on-demand to the team members.

- Team members should be evaluated through assessments and quizzes, after completing the training. The evaluation process ensures the effectiveness of the training.

- Team members should be encouraged to take the trainings. Project managers can provide time off and other incentives to ensure that each team member attends the needed trainings.

The Process Improvement Plan

The process improvement plan is an ongoing activity that explores all improvements to processes. It helps bring continuous and iterative optimization to each project.

Key Points of the Plan

The process improvement plan should cover these salient points:

- Developing a defect prevention plan is one of the main activities of the process improvement plan. The project manager has to analyze the defect trends using root cause analysis, analysis based on the severity and defect type of the errors, pareto analysis (involves analyzing 20% of the causes leading to 80% of the defects), and causal analysis to gain insights into the defect trend. Based on these insights, the project manager has to develop a defect prevention plan (described in Chapter 7). Based on the key focus areas identified from these insights (directives such as improve documentation, improve test cases, elaborate on requirements, and define roles and responsibilities), the project manager must take measures to address these potential issues. We elaborate on the defect prevention plan in Chapter 7.

- The productivity improvement plan (described in chapter 7) is another process improvement area. The project manager has to plan for reusable tools, open source frameworks, and automated processes to improve productivity iteratively.

- Improving the user satisfaction and application usability can also be part of the process improvement plan. Based on user feedback, the project manager has to plan for improving the overall usability and user satisfaction. This includes introducing features such as self-service, accessibility, omni-channel enablement (rendering the application seamlessly on various devices such as mobiles, tables, desktops, etc.), self-help, search capability, and so on.

- For support and maintenance projects, the project manager has to plan to iteratively reduce ticket volumes and reduce the average ticket resolution time.

- The project manager has to plan for continuous quality improvement by using checklists. Automated code analysis, continuous integration, centralized knowledge repository, and iterative testing are some of the measures you can use to enforce continuous quality improvement.

Drivers of the Process Improvement Plan

The key drivers of the process improvement plan are as follows:

- Reduce the development and operation costs on an iterative basis.

- Increase the time to market on an iterative basis.

- Improve the quality and productivity on an iterative basis.

- Improve user satisfaction and user adoption rate.

Key Success Factors

The key success factors of the process improvement plan are as follows:

- Introduce quantifiable improvements over each iteration.

- Continuously look for leveraging open source tools and frameworks to improve the project management processes. The current processes should be benchmarked against industry standards on a periodic basis and any gaps should be addressed.

Communication Plan

The project manager has to define and use a communication plan to communicate the status updates, risks, and milestone-related information to all concerned stakeholders.

Key Points of a Communication Plan

The communication plan should cover these topics:

- The communication plan should create the communication mode (e-mail, call, report, etc.) for each interested stakeholder and for the communication frequency.

- The communication plan should also define the expected input from each stakeholder.

- The plan should also define the escalation process and the related SLAs.

Drivers of the Communication Plan

The main drivers for a project management plan are given here:

- Periodically update the project status, risks, and other information needed from concerned stakeholders.

- Minimize any last-minute surprises and related impact on the project.

- Secure support from relevant teams and stakeholders through timely communication.

Key Success Factors

The key success factors for the communication plan are:

- During the requirements elaboration phase, the project manager has to create a stakeholder matrix along with their roles and interest areas. The project manager then creates the communication plan based on the stakeholder matrix.

- The communication method (e-mail, online dashboard, report, call, etc.) and communication frequency should be agreed upon by all stakeholders.

- While communicating risks and actions, the communication plan should clearly define the ownership and dates.

Risk Management Plan

A risk management plan is prepared to proactively identify the potential risks during the course of a project's execution. Though the first version of the risk management plan is prepared during the initial stages of project execution, the plan is continuously updated and risks are identified on a continuous basis throughout execution.

Key Points of the Plan

The risk management plan should cover these salient points:

- Provide a list of all foreseen risks along with their probability of occurrence, impact on project, and risk mitigation. The risk mitigation plan is part of the risk management plan and it details various options to address the risks.

- The risk mitigation plan should provide all corrective actions needed to minimize the impact of the risk.

- Periodically update the risk management plan based on its likelihood and impact.

- Communicate the risk and the mitigation plan to all concerned stakeholders.

- Categorize the risk for a better mitigation plan. The main risk categories include:

  - People-related risks, including attrition, gaps in skillset, and lack of key resources.

  - Process-related risks, including an incomplete planning process and an inaccurate estimation process.

  - Requirements-related risks, such as incomplete requirements gathering process, undefined integration requirements, undefined nonfunctional requirements such as scalability, security, performance, quality, reliability, and modularity.

  - External risks, which datacenter failure, natural disasters, changes to legal regulations and compliances, changes in market conditions, and macro-economic changes.

The main steps of the risk management process are defined in Figure 3-8.

Figure 3-8. *Risk management process steps*

As depicted in Figure 3-8, the risk management process starts with identifying the main risks. Once these risks are identified, they are categorized into one of the main categories (people related, process related, requirement related, or external) and are prioritized based on risk likelihood and impact. The project manager then defines the mitigation plan for each identified risk. The project manager tracks the risk during each project stage and communicates any updates to all the stakeholders. The key risks and mitigation plan for each project management stage are listed in Table 3-1.

Table 3-1. *Sample Risk and Mitigation Plan Across Project Stages*

Project Lifecycle Stage	Key Risks	Mitigation Plan
Project Initiation	• Incomplete requirements gathering • Inadequate planning • Absence of system and functionality documentation	• The project manager has to plan for an elaborate requirements gathering exercise covering all functional and nonfunctional requirements. • Review and get sign off on finalized scope and requirements from all stakeholders.
Project Execution	• Change in scope and requirements • Resource attrition • Lack of project sponsorship	• Project manager has to create a change request management process and use it to manage scope changes. • Create a knowledge base to capture all SME knowledge, best practices, and lessons that can be used for training.
Project Closure	• Specified SLAs are not met • Lack of application adoption	• Acceptance criteria should be defined and signed off on. • Continuous monitoring and notification setup should be done. • All business stakeholders should be periodically notified to secure their sponsorship and enhance adoption rate.

Drivers of the Risk Management Plan

The main drivers of a risk management plan are given here:

- Early identification of risk and defining its mitigation plan reduces the negative impact of the risk on the overall project.

- One of the main drivers of risk management plan is to reduce the deviation of planned effort, cost, and schedule. The risk management plan also ensures that specified functionalities are properly implemented.

Key Success Factors

The key success factors for the risk management plan are:

- Each risk should define the probability of occurring and its impact on the project (effort, time, and quality). This helps to accurately prioritize the risk.

- The risk should be continuously monitored across all project stages.

- Risk identification should be an ongoing activity during each project stage.

Other Project Plans

This section looks generally at other plans used for overall project planning purposes. Only the main points are covered for each of these plans.

Release Management Plan

The release management plan consists of processes that release the software modules to various environments. The plan provides optimal processes related to software operations. The plan details version management, source control processes (code check-in, versioning, code check-out, and source control structure), build processes, deployment processes, code promotion processes, and DevOps processes.

Test Plan

The QA/validation team develops the test plan. It typically defines test scope, needed test tools, and testing types (unit testing, functional testing, integration testing, system testing, regression testing, security testing, performance testing, etc.) that will be carried out. Based on the business needs, the test plan has to define the processes for testing the application on supported devices and for supported standards (such as accessibility standards, HTML standards, etc.). The test plan should map test cases to each of the baseline requirements in the traceability matrix.

Configuration Management Plan

The configuration management plan defines how you manage the work items that needs to be configured. It defines the version management and archival for items such as code and project artifacts. A configuration management plan is needed to release the right set of project artifacts. We elaborate on the configuration management plan in Chapter 7.

Delivery Acceptance Plan

This plan should clearly define the success criteria for each iteration and the acceptance criteria for each deliverable. The acceptance criteria should specify test data and quantified SLAs that can be used for acceptance of the deliverable and should define the ownership of the verifying the deliverable. The acceptance criteria should be reviewed by all business stakeholders and should be signed off on before the commencement of project iterations.

Summary

In this chapter, we discussed various aspects of digital project management:

- A project manager defines the processes and the governance structure for the future phases as part of the project planning process.

- The project management plan details all the tasks, task dependencies, ownership, and timelines.

- The project management plan should contain a detailed list of activities and sub-activities assigned to resources and timelines. The milestone dates should be marked for easier understanding.

- The project activities and deliverables are dependent on the nature of the digital project.

- The collaboration plan defines the collaboration methods, tools, and metrics used for team collaboration.

- In the collaboration plan, the digital project manager has to identify the key collaboration tools, such as wikis, forums, communities, shared calendars, centralized knowledge bases, chats, and such.

- A quality management plan outlines the main quality and governance processes for the project.

- The staffing plan provides details about the human resources needed for the duration of the project.

- The process improvement plan is an ongoing activity that explores all improvements to the processes.

- The project manager has to define and use the communication plan to communicate status updates, risks, and milestone-related information to all concerned stakeholders.

- A risk management plan is prepared to proactively identify the potential risks during the course of project execution.

- The release management plan consists of processes that release the software modules to various environment.

- The testing plan defines the test scope, test tools needed, and testing types used on the project.

- The configuration management plan defines the plan for managing the work items that need to be configured.

- The delivery acceptance plan should clearly define the success criteria of each iteration and the acceptance criteria of each deliverable.

CHAPTER 4

Digital Project Estimation and Pricing

Effort estimation is an important aspect of project planning, as it helps the project manager to accurately staff and allocate resources. An accurate effort estimation for the end-to-end digital project activities helps with right staffing and helps estimate the overall cost and project margin. Once the project plan and high-level activities are finalized, the digital project manager has to estimate the effort needed to complete each of the project activities. We can use various estimation modules such as function point estimation, use case based estimation, SMC (simple, medium, and complex) estimation, etc. Based on the project execution model, the project manager has to select the most appropriate estimation model suitable for the project. After estimation, the project manager has to use the appropriate pricing model to arrive at the overall project cost.

This chapter explores various estimation models and their suitability to digital projects. We also briefly discussed some of the popular pricing models that can be used in various scenarios.

Project managers, account managers, and program managers will find this chapter useful.

Estimation Framework

The software sizing and estimation was done through simple and straightforward ways, such as using Lines of Code (LoC) or using number of modules in the initial stages of software development. With the increase in complexity of software applications, we need to consider various factors such as user interface complexity, integration complexity, execution models, data requirements, and complex testing effort for

© Shailesh Kumar Shivakumar 2018
S. K. Shivakumar, *Complete Guide to Digital Project Management*,
https://doi.org/10.1007/978-1-4842-3417-4_4

accurate estimation and planning. A robust estimation framework has to consider all these factors to come up with a comprehensive effort estimation. This section defines an estimation framework and discusses the key risks and best practices related to effort estimation.

The digital project manager has to establish the estimation framework that can be used for the digital project. The key components of the estimation framework are depicted in Figure 4-1.

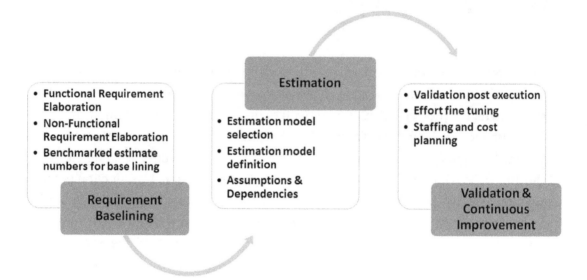

Figure 4-1. Estimation framework

The initial phase of the estimation framework is the Requirements Baselining phase, wherein all the requirements are properly defined. For waterfall models, the complete requirements for the entire project are defined. For Agile models, the requirements for the current sprint are defined. The business rules, use cases, business flows, and exception scenarios related to functional requirements should be fully defined. The SLAs and testing scenarios for non-functional requirements such as security, performance, etc. should also be completely defined. The effort estimates from similar projects are taken as baselines for the next stage in the estimation framework.

During the Estimation phase of the framework, the digital project manager selects the most appropriate estimation model needed for the project. Depending on the project's execution model and requirement type, the project manager has to select the most appropriate estimation model. Prominent estimation models include function point estimation, SMC estimation, use case estimation, user story based estimation, etc. The next section explains the definition process for the estimation model for each of the prominent estimation models. The project manager also should document the assumptions and dependencies used in the estimation process.

During the Validation phase, the planned effort values are compared with the actual effort values once the project is completed. The effort deviations are used to update and correct the estimation guidelines for future project iterations. This process is repeated across various iterations and projects to continuously improve the estimation model. The estimation model is used for staffing and costing purposes.

Risks in Effort Estimation

All estimation models leverage historical effort estimation data and SME experience to arrive at accurate estimations. That means that any estimation carries these risks:

- Overestimation or underestimation of some of the activities due to inadequate requirement understanding or lack of subject matter experts leading to inaccurate effort and cost estimates. Inaccurate effort later leads to effort overruns in the project.

- Effort estimation of complex activities (with no prior execution history) or activities involving unproven niche digital technologies.

- Effort optimization to achieve the timeline targets or to force fit the estimation numbers to a predetermined value.

- Subjectivity in assessing the complexity of a given task varies from person to person might lead to differences in estimates.

- Absence of baseline efforts to compare the effort values.

- Absence of an effort review process.

Here are some of the risk mitigation measures to tackle these challenges:

- For all the unknown and unproven complex activities, the project manager has to understand the involved tasks in greater detail to fine tune the estimates.

- For activities involving niche and unproven digital technologies, it is necessary to understand the estimates through a proof of concept (PoC).

- The digital project manager has to add all the necessary estimation assumptions (such as web pages estimated, content volume assumed, number of web services assumed, number of enterprise interfaces assumed, etc.).

- The project manager can cross-verify the estimation numbers by applying multiple estimation models. This ensures the accuracy of estimates and normalizes the estimates.

- Analyze the business processes and model the flow diagrams to capture the business rules and review them with business SMEs.

- Develop early prototypes to depict the user experience, navigation model, information architecture, and iteratively review with all concerned stakeholders.

- Frequently conduct requirements elaboration workshops to clarify the requirements and to demo the requirement artifacts.

- Establish the requirement review process and get the review and sign-off from all stakeholders.

- Capture the non-functional requirements related to availability, performance, security, scalability, modularity, extensibility, localization, accessibility, etc.

- If the project is heavy on integrations, create a separate interface specification document to capture the integrations-related requirements.

Best Practices in Effort Estimation

Here are the common best practices to obtain accurate effort estimations.

- A robust requirement elaboration process is needed to ensure that all functional and non-functional requirements are fully defined. Thoroughly defined requirement items translate into a more accurate estimation. The estimators need to have an in-depth understanding of the system to increase the accuracy of the estimates.

- For complex and large projects, estimate the items using multiple estimation methods to normalize the results. Wherever possible, get independent estimations by experts to minimize subjectivity. Compare the estimates with the previous projects of similar complexity to identify any gaps.

- For large digital projects, the estimators should provide detailed assumptions and should be able to justify their values with necessary data points. Estimators can attach a confidence level to their estimates. After estimation, the project team should discuss the details to identify any gaps and missing information.

- The estimation template should cover all the necessary items along with regular functional requirements. The template should cover non-functional items such as performance, security, scalability, and availability and should cover project-specific needs such as documentation, user training, knowledge transition, project management effort, integration effort, localization effort, environment setup effort, data migration effort, configuration management effort, user experience design effort, warranty support effort, release management effort, support effort, change management effort, vendor management effort, and so on.

- When estimating under uncertainty or if the requirements are very ambiguous, the estimators can provide a range value instead of a fixed estimate value.

- Use the Delphi technique (that uses independent estimation views and assumptions) to get multiple views on estimation. All the individual estimates are discussed and reviewed in a group to eliminate any estimation related biases. During the discussion, all reviewers should agree on a highest estimate, median estimation, and lowest estimate to improve estimation accuracy.

- The estimators should recommend a proof-of-concept (PoC) for complex or unknown activities where estimation cannot be done meaningfully. PoC outcomes can be used to fine tune estimates.

Estimation Models

This section discusses various estimation models, such as function point estimation, SMC/complexity based estimation, use case estimation, user story based estimation, and packaged product estimation.

Function Point Estimation

Function point is an improvement over the software size based estimation model (which uses lines of code to estimate the software size). A function point is a logical unit of requirement that is used by the end user. The function point (FP) estimation model uses various factors such as external inputs, external outputs, external queries, internal logical files, and external logical files.

When to Use the Function Estimation Model

Function point based estimation is used for custom developed software to identify function points. The estimation model is well suited for functional oriented architecture.

Estimation Model Details

The function point estimation model uses the following components:

- *External inputs (EI)*: EI depicts the data coming from the outside to the system.

- *External outputs (EO)*: EO depicts the data going out from the system to external interfaces.

- *External query (EQ)*: EQ depicts the queries for data retrieval from file systems or databases.

- *Internal logical files (ILF)*: ILF depicts a logical related data that is a part of the application. ILF consists of structured data that is used within the application boundary. For instance, the information related to web users (including name, address, email, phone, etc.) qualifies as ILF.

- *External interface files (EIF)*: The logical related data that is outside of the current application.

The application components are classified into these categories and scored to get the Unadjusted Function Points (UFP). The value adjustment factor (VAF) is calculated based on the 14 system characteristics. The final function point is calculated by multiplying UFP with VAF:

```
FP = UFP * VAF
```

We have detailed an example in the next section to illustrate the calculation.

Identification Rules for Application Components

This section explains are rules for identifying ILF, EIF, EI, EO, and EQ. The digital project manager can use them as rules:

- ILF consists of logically related semantic data within the application boundary. Identification rules are as follows:

    - The data should be logically related and should be recognizable by the user. For instance, a customer name, custom e-mail, and customer phone number are logically related to a customer and hence can be grouped as ILF.

    - The data should be within the boundary of the application being estimated.

- EIF consists of logically related semantic data of another application. The logically related data that resides outside the application boundary, such as bank branch details (branch location, branch ID, branch manager, etc.), can be categorized as EIF. Identification rules are as follows:

  - The data should be logically grouped and be recognizable by the user.

  - The data should be referenced by the application being estimated; for instance, the customer application should reference branch details to qualify the branch data as EIF.

  - The data should be recognized as an ILF of another application.

- External input includes the incoming data from outside the application boundary.

- External output depicts the data sent outside of application boundary. Identification rules are as follows:

  - The data should be sent outside the application boundary.

  - The entity sending the data outside the application boundary should have at least one ILF. For instance, a customer maintenance application (that has customer details as ILF) requesting branch details from an external interface by sending a customer ID satisfies this scenario.

- External queries consists of input-out that is needed in query-based data retrieval. Identification rules are as follows:

  - The data is retrieved from ILF or EIF.

  - The entity sending the external queries does not maintain or update the ILF or EIF. For instance, a user interface screen that displays both customer details (ILF) and branch details (EIF) without updating them satisfies this scenario.

Example of FP-Based Effort Estimation

This section looks at a simple example for function point estimation. Consider a simple requirement that states "management of books". A book management application needs to have a user interface for end-to-end management of books online. The requirement has the following components:

- *Internal Logical files (ILF)*: There will be two internal files (configuration file and master book list file) for achieving this functionality.

- *External Interface files (EIF)*: There will be three external interface files (report, mail, and audit) for achieving this functionality.

- *External inputs (EI)*: There will be three external inputs (add books, update books, and delete books) to manage the book data.

- *External outputs (EO)*: There will be one outgoing data point to mail interface.

- *External query (EQ)*: There will be three queries for mail, configuration, and language needed for localization functionality.

- *Value Adjustment factor (VAF)*: This consists of 14 factors, listed in Table 4-1. For each of the factors, you assign a value 0 (for absence of factor), 1 (for minor impact), 2 (for average impact), 3 (for above average impact), 4 (for high impact), or 5 (for significant impact for the entire duration). The impact of each factor is compared to the usage of the factor; for example, if the performance is heavily used in the application, its value is 4. The value assigned to each adjustment factor is shown in Table 4-1.

Table 4-1. *Value Adjustment Factor (VAF)*

Factors That Influence the FP	Value (0-5)
Data communications	4
Distributed data processing	4
Performance	4
Heavily used configuration	3
Transaction rate	3
Online data entry	4
End user efficiency	3
Online update	4
Complex processing	3
Reusability	3
Installation ease	1
Operational ease	3
Multiple sites	1
Facilitate change	3
Total	**43**
VAF ((Total * 0.01) + 0.65)	**1.08**

Note   The VAF formula calculates the final value by multiplying the total value by 0.01 and adding the result to 0.65.

- *Unadjusted function points*: In the final step, you define the estimation guidelines for estimation categories and use the estimation guidelines to can calculate the base effort. You then assign a multiplier value based on the complexity of the components (ILF, EIF, EI, EO, and EQ). A higher value indicates higher complexity. For instance, Table 4-2 shows that for a "simple" complexity ILF component, the multiplier value is 7. So if there are two "simple" complex ILF files, the net value is 14 (7 x 2, the number of such components with that complexity).

The sample unadjusted function points are listed in Table 4-2.

Table 4-2. *Unadjusted Function Points*

Types		Simple	Medium	Complex
Internal Logical Files	(ILF)	7	10	15
External Interface Files	(EIF)	5	7	10
External Inputs	(EI)	3	4	6
External Outputs	(EO)	4	5	7
External Queries	(EQ)	3	4	6

Based on these guidelines, the function point effort is calculated as explained in Table 4-3.

Table 4-3. *Base Effort Calculation*

FP Items	S	M	C	Computation	
ILF	0	2	0	10x2= 20	
EIF	0	3	0	7 x 3= 21	
EI	0	3	0	4 x 3= 12	
EO	0	1	0	5 x 1= 5	
EQ	0	3	0	4 x 3 = 12	
Total Unadjusted FP **(ILF+EIF+EI+EO+EQ)**				**70**	
VAF				1.08	
Total Adjusted FP **(Total Unadjusted FP * VAF)**				**75.6**	
Effort (Total Adjusted FP * Hours/FP)		10	Hrs/FP	**756**	PHours

SMC Estimation Model/Complexity Based Estimation Model

The SMC estimation model is basically a bottom-up approach for estimation, wherein you categorize the requirements and functional items into simple, medium, and complex categories based on its implementation complexity. You use the historical effort data to assign an effort value for each category.

When to Use the SMC Estimation Model

The SMC estimation model can be used in a wide variety of scenarios. Wherever it is possible to create a logical group of categories consisting of activities, you can assign a complexity factor to each of those activities and calculate overall effort based on that. The SMC estimation model can be used with custom application development, support, and maintenance projects.

Estimation Model Details

This section discusses the SMC model in greater detail. It looks at an end-to-end estimation example and shows how to leverage the SMC model for maintenance projects and for complexity-based bucketed estimation.

End-to-End Estimation Using the SMC Model

The effort needs to be computed for all the activities that are involved in end-to-end execution of the project. For each of the effort items, the effort is distributed across various activities spanning across the entire project. A typical effort distribution of a single activity across various project phases involved in an end-to-end project is depicted in Table 4-4. The effort distribution is based on the average effort spent over 10 or more digital projects.

Table 4-4. *Average Effort Distribution of a single activity Across Various Project Phases*

Project Phases	Percent Effort Distribution
Requirements	9%
Architecture	5%
Design	10%
Build	39%
Test	13%
Non-functional requirements	3%
Project management	12%
Training	0.5%
Contingency	2%
Build Effort	**93.5%**
User training	0.25%
Deployment	0.5%
UI design	1%
Defect fixing	1%
Integration effort	1%
Vendor management	0.25%
Change management	0.25%
Integration Effort	**97.75%**
Review effort	0.25%
Testing support	1%
Release management	0.25%
Automation effort	0.25%
Infrastructure setup	0.5%
End-to-End Effort	**100%**

Note   Not all the activities under "Integration Effort" and "End-to-End Effort" are applicable to all projects. In such cases, you can add a higher percentage effort to "Contingency" or other relevant categories under the "Build Effort" section.

You need to define the values for simple, medium, and complex tasks. The values for simple, medium, and complex are based on the baseline numbers and historical data for similar projects executed in the past. An example of simple, medium, and complex for requirements, design, and build activities is shown in Table 4-5.

Table 4-5. *Sample SMC values for Requirements, Design, and Build Activities*

	Simple (Person Days)	Medium(Person Days)	Complex (Person Days)
Requirements	2	5	10
Design	3	6	10
Build	5	10	15

Leveraging the SMC Model for a Support and Maintenance Project

A variant of the SMC model is used to handle the production tickets during the production support phase post go-live. The average effort needed to solve each of the complex levels (simple, medium, complex) tickets is calculated through historical analysis of tickets. In the absence of historical data, the effort values can be based on sample values and then iteratively fine tuned based on the actual effort spent. Once you analyze the ticket volume and the corresponding effort needed for the past six months, the numbers can be used for future effort planning purposes and the project manager can staff the support resources. A sample calculation of human support resources needed is shown in Table 4-6, based on six-month historical ticket data.

Table 4-6. *Ticket Volume Distribution*

Area	Total number of Tickets per month during first six months	Simple	Medium	Complex	Resources for handling Simple complexity tickets (80 tickets per resource per month)	Resources for handling Medium complexity tickets (40 tickets per resource per month)	Resources for handling Complex complexity tickets (13 tickets per resource per month)	Team size
Web application support	76	45	23	8	0.56	0.57	0.61	1.74

Table 4-6 determines that one support person can handle 80 simple-level tickets per month. So if you get 45 simple-level tickets, you need 0.56 resources to handle them. With similar calculations for medium-level and complex-level tickets, you arrive at 1.74 resources needed to handle the total ticket volume of 76 tickets per month of all complexities. So you can staff about two persons on a monthly basis for ticket handling.

The historical data during the support/maintenance phase can be similarly analyzed into simple, medium, and complex categories and can be used to estimate the effort needed in future support phases for a given number of enhancements. Normally, the simple-level activities take less than four days, medium-level activities take five-seven days, and complex-level activities take eight-fifteen days.

Leveraging the SMC Model to Create a Bucketed Estimation

Modern digital projects use 4-5 key requirement buckets such as user interface, integration, business logic, and testing. High-level requirements are broken down into estimation items for each of these buckets. Under each bucket, you list the estimation items belonging to that bucket and categorize them into simple, medium, or complex. A sample bucket model is shown in Table 4-7.

Table 4-7. *Sample Buckets/Categories for Digital Projects*

Buckets/Categories	Estimation Item	Simple	Medium	Complex
User interface	Page complexity			
	Number of navigation elements			
	Prototype design			
	UI validations			
	Widgets			
Integration	Integration complexity			
	Number of interfaces			
	Custom integrators/adaptors			
Business logic	Number of services			
	Complexity of services			
	Number of business rules			
Testing	Testing complexity			
	Number of test cases			
	Test data setup			

You could also create buckets based on activities (coding, testing, deploying, documentation, etc.) and add activities to each of those buckets. Overall effort estimation calculation involves these steps:

1. Define an effort estimation guideline for simple, medium, and complex tasks for each activity in all the buckets.

2. Once you identify the actual count for simple, medium, and complex activities, multiply the count by the estimate to arrive at the total effort estimate.

3. The sum of the estimate for all the activities in all buckets becomes the overall effort value.

Use Case Estimation

A use case defines the process or activities and all the actors (users) involved in that activity. Use case based estimation is a top-down estimation technique that defines the overall effort based on use case complexity, actor complexity and other technical weighting factor and environmental weighting factor.

When to Use the Use Case Estimation Model

The use case estimation model is mainly used for projects (such as object-oriented projects) where requirements are defined in use cases.

Estimation Model Details

The detailed process of use case based estimation is depicted in Figure 4-2.

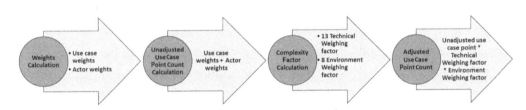

Figure 4-2. *Use case based estimation*

Once the business requirements are defined as use cases, the first step is to calculate the use case weights and actor weights. Each of the use case actors is identified and each of the actors is assigned a weight based on the complexity factor associated with those actors. For instance, an actor depicted by an end user or a system with a structured interface can be categorized as "simple," as there is not much complexity involved here. An actor depicted by a system with a complex interfacing method (such as integration with backend ERP) can be categorized as "complex," as it has complex interfacing needs. The overall actor weight is the weighted sum of all actor weights. Similarly, use case weights are calculated based on the weighted sum of individual use cases. You can define the complexity levels for each use case. One of the ways to categorize the complexity level of a use case is to use the transaction count (total number of handled transactions) or class count (total number of implementation classes) to decide the complexity level (for instance, if the use case handles fewer than two transactions, it can be categorized as "simple" and if the use case handles more than five transactions, it can be categorized as "complex"). The "Unadjusted Use Case Point Count" is the sum of the actor weight and the use case weight.

In the next step, you calculate the Complexity Factor, which is the sum of the 13 technical weighing factors and the eight environment weighing factors. The 13 technical weighing factors are distributed system, response of throughput performance objectives, end user efficiency, complex internal processing, code reusability, ease of install, portability, ease of change, support for concurrent-ness, need for specialty security features, need for direct access to third parties, need for user training. The eight environment factors are familiarity with the process modeling, application experience, object-oriented feature experience, motivation, environmental stability, complexity of the programming language, subject matter expertize, and need for partial/full time resources.

The "Adjusted Use Case Count" is the product of unadjusted use case count, the 13 technical weighing factors, and the eight environment weighing factors.

User Story Based Estimation

Modern digital projects adopt an Agile execution approach, wherein the project is delivered in sprints. User stories are defined and addressed during each sprint. The estimation model can be used for estimation either in each sprint or at the beginning of the project in sprint 0 if all user stories are defined. The user story based estimation model uses user stories as the unit of estimation and considers user story factors such as requirements complexity, solution components, external interfaces, and quality attribute complexity to arrive at the overall estimate.

When to Use User Story Based Estimation

User story based estimation can be used with sprint-based Agile projects, wherein each sprint includes various user stories.

Estimation Model Details

Prior to the user story based estimation model, the project team should define all the user stories needed for the sprint. The user stories should clearly define the business logic, integration details, and non-functional attributes (such as performance, security, and modularity). Figure 4-3 depicts the steps involved in the user story based estimation model.

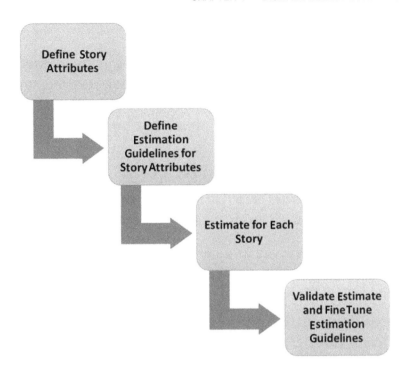

Figure 4-3. *User story based estimation model*

The first step in defining the user story estimation model is to define the attributes needed for the story. The user story attributes include factors such as requirement complexity, solution components, external interfaces, etc. In the next step, you need to define the estimation guidelines for each of the user story attributes. The estimation guidelines define the criteria to assign the attribute to an estimation category (such as simple, medium, and complex). Once you have the user story estimation model ready, you can use it to estimate each of the user stories. Once each user story is delivered, you need to compare the actual effort spent to the planned effort determine the deviation. The error caused by the deviation should be used to fine tune the estimation model and continuously improve it.

The next sections define a sample user story framework to explain this estimation model.

Step 1: Define the Attributes of the User Story

This sample user story estimation model uses the following user story attributes. The attributes may be updated based on the user story needs. The attributes vary based on the solution scenario. Each user story should be validated to ensure that the user story attributes are defined in detail to ensure accurate usage of the estimation model. Here is a generic set of attributes used:

- *Requirements complexity*: This attribute indicates the complexity of the user story requirement. If the requirement involves complex business rules or has complex flow steps, it is considered highly complex.

- *Solution components*: This attribute indicates the number of solution components that will be developed to implement the user story.

- *External interfaces*: The attribute provides a list of external integrations needed to implement the user story. The complexity increases with an increase in the number of external interfaces.

- *Quality attribute complexity*: This attribute indicates the non-functional requirements such as performance, scalability, and modularity needed.

Based on the scenarios and user story needs, you may also include other attributes such as test case complexity, technology complexity, business transaction complexity, and data volume (for migration projects) in the list of attributes.

Step 2: Define the Estimation Guidelines for Story Attributes

In this step, you define the estimation categories needed for the user story and define the qualification criteria for each of the estimation attributes. Table 4-8 shows sample estimation guidelines for the story criteria discussed earlier.

Table 4-8. *Estimation Categories for Story Attributes*

Attribute/Estimation Category	Simple	Medium	Complex
Requirement complexity	If number of business rules < 5 Or If user story has simple steps that can be done in a single layer	If number of business rules < 10 Or If user story impacts multiple solution layers	If number of business rules > 11 Or If user story has multiple steps impacting all layers of the solution
Solution components	If user story needs < 2 solution components	If user story needs < 4 solution components	If user story needs > 5 solution components
External interfaces	If the application needs to be integrated with < 2 external interfaces	If the application needs to be integrated with < 4 external interfaces	If the application needs to be integrated with > 5 external interfaces
Quality attribute complexity	If performance, scalability, and modularity requirements can be addressed easily or using out of the box/built-in features	If performance, scalability, and modularity requirements can be addressed through configuration	If performance, scalability, and modularity requirements can be addressed through heavy code customization

You then give a value to the effort of each of the estimation categories (simple, medium, and complex). You can use the historical analysis of the effort value for similar user stories in past projects. Some of the attributes get more weight based on their importance to the user story.

Step 3: Estimate Each User Story

Once the user story estimation model is ready, the project manager can use this model to estimate each user story. The overall effort will be a weighted sum of story attributes for each of the user stories. The value can then be used for costing and staffing purposes.

Step 4: Validate and Fine Tune Estimation Guidelines

At the end of the user story execution, the project manager compares the estimated effort values to the actual effort spent. The difference indicates the error margin. The project manager has to continuously update the effort guidelines based on this analysis.

Packaged Product Estimation

The packaged product estimation model is used when digital projects heavily use package tools and products. In such scenarios, most of the effort is driven by the digital tool's capability and hence the overall effort mainly depends on the effort needed to execute the task in the corresponding tool. The packaged product estimation uses the tool estimation guidelines and defines the estimate to calculate the overall effort.

When to Use Packaged Product Estimation

Project managers can use this model if more than 70 percent of development effort is done through the tool. Many projects related to analytics, data migration, reporting applications, business intelligence (BI), and such digital projects heavily rely on tools and these are good examples where this estimation model can be used.

Estimation Model Details

This model has three main steps for estimation, as depicted in the Figure 4-4.

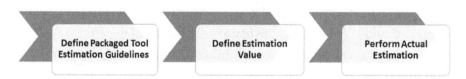

Figure 4-4. *Packaged product estimation model*

Define Packaged Tool Estimation Guidelines is the first step, wherein the project manager defines the estimation guidelines that place the estimation item in a particular estimation category (categories such as simple, medium, and complex). In the next step, the digital project manager, with the help of SMEs, defines the estimate (in terms of person days or person hours) for each of the defined estimation categories. The last step is the actual estimation, wherein the project manager provides values for estimation items and calculates the overall effort.

Details of this estimation model are explained with examples in the next sections.

Step 1: Define Packaged Tool Estimation Guidelines

In this step, the project manager defines the estimation categories and the qualification criteria. The qualification criteria is based on the analysis of the effort spent in previous projects and on the SMEs with rich experience using these tools.

This section looks at two scenarios to illustrate this. Table 4-9 shows the estimation guidelines for estimating using a reporting tool for a BI application.

Table 4-9. *Estimation Guidelines for a Reporting Tool*

Functional Module\ Category	Simple	Medium	Complex
Report Modules	Number of database tables used <=3	Number of database tables used <=5	Number of database tables used >=6
Transaction Modules	Maximum of one business transaction supported in the function module	Maximum of two business transactions supported in the function module	Maximum of three business transactions supported in the function module

These guidelines define three categories for estimation: simple, medium, and complex. Two functional modules define their fit into one of these three categories. If the report module uses fewer than three tables, it qualifies as "simple". Similarly, if the transaction module supports maximum one business transaction, it is qualifies as "simple". Optionally, the project manager can assign weights to these parameters.

For a data migration project, Table 4-10 lists some sample estimation guidelines for a data migration tool.

Table 4-10. *Sample Estimation Guidelines for a Data Migration Project*

	Parameter	Simple	Medium	Complex
Master data	No. of source legacy systems	1	2 to 3	>3
	Average volume of database records	<10K	10K-50K	> 50K
	Percent of fields requiring conversion/data transformation	<10%	10%-30%	>30%
	Percent of fields requiring cleansing (normalization, duplicate removal, fixing incorrect data)	<10%	10%-30%	>30%

In Table 4-10, you use the volume of data records to categorize migration data into three categories: simple, medium, and complex. A project manager can also define point-based categories similar to the simple, medium, and complex categories.

Step 2: Define the Estimation Value

Once you define the estimation guidelines, the next step is to define the effort of each of the defined categories. The project manager uses the historical effect trends of similar projects and leverages tools and SME expertise to define effort values. A sample effort value for the functional modules defined previously is shown in Table 4-11 (all effort values are in person days).

Table 4-11. *Effort Values for Functional Modules*

	Simple	Medium	Complex
Report Modules	5	9	12
Transaction Modules	6	10	15
Master Data	10	20	30

Table 4-11 indicates the amount of effort needed (in person days) to develop the module. In some cases, the effort number will include the design effort, build effort, test effort, and deployment effort.

Step 3: Perform the Actual Estimation

In this step, the project manager calculates the final numbers. The project manager has to identify the categorized count of functional modules, as depicted in Table 4-12.

Table 4-12. *Categorized Count of Functional Modules*

Use Case Requirement	Functional Module Mapping	Simple	Medium	Complex
Sales Report	Report Modules	0	2	0
Purchase Functionality	Transaction Modules	0	1	0

In this table, we define that development of a sales report use case that needs a medium category of effort. Based on the defined effort values, the total effort for this sales report will be 18 person days of effort. Similarly, the development of the purchase functionality needs 10 person days of effort. The overall effort will be 28 person days.

Comparison of Various Estimation Models

Table 4-13 compares the various estimation models.

Table 4-13. *Comparison of Estimation Models*

Estimation Model	Scenario	Execution Model	Key Strengths	Key Weakness
SMC/complexity based estimation	Bottom up approach that is mainly used for custom application development when low-level details are known.	Agile, iterative, or waterfall	Can be used in a wide variety of scenarios, such as production support, maintenance, and custom application development.	The estimation model may miss system setup and tasks such as continuous integration. The model is inaccurate if low-level requirements are unknown. Risk of subjectivity or biases in estimating task complexity.

(continued)

Table 4-13 (*continued*)

Estimation Model	Scenario	Execution Model	Key Strengths	Key Weakness
Packaged product estimation	Mainly used for packaged tool-based application development.	Agile or iterative	Covers various aspects of packaged implementations.	Cannot be used for non-product driven project such as custom application development or maintenance.
Use case-based estimation	Top-down approach mainly used for project requirements defined through use cases.	Agile or iterative	Provides comprehensive estimation model for use case-driven projects. The model can be used when high-level requirements are known.	Prone to subjectivity bias when there's a lack of historical data. Tends to ignore low-level implementation details. Risk of subjectivity or biases in estimating actor and factor (technical and environmental) complexity.
Function point	Can be used in a wide variety of scenarios, including custom application development.	Agile, iterative, or waterfall	Variations of the model can be used for production support, maintenance, and reverse engineering projects.	Cannot be used for support and maintenance. Prone to subjectivity bias when there's a lack of historical data.
User story-based estimation	Mainly used for Agile projects where requirements are defined by user stories.	Agile or iterative	Provides flexible options and comprehensive estimates for user stories.	Cannot be used with non-Agile projects.

Pricing Models

After estimating the work items, the project manager has to use the appropriate pricing model to calculate the total cost and staff the resources. This section introduces and discusses various pricing models. There are two main models: linear pricing models, which calculate cost uniformly for the work unit/effort value, and nonlinear pricing models, which use various nonlinear cost drivers. The fixed price model and the time and material model are popular linear pricing models. Work unit based pricing, outcome based pricing, and transaction based pricing are examples of nonlinear pricing models.

Linear Pricing Models

This section discusses the fixed price model and time and material model.

Fixed Price Model

The fixed price model provides a fixed price for a given set of requirements. The project manager has to calculate the effort needed for a given set of requirements using one of the estimation models discussed earlier. Based on the calculated effort, the overall cost will be calculated along with a buffer cost to handle any contingencies. The fixed cost covers all the scope activities for the duration of the program. The project manager has to ensure robust project governance, robust requirements management, and robust quality governance processes to ensure successful delivery of fixed priced projects.

When Do You Use This Pricing Model?

Project managers can use the fixed price model when the scope of the project is clearly defined and has highly detailed requirements with little or minimal change requests.

Strengths and Weakness

Fixed price projects provide good control and clarity to the overall project cost and delivers predictability to the customers. This pricing model is most suitable when you have strict budget constraints. It greatly reduces the cost-related risks to an organization. Any change in scope or requirements can be difficult to accommodate and will need a separate change requirement management process. When the requirements are constantly evolving or when you need to incrementally build the solution based on feedback, it is difficult to achieve it using a fixed price model. Any unforeseen risks or contingencies will greatly impact the project margin, as there is no scope for altering the cost.

The Time and Material (T&M) Model

Also known as the cost and material model, the cost is calculated based on time units (usually on hourly basis) using the rate card of the staffed resources. The model is used when the project gets continuous requirements or ad hoc requirements on a regular basis and the project should be staffed to handle the incoming requirements. The T&M model can also be used by organizations to augment their in-house team with additional skilled resources for a task that has a specified duration.

When Do You Use This Pricing Model?

Project managers can adopt this model if the scope is unclear or if there is a steady stream of requirements.

Strengths and Weakness

The time and material model helps the project manager absorb any number of requirements with appropriate staffing. Based on the scope and requirements, the project manager can appropriately ramp up or ramp down the resources on-demand. This model provides staffing flexibility and makes it easy to accept new requirements and change requests. The key drawback to this model is that the overall cost is directly proportional to the total resource hours and is not directly related to the business value or the business outcomes. Improper estimation leads to waste.

Nonlinear Pricing Models

This section looks at some of the nonlinear pricing models, such as work unit based pricing, outcome based pricing, and transaction based pricing.

Work Unit Based Pricing

The pricing is set based on work units (a quantum of scope such as tickets, defects, or a business flow). The model is well suited for structured, quantifiable, and predictable work units-based activities such as enhancements, production incident handling, defect fixes, and so on.

When Do You Use This Pricing Model?

This pricing model is best when the work units are properly defined.

Strengths and Weakness

The work unit based pricing model provides optimal cost as the organization is billed only for the work units. This can reduce the operational and maintenance costs, such as production support, production fixes, etc.

Outcome Based Pricing Model

Pricing is directly associated to the business value and the business outcomes. For instance, the business outcome is based on metrics such as ROI, average order value (for e-commerce applications), and so on. In this model, service providers have incentive to optimize business outcomes through optimized processes and intellectual property. Service providers also need to have the complete idea of business processes and they should have a thorough understanding of painpoints and challenges.

When Do You Use This Pricing Model?

This is an innovative pricing model that can be used when business outcomes (such as percent increase in revenue, increase in site traffic, increase in order value, increase in conversion rate, etc.) are critical to program success.

Strengths and Weakness

The service provider can use innovations and intellectual property (IP) to influence the business outcomes, thereby optimizing the development effort and time to market. The organization enjoys minimal risk, as the total cost is tied to the business outcome.

Quantifying the business value and business outcome is challenging and the pricing model may get complicated. The pricing model carries risk for to service provider if the business outcomes are not properly quantified and tracked.

Transaction Based Model

This model is similar to an outcome based model, wherein the cost is attached to the total number of business transactions.

When Do You Use This Pricing Model?

This model is mainly applicable to transactions-based businesses, such as e-commerce systems, retail systems, and finance systems, wherein the transactions are the key business metrics.

Strengths and Weakness

Organizations only pay based on the volume of successful transactions, which optimizes their investment.

Summary

In this chapter we discussed various aspects of digital project estimation and pricing:

- A robust estimation framework has to consider various factors such as interface complexity, integration complexity, execution models, data requirements, and complex testing efforts for accurate estimation and planning.

- The estimation framework consists of three key phases: requirements baselining, estimation, and validation. The initial phase of the estimation framework is the Requirements Baselining phase, wherein all the requirements should be properly defined. During the Estimation phase of the framework, the digital project manager selects the most appropriate estimation model. During the Validation phase, the planned effort values are compared to actual effort values once the project is completed.

- The key risks in effort estimation are overestimation or underestimation, inaccurate effort estimation of complex activities, force fitting estimation numbers, estimator subjectivity, absence of baseline effort values, and absence of an effort review process.

- Key risk mitigation measures are having a greater understanding of requirements, PoC based effort validation, documentation of effort related assumptions, and cross-verification of effort numbers through multiple methods.

- The key best practices for effort estimation are robust requirement elaboration process, cross-validation of estimation through multiple methods, detailed documentation of estimation assumptions, discussion of estimation numbers to identify any gaps, a thorough estimation template covering functional and non-functional and project specific requirements, and using the Delphi method.

- The function point (FP) estimation model uses various factors such as external inputs, external outputs, external queries, internal logical files, and external logical files.

- The SMC estimation model is basically a bottom-up approach for estimation, wherein you categorize the requirements and functional items into simple, medium, and complex categories based on complexity.

- Use case based estimation is a top-down estimation technique that defines the overall effort based on use case complexity, actor complexity, and other technical weighting and environmental factors.

- User story based estimation incorporates user stories as the unit of estimation and considers user story factors such as requirements complexity, solution components, external interfaces, and quality attribute complexity to arrive at the overall estimate.

- The packaged product estimation uses the tool estimation guidelines and defines the estimate to calculate the overall effort.

- Linear pricing models calculate cost uniformly for the work unit/ effort value and nonlinear pricing models use various nonlinear cost drivers.

- The fixed price model provides a fixed price for a given set of requirements.

- In the cost and material model, the cost is calculated based on time units (usually an hourly basis) using a rate card of staffed resources.

- In the work unit based pricing model, pricing is set based on the work units (a quantum of scope such as tickets, defects, or a business flow).

- In the outcome based model, the pricing is directly associated with the business value and the business outcomes.

- In the transaction based model, the cost is attached to the total number of business transactions.

PART II

Execution of Digital Projects

CHAPTER 5

Models, Tools, and Templates Used in Digital Project Management

Digital project managers need to efficiently use project management tools and proven models and templates for efficient project management. Tools, models, and templates ensure that project managers use the proven techniques and best practices, thereby improving the overall delivery quality and productivity.

This chapter covers the proven tools, models, and frameworks that digital project managers can use for efficient project management.

Project managers and program managers will find this chapter useful.

Models Used in Digital Project Management

This section covers two main models related to earned value management and the digital maturity model that can be used for effort/cost forecasting and digital maturity assessment, respectively. We already detailed estimation models and pricing models in Chapter 4; in this section, we look at other two models related to forecasting and assessment.

© Shailesh Kumar Shivakumar 2018
S. K. Shivakumar, *Complete Guide to Digital Project Management*,
https://doi.org/10.1007/978-1-4842-3417-4_5

Earned Value Management

Earned value management helps digital project managers effectively monitor and forecast project performance. The earned value analysis technique needs a structured definition and assignment of work items (or work packages) with clearly defined timelines.

The key advantages of the earned value technique are:

- Helps project managers measure the project's progression and identify variances in cost and schedule. Project managers can manage the critical path more effectively.

- Helps project managers forecast, monitor, measure, and report the cost and schedule more effectively. Can be used for data-driven decision making.

- In earned value management, you compare the completed work (the earned value) to the planned work and quantify its value in dollars and in person hours. Based on the variations, digital project managers can take course-corrective steps and control schedule delays and cost escalation.

- Provides an accurate progress of the project status by rolling up the status of the individual tasks to the overall project level.

- Provides an early warning mechanism for indicating project performance.

- Can be used to communicate status to all stakeholders.

- Can be used to minimize the cost and schedule related risks.

Main Terms Used in Earned Value Management

The main terms used with earned value management are listed in Table 5-1.

Table 5-1. *Key Terms of Earned Value Management*

Term	Brief Details
BCWS (PV) Budgeted Cost of Work Scheduled	Indicates the budgeted total cost of scheduled work items until the status date.
BCWP (earned value/EV) Budgeted Cost of Work Performed	Indicates the planned total cost of completed work items until the status date.
ACWP (actual cost = AC) Actual Cost of Work Performed	Indicates the actual total cost of completed work items until the status date.
SV Earned Value Schedule Variance	The cost difference between current work completed and work planned. SV = BCWP – BCWS
CV Earned Value Cost Variance	The cost difference between budgeted and actual cost. CV = BCWP – ACWP
EAC Estimate at Completion	The total schedule cost of a task. It forecasts the total project cost using current project cost.
BAC Budget at Completion	Indicates the total cost planned for all the tasks for the entire project.
VAC Variance at Completion	The difference between budgeted cost and the total cost for a given task. Indicates the task-specific cost slippage.
ETC Estimate Time to Complete	The estimated cost to complete the remaining work.
SPI Schedule Performance Index	The planned progress rate indicating the schedule efficiency. SPI = EV/PV

Process Steps in Earned Value Management

The detailed steps in performing earned value management are as follows:

- *Step 1: Work package definition*: The project manager has to clearly define the work items in the form of a work breakdown structure (WBS). WBS should convert the scope items into logical and mutually exclusive work items. For each of the defined work items, the project manager has to assign owners and define the start and end dates to baseline the project. A sample work breakdown structure depicting the deliverables and timeline is depicted in Figure 5-1.

Phases + Low Level Breakdown	Deliverables	Month 1	Month 2	Month 3	Month 4	Month 5
Project Kick off						
Project Kick off	Project Charter	▓				
Orientation & Onboarding of Project Team	Project Kick Off presentation	▓				
Onsite and Offshore Resource Connectivity Setup	Communication Plan	▓				
Planning						
Project Planning and Strategy	RACI (Responsible, Accountable, consulted, Informed) Matrix , Risk Log Tracker , Change Management Plan	▓				
Prepare Master Project Plan , Review & Sign off	Weekly Status Report , Project Control Steering Report					
Technical Assessment Workshop Planning	Requirement Workshop Plan					
Technical Assessment						
Assessment of the Existing Application Landscape	Infrastructure Landscape Document	▓	▓			
Study existing business processes	As-Is Business Process Document	▓	▓			
Study existing customizations	Feasbility Analysis Document	▓	▓			
Documentation Study	Process Workflow Recommendations	▓	▓			
Feasibility Analysis	Business Requirement Specification ,	▓	▓			
Requirements Elaboration (process modeling, workshops, interviews, documentation review, prototyping, scenario walkthrough, use case modeling, white boarding, brainstorming)	Business Requirements document, Use case document	▓	▓			
Conduct boot camp session	Meeting Minutes & Agenda for Boot Camp/Workshops	▓				
Conduct Requirement Gathering workshops	Functional Requirement Specification	▓				
Document , Study & Prepare Business Requirement Specification	Business Requirement Specification	▓				
Solution , Design & Architecture						
Prepare Holistic Application Solution	Complete Technical Solution & Architecture Document			▓	▓	▓
High Level Design & Architecture	High Level Design Document				▓	▓
Low Level Design	Low Level Design Document				▓	▓
Design Review & Sign off	Design Review - Sign off Evidence					
Built + Unit Testing						
Prepare for Development of Modules	Code Setup , Code Build Methodology				▓	▓
Build Modules	Unit Test Cases , Build Plan				▓	▓
Build & Consume Integration Interfaces	Code Implementation & Check In				▓	▓
Unit Testing Modules	Unit Test Case Execution results					
Integration Testing Modules	Integration with backend services results					
Code Review & Finalize Work Package	Code Quality Reports , Code Review & Rework Reports				▓	▓

Figure 5-1. *Sample WBS*

- *Step 2: assigning value to work items*: The project manager has to assign a value (monetary value or person hours) to each of the work units.

- *Step 3: define calculation rules*: The project manager has to determine a way to calculate the work item value. The calculation rules can be based on percent of task completion, milestone completion, etc.

- *Step 4: project execution*: The project manager can execute the project and update the progress against each work item.

Earned Value Management Example

This section explains an example of earned value management. The status of various project activities at the end of five weeks is shown in Table 5-2.

Table 5-2. *An Example of Earned Value Management*

Activity	Budgeted Cost ($)	Planned Duration (Week)	Current Status	Actual Cost ($)
Elaboration of requirements	1000	1	100% Completed	1000
Architecture definition	1000	2	100% Completed	1500
Development	3000	3	60% Completed	3400
Validation	2000	2	Yet to start	TBD
Acceptance and Implementation	1000	1	Yet to start	TBD

The calculations for earned value management at the end of week five are listed in Table 5-3.

Table 5-3. *Earned Value Analysis by the End of Week 5*

Value	Calculation	Value	Remarks/Impact on Project
PV	1000+1000+3000	5000	Work in the amount of $5000 should have been completed
EV	1000+1000+1800	3800	Actual work completed is $3800
AC	1000+1500+3400	5900	Actual amount spent is $5900
BAC	1000+1500+3000+ 2000+1000	8500	$8500 is the total project cost
CV	3800-5900	-2100	$2100 over budget at end of week 5
SV	3800-5000	-1200	Behind schedule
SPI	3800/5000	0.76	76% is the planned progress rate

(*continued*)

Table 5-3. (*continued*)

Value Calculation		Value	Remarks/Impact on Project
CPI	3800/5900	0.64	The team is getting 64 cents for every one dollar spent
EAC	8500/0.64	13281	$13281 will be the total project cost based on current project performance
ETC	13281-5900	7381	Need $7381 to complete the project
VAC	13281-8500	4781	The project is over budget by $4781

Best Practices of Earned Value Management

Here are the key best practices of the earned value management process:

- All work items should be clearly defined and assigned along with start and end dates.

- Resource cost should be defined and milestones should be defined.

- Baseline budget and base schedule should be defined.

Digital Maturity Model

One of the initial steps in the digital transformation journey is the digital maturity assessment step. During the digital maturity assessment step, the digital consultants assess the current capabilities and processes of the organization. The digital maturity assessment provides insights into the gaps in the existing processes. The digital maturity model is used to assess the current maturity level for the organization. Digital project managers can use the digital maturity model to assess and define a digital roadmap.

The digital maturity model defines various phases in the digital transformation journey and each phase has a defined set of features, challenges, and digital elements. This is depicted in Figure 5-2.

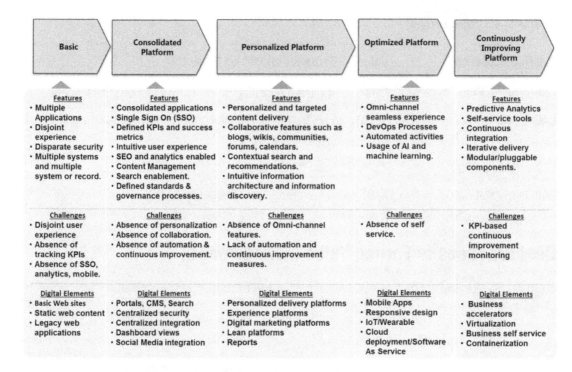

Figure 5-2. *Sample digital maturity model*

Various Stages of the Digital Maturity Model

The stages of the digital maturity model as defined in Figure 5-2 are described next:

- *Basic stage*: During this stage, the organization is maintaining multiple web applications mainly for static information delivery. Each of the web applications has its own user experience, leading to a disjoint experience for the end users navigating across web applications. In this stage, the technical ecosystem will not have centralized systems or records. Data, functionality, and concerns are distributed across various systems. The main challenges at this stage are inconsistent user experience with absence of single sign on (SSO) and tracking key performance indicators (KPIs). The main digital elements at this stage are static web sites, legacy web applications, etc.

- *Consolidated platform*: During this stage, all disparate web applications are consolidated into a single platform. For instance, various internal web applications such as HR application, leave application, and travel application are consolidated into an intranet portal. The integrated experience is enabled by single-sign-on (SSO), which provides seamless access to all secured applications. The digital platform mainly consists of portals, content management systems, and enterprise searches. Search Engine Optimization (SEO) and analytics are enabled for the applications. Standards and governance processes are defined for the key business processes. Personalization, collaboration, and automation are not implemented as part of this stage. The main digital elements used in this system are portals, CMS, search, and centralized integration (such as ESB and API gateways).

- *Personalized platform*: At this stage, the information and functionality are personalized based on user preferences and behavior. Based on contextual information, targeted information is presented to the users. The digital platforms at this stage have intuitive information architectures (including menus, site hierarchy, and navigation elements) and provide user-friendly information discovery features, such as search, saved searches, top downloads, popular topics, etc. Omni-channels and automation are yet to be implemented at this stage.

  At this stage, personalized presentation platforms, digital experience platforms, digital marketing platforms, lean portals, and reports are used.

- *Omni-channel platform*: At this stage, the digital platforms are optimized for all channels such as web, mobile, tables, and PDAs. Users have a seamless experience across various touch points. Many of the business processes are automated and artificial intelligence (AI) techniques such as chat bots and machine learning are employed for enhanced user engagement. DevOps processes are used to optimize the release management and deployment processes. The key digital elements at this stage are mobile apps, wearable systems, responsive design techniques, and cloud enabled systems.

131

- *Engagement platform*: At this stage, the digital platform provides many features to actively engage the users. This includes self-service tools, decision-making tools, and predictive analytics that actively engage the end users. At this stage, the digital platform and ecosystem implement continuous integration continuous testing, and iterative delivery. The components are developed as pluggable and modular components. The main digital elements are business accelerators, virtualization, business self-service, and containerization.

Quantitative Risk Management Model

Risks impact the project metrics (quality, schedule and cost) and affect the success factors of the digital project. There could be numerous reasons for project risks, such as ineffective tracking, external dependencies, skillset gaps, resource issues, scope creep, absence of continuous integration, etc. A quantitative risk management plan helps project managers make informed decisions in uncertain situations and enhances delivery predictability. A digital project manager has to identify potential risk and continuously track it to closure. This section discusses the risk management model. The quantitative risk management model is depicted in Figure 5-3.

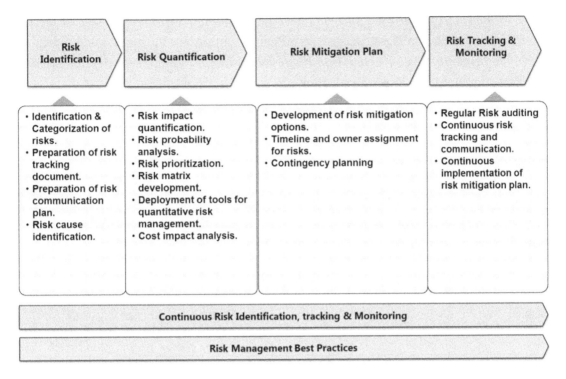

Figure 5-3. *Quantitative risk management model*

Various phases of the quantitative risk management model are covered next. Risk identification and tracking and application of risk management best practices are carried out continuously and iteratively across all project phases.

Risk Identification

Proactively identifying potential risks is done in the initial stages of project management. A project manager involves all stakeholders to compile a list of all potential risks. The project manager can use various tools and techniques for risk identification. This might include interviews (discussing with the team and stakeholders), SWOT analysis (creating a matrix of strengths, weakness, opportunities, and threats), brainstorm sessions (group discussion of ideas), root cause analysis (identification of the problem's root cause), etc. The project manager also has to validate the assumptions and constraints of the project to understand the possibility of project risk in those areas. Risks are also categorized during the exercise and the project manager maintains a list of risks in a "risk registry". The common risk categories are technology-related, resource-related, external dependency-related, and requirements-related. The root cause of the risk (such as skillset gap, resources, project phase, or dependencies) is used to categorize the risk. The project manager secures the budgetary support of business stakeholders for risk management. For efficient tracking of risk, the project manager prepares a risk tracking document and a communication plan.

Risk identification is a continuous and iterative process that is carried out throughout all the project phases.

Risk Quantification

The probability (likelihood of risk occurrence) and impact (impact on cost, quality, schedule, and effort of the project) are defined in a matrix format. A sample risk probability-impact matrix is shown in Table 5-4.

Table 5-4. *Sample Risk Probability Impact Matrix*

Risk	Probability	Impact	Risk Priority
Availability of digital resources	0.7	0.25	High
Lack of proper documentation of existing systems	0.4	0.02	Low
Delay in infrastructure setup	0.5	0.1	Medium

The impact value determines the overall impact on project cost, quality, and schedule. A project manager can define categories for these impact values. (This involves calculating the impact cost and using the impact cost to categorize the impact category, such as an impact value < 0.1 or an impact cost that's less than 5000 USD indicates a low impact. An impact value between 0.1 and 0.2 and an impact cost between 5000 and 10000 USD indicates a medium impact and an impact value > 0.2 or a cost that's more than 10000 USD indicates a high impact.)

The probability and impact values are used to determine the overall risk. For instance, the risk of "availability of digital resources" has a high probability and a high impact value and hence it has a high priority. The risk item "Lack of Proper Documentation of Existing Systems" has a low probability value and a low impact and hence is given a low priority. High priority risks are further analyzed for their impact and response planning.

The digital project manager can use the following variations of the probability-impact matrix:

- The project manager can assign three categories of probability values: optimistic probability, pessimistic probability, and most likely probability. This technique is referred to as a three-point quantification.

- The project manager can define the impact factors separately for cost, schedule, quality, and other key project attributes.

These variants can be used to better analyze risk impact, perform cost-impact analyses, and gain insights into high-priority risks. The project manager can do a deep dive analysis of all high-priority risks.

Various tools and techniques such as simulation and risk modeling (using the historical risk data and creating a mathematical model of the risk and then attaching a probability and impact), monetary impact analysis (identifying various risk impact scenarios and their associated cost), and decision tree analysis (creating a tree of risk-related decisions and their associated impact cost) can be used for risk quantification.

Risk Mitigation

The project manager has to come up with risk response and risk mitigation plans for all the high priority risks and for the risks that have a high impact. The project manager has to discuss with business and technical stakeholders their risk tolerance for each of these risks. Some of the risks can be avoided through proven governance processes and best practices; for instance, the Incomplete Requirements risk can be avoided with a robust requirements gathering process. Some risks can be accepted if they have a low priority and if the business users are willing to accept that risk.

A few risks can be transferred to other groups, which then own and track those risks. For all the remaining risks, the project manager has to come up with detailed mitigation plans.

The ownership and timelines are assigned to each risk owned by the team. The project manager has to define a contingency plan needed to mitigate the risk; for instance, a buffer resource should be maintained throughout the project to absorb any unavoidable scope creep.

Risk Tracking and Monitoring

The project manager has to track all the identified risks continuously throughout the project phases. The mitigation plan has to be implemented during the appropriate project stages. The project manager has to communicate the risk updates, as per the defined communication plan, to all the stakeholders. The project manager has to conduct regular risk audits and proactively adopt preventive measures. Sometimes the risk mitigation plan has side-effects leading to secondary risks, which also need to be tackled.

The Continuous Execution Model

The continuous execution model provides frequent and iterative releases through continuous builds, testing, integration, and deployment. Continuous delivery is a key tenet of the Agile-based execution model. Continuous delivery not only reduces the time to market through iterative deliverables, it also enhances the quality and stability of the overall delivery. The continuous execution model helps project managers make faster, iterative releases that incrementally add the business capabilities and values to the system. The continuous execution model helps project managers incorporate the feedback and change requests more quickly in the project. The continuous execution model employs tools, automation, and productivity improvement processes to achieve these goals.

Key Elements of the Continuous Execution Model

The main process elements of the continuous execution model are depicted in Figure 5-4.

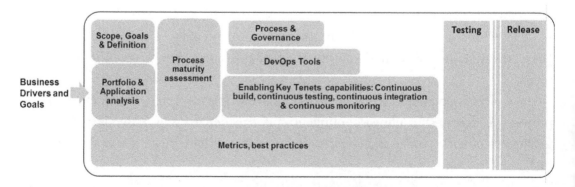

Figure 5-4. *Major elements of the continuous execution model*

In the initial stages, the project manager has to understand the scope and goals of the execution model. The project manager has to translate the business vision elements into the scope, goals, and metrics that are applicable for execution. During this translation process, we create comprehensive requirement artifacts such as use case documents, user stories, and process flow diagrams to capture the requirements. For instance, if the business wants to be hyper-responsive to changes, the project manager can translate this desire into goals such as frequent releases, quicker time to market, and iterative and incremental addition of capabilities.

As part of the Portfolio and Application Analysis stage, the project manager has to analyze the existing gaps in current capabilities. The project manager can identify the applications (known as "early adopters") that can be taken up for continuous execution model during the initial phases. The project manager has to assess existing processes and determine their maturity level. The common gaps in release management and execution processes are too much manual effort in release management, lack of automation, lack of centralized knowledge repository, traditional release management processes, absence of metrics, and absence of standards and well-defined processes.

The project manager has to define the processes for the continuous execution model. The processes include Agile delivery, continuous delivery, release management, continuous integration, and so on. The project manager also has to identify all the DevOps tools that are needed to implement the continuous execution model. The tools are used to automate the processes and to introduce productivity improvements. The project manager has to enable the key capabilities related to continuous build, continuous integration, continuous testing, and continuous monitoring to implement the continuous execution model. As this element is the core feature of the model, it's discussed in detail in the next section. Throughout the project execution, the project manager has to track the improvements and quantify them against the baselined goals and metrics. The changed process is thoroughly tested before the final release is made. The common metrics used to measure success of the continuous execution model are listed in Table 5-5.

Table 5-5. *Sample Metrics in the Continuous Execution Model*

Category	Metric	Formula	Proposed Usage
Build	Build failures	Number of failed builds/ total number of builds per day	To understand the impact of the model on build quality and success rate
	Total build time	Average total time for the build	To understand the improvement in build times due to automation
Release Frequency	Deployments/day	Total number of deployments/ number of days	To understand the improvement in deploying a feature
	Releases/week	Total number of releases/ week (by environments)	To understand the improvement in agility
Agility	Change lead time	Total time needed to release a change request in production since the change request was made	To know the improvement in lead time to release a change request and to understand improvement in responsiveness
Quality	Code coverage	Percent of code covered through the test cases	To know the testing effectiveness
	Release efficiency/ repeatability	Percent of successful releases over a period of time	To understand improvement in release quality
	Production defect matrix	Average percent of defects released into production	To understand improvement in quality processes
Performance	Availability	Percent availability of service or system	To understand the improvement in availability SLA and release stability
	Outage	Outage per day/week/ month	To understand the improvement in availability SLA and release stability
Reliability	Mean time to recover	Time required to recover from outages	To understand improvement in mean time to recover
Efficiency	Cost or effort per release	Initial effort/cost per release	To understand the improvement in operational costs

Key Capabilities of the Continuous Execution Model

The key capabilities of the continuous execution model are depicted in Figure 5-5.

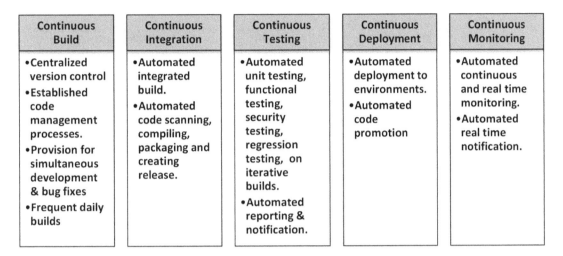

Figure 5-5. *Key capabilities of the continuous execution model*

The continuous execution model needs to adopt the continuous concept for all stages of the release, including the build stage, testing stage, deployment stage, and monitoring stage. Requirements are also elaborated in an iterative way to elucidate the requirement details.

Continuous Builds

To enable continuous builds, the project team has to use a centralized version control system. All developers should check in the code to this centralized code repository. The code management process should allow for simultaneous development, continuous development, and defect fixes. Most of the modern source control systems such as SVN (Apache Subversion) and Git support features such as locking, checkin, checkout, versioning, and tagging to enable continuous builds.

Continuous Integration

In continuous integration, the code from the centralized source control system is used to create continuous builds. During the build process, you can also analyze the code quality (through static code analysis tools) and compile and package code artifacts for testing.

Continuous integration increases collaboration among various teams. A DevOps tool like Jenkins can be used to implement continuous integration.

Continuous Testing

When the code package is ready, a continuous integration (CI) tool can automatically execute the unit test cases, functional test cases, security test cases, performance test cases, and regression test cases to identify defects with the build. The test reports can be sent to the development team for further action. The testing team has to ensure that the test suite and functional test cases are aligned with the latest requirements.

Continuous Deployment

Continuous deployment involves the deployment of tested code artifacts to various environments. This includes remotely copying files or using the admin interfaces for remote deployment. Automated continuous deployment enables faster deployment and reduces the overall risk with the delivery.

Continuous Monitoring

Continuous monitoring involves real-time monitoring of system resources, system health check metrics, and the application attributes (such as performance, availability, and scalability) at runtime. The monitoring infrastructure allows administrators to configure the triggers and threshold values for the metrics. They indicate whether the actual values exceed the configured threshold values.

Benefits of the Continuous Execution Model

The key benefits of the continuous execution model are as follows:

- *Increased responsiveness*: Organizations can absorb change requests and feedback more efficiently and increase their competitive advantage. Organizations can incrementally add capabilities and value to the system.

- *Faster time to market*: The features, bug fixes, capabilities, and change requests can be deployed to production quickly due to increased automation.

- *Enhanced release quality*: The release quality is better due to automated testing and automated code analysis at various levels (unit testing, functional testing, integration testing, and regression testing).

- *Efficient risk management*: Due to increased and iterative testing, the delivery risk at production time is greatly reduced.

- *Improved efficiency and productivity*: Due to improved release management processes and automation, manual effort will be greatly reduced, leading to more consistent builds.

Tools Used in Digital Project Management

This section introduces a few tools that can be effectively used for digital project management. These tools complement the regular project management tools, such as Microsoft Project. Table 5-6 lists the main tools used in various digital project management functions.

Table 5-6. *Sample Tools Used in Digital Project Management Functions*

Project Management Function	Tool
Project planning	Microsoft Project
Collaboration	Microsoft SharePoint, portals
Test tools	JUnit, SOAPUI, Cucumber, JMeter, LoadUI, Selenium, Fortify, KARMA, TestNG, AppScan
DevOps and continuous integration (CI)	Jenkins, Docker, Puppet, Chef, Ansible, Bamboo
Reporting	Microsoft Excel, Microsoft PowerPoint
Risk management	Project management dashboard, WBS
Agile project management	Jira, Agilo, Ice Scrum, scrumy.com

(*continued*)

Table 5-6. (*continued*)

Project Management Function	Tool
Defect tracking/issue management	Jira, BugZilla
Build tools	Jenkins, ANT, Maven, Gradle, Grunt
Test management	Tarantula, Jataka Testcube, Jira
Requirements management	Requirement traceability matrix, Jira, CASE tools, IBM Rational DOORS, etc.
Status tracking	Project management dashboard
Deployment and release management tools	Jenkins, Buildbot, Travis
Source control tools	Git, Subversion, CVS, Perforce, Bitbucket
Source code quality control tools	SonarQube, PMD, Checkstyle, FindBugs, JSHint, Fortify, Crucible, EMMA, Cobertura, JProbe, JaCoCo, Clover
Monitoring	Nagios, Splunk, App dynamics, logstash

Issue Management Tools

Issue management tools such as Jira are essentially defect-tracking tools that provide intuitive dashboards and other project management features. Project managers can create sprint plans, prioritize activities, distribute the tasks, and monitor the project status.

DevOps and Continuous Integration Tools

Jenkins is mainly a continuous integration tool. However, Jenkins can also be used for effective project management. Jenkins CI can be used to automate many of the project activities, such as deployment, code review, testing, code review, and so on. The dashboard view of Jenkins CI can be used to get a holistic view of the project's overall health. Project managers can track the project's KPIs, such as code coverage, defect age, average release time, and so on, using the CI tools.

Project Planning Tools

Project planning tools are mainly used for resource allocation, task management, milestone tracking, and so on. Project planning tools enable finer control over dependency tracking. Other functionalities of the project planning tools are project scheduling and tracking, Gantt chart views for dependency tracking, critical path tracking, and progress monitoring. Microsoft Project is one of the most popular tools in this category.

Collaboration Tools

Project collaboration tools such as Microsoft SharePoint are used to store the project documents with controlled access. The collaboration tools also provide features such as calendars, document management, knowledge management, cross-team collaboration, reporting, auditing, fine-grained folder/document level permissions, and artifact checkin/checkout/locking.

Agile Project Management Tools

Most of the modern digital applications use Agile project delivery to become responsive to change and to deliver the solution faster to market. Agile project management tools such as Jira and Scrumy help the project managers to create scrums, plan and assign user stories, and create tasks for user stories. These Agile project management tools also provide dashboards for efficient tracking of Agile projects.

Test Management Tools

Test management tools provide features such as test case creation, test suite creation, test case execution, mapping test cases to requirements, test dashboards, test automation, test reporting, and test data management. Test management tools are used to increase test coverage and for efficient management of the test process.

The Project Management Dashboard

The project management dashboard provides a holistic snapshot of the digital project at any given point. The project manager can also use the dashboard report for structured communication with all stakeholders. A sample project dashboard is depicted in Figure 5-6.

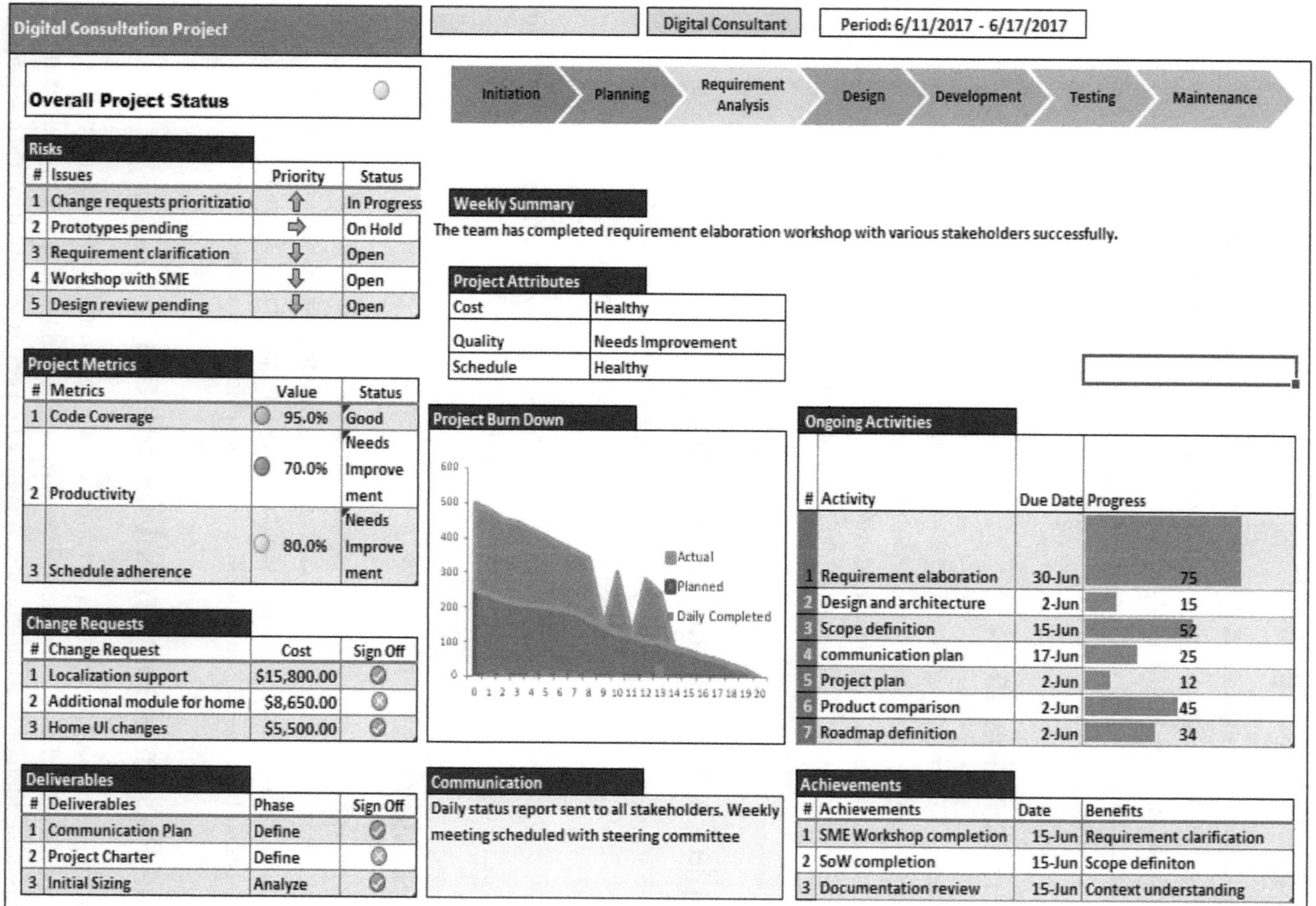

Figure 5-6. Sample project management dashboard

As depicted in Figure 5-6, a typical project dashboard provides insights about ongoing activities, top risks, key metrics, project burn rate, milestone status, and more. At the top of the dashboard are the project phases, with the current phase highlighted in yellow. The dashboard also reminds the project manager about upcoming deliverables, slipped targets, and more, so that the project manager can take corrective actions. The main elements of the project management dashboard as depicted in Figure 5-6 are as follows:

- *Risk*: Risk details along with its priority and status. This helps the project manager manage the risk effectively. You can also capture other details such as impact, probability, etc.

- *Metrics*: All key project metrics are tracked on the dashboard. In Figure 5-6, the metrics related to code coverage, productivity, and schedule adherence are tracked. Based on project needs, you can also track other key project metrics such as defect age, effort variance, reopen percentage, performance times, etc.

- *Activities*: Provides a list of all activities along with their due dates and current completion percentage. The project manager gets the overall status of all ongoing activities and can see any deviation from scheduled timelines.

- *Deliverables*: All committed deliverables for the time period are listed along with their review and sign-off status.

- *Milestones*: The planned and upcoming milestones are depicted visually. The project manager can track the actual date of milestone completion against the planned date.

- *Change requests*: Details of change requests (CR) such as date, priority, cost impact, and approval status, are tracked.

- *Project burndown*: The project manager can track the actual effort burndown rate against the planned burndown rate.

- *Achievements*: The project manager can document all key achievements and the realized benefits for the time period.

- *Project attributes*: The project manager can track the key project attributes such as cost, quality, and schedule on the dashboard.

Based on the project's specific needs, you can include other topics in the project dashboard such as code quality reports, build reports, stakeholder communication status, and dependency status.

Templates Used in Digital Project Management

This section looks at some of the common templates that digital project managers can use for various project management activities.

Resource Induction Template

To induct new human resources into a project, the project manager has to define an induction process. Induction process typically consist of completing several on-boarding formalities, such as interviews, training, access assignments, NDA signing, etc. Table 5-7 provides a sample template to capture all the induction-related activities. The induction activities are categorized and the owners are listed.

Table 5-7. *Sample Induction Template*

S.No.	Category	Induction Topic	Owner	Planned Date	Start Time	End Time
1	Business domain	Overview of business domain	Business SME			
		Business drivers and metrics	Business SME			
2	Process	Governance and processes	Project manager			
		Source control system overview	Project manager			
		Security and regulations related information	Project manager			
		Security audit awareness	Project manager			
		Resource on-boarding process (SLA/NDA agreements, background checks, interviews)	Project manager			
3	Training	Skill related training	Project manager			
		Behavioral related trainings (if any)	Project manager			
4	Project related	Overview of modules	Project manager			
		Set up of needed software and infrastructure	Project manager			
		Expectations and responsibility	Project manager			

(*continued*)

Table 5-7. (*continued*)

S.No.	Category	Induction Topic	Owner	Planned Date	Start Time	End Time
5	Technology related	Project specific guidelines, checklists	Technical SME			
		Project related best practices	Technical SME			
		Technical training	Technical SME			
		Overview of technical frameworks and accelerators needed	Technical SME			
		Overview of technology tools, plugins	Technical SME			
		Overview of all software used in the project	Technical SME			
6	Access	Project area	Project manager			
		source control	Project manager			
		Network	Project manager			
		Account setup	Project manager			
		Collaboration area	Project manager			
		Application access	Project manager			

The induction template is mainly used for inducting and orienting the newly on-boarded human resources to the project. The induction template can be customized based on project needs. Some projects need language training, mandatory certifications, medical checkups, and such. They can be added to these activities in the appropriate category. The digital project manager can create an induction kit that packages the key resources for easier and faster on-boarding of resources, using a predefined set of on-boarding processes.

RACI Template for Project Governance

RACI (Responsible, Accountable, Consulted, Informed) is a structured way of defining roles and responsibilities for various project activities. Project managers use the RACI matrix to communicate the expectations and deliverables of various team members. A variation or a part of the RACI matrix is used in communication. The parameters for RACI are defined here:

- *Responsible*: A team member who works on a particular project activity with individual contributions is said to be "responsible" for that project activity. A developer is responsible for a web service used in a project module.

- *Accountable*: A team member who takes the ownership of the project activity is said to be accountable. For instance, a module lead is accountable to the design of the entire module.

- *Consulted*: A team member who is consulted on a project activity is added to this category. Domain experts or SMEs are often consulted to get their expert opinions or to validate the design decision or review an artifact.

- *Informed*: People who should be kept informed about progress are added to this category. This is typically program managers and business stakeholders.

Table 5-8. *Sample RACI Template*

Project Phase	Action	Responsible	Accountable	Consulted	Informed
Initiation	Business requirements elaboration	Business analysts	Business analysts	Infrastructure SME, security SME, functional domain expert	Project manager, Business stakeholder
Initiation	test case preparation	QA team	QA lead	Development lead, architect, project manager,	Project manager, business stakeholder
Development	build and application development	Development team	Development lead	technical architect, test lead	Project manager, business stakeholder
Development	unit testing	Development team	Development lead	Technical architect, test lead	Project manager, business stakeholder
Development	code porting from dev to QA environment	Release team	Release manager	Technical architect, Test lead	Technical architect, Test lead
Testing	System testing	QA team	QA lead	Development lead, architect, project manager	Project manager, business stakeholder
Testing	User acceptance testing	Business users	Business SME	Development lead, architect, project manager	Development lead, architect, project manager

Requirements Elaboration-Related Templates

The requirements elaboration exercise documents the business requirements in detail. The requirements gathering template should document all the key flows, business rules, exceptions, constraints, pre-conditions, post-conditions, and so on. The following sections define the templates related to user stories (used for agile model) and use case templates (used for use case based requirement gathering).

User Story Template

User stories are mainly used in Agile projects. A user story represents a user-centric logical unit of work in Agile delivery. User stories capture the end user requirements and document the goals, value delivered, and objectives of the user story. The user stories should be testable and should provide estimates based on user stories. A long-running (usually more than a week) user story is called an epic or a theme. It captures the sample user story template, as listed in Table 5-9. The story description provides the key value delivered by the story and the acceptance criteria describes the main conditions for acceptance of the user story. The "Definition of Done" defines the quality criteria and standards that will be used to validate the user story.

Table 5-9. *Sample User Story Template*

User Story	Details
Story description	Web users should be able to search the product based on product name and model number and select the product they want.
Acceptance criteria	Users should get a product search field. Users should be able to enter a product name with a maximum length of 200 characters. Once the users click the Search button, the system should return the matching products. If there are more than 10 products matching the criteria, the results should be shown in a paginated view. The Search function should provide an appropriate error message if no results are found.
Definition of done	The UI should match the search UI design. All test cases related to search product should pass. The search should execute within five seconds. The search should execute with maximum use traffic of 100 concurrent users.

Use Case Template

Many of the business analysts leverage use cases to capture requirements. The use case documents the actors (users of the flow), flow steps, pre-conditions (the conditions that need to be satisfied before the use case begins), post-conditions (result of the use case execution), and exception flow. A sample template for the Search Products use case is shown in Table 5-10.

Table 5-10. *Sample Use Case Template for Search Products use case*

ID: UC_1		Name: Search Products	
Priority:		High	
Source:		Requirements document	
Goal:		Search for products matching entered search criteria	
Primary Actors:		Web user, admin	
Pre-Conditions:		Actor is logged in to the system	
Post Condition:		Actor can view the list of products based on the search criteria	
Basic Flow			
Step	**Actor Action**	**Step**	**System Response**
1	Use case begins when the actor clicks on Search	2	System displays the search screen
3	Actor enters the search criteria		
4	Actor clicks Search	5	Use case ends when the system displays the search results
Exception Flow (EC1): No Search Results returned			
Step	**Actor Action**	**Step**	**System Response**
		5a	The system displays a message "No products match your search criteria. Please change your search criteria and try again."
5b	Actor rejoins the basic course at Step 3		

Summary

This chapter covered the models, tools, and templates used in digital project management:

- Earned value management helps digital project managers effectively monitor and forecast a project's performance.

- The earned value technique helps project managers forecast, monitor, and measure the project's progression and effort/cost variance, and serves as an early warning mechanism.

- The main steps in earned value management are defining the work package, assigning value for work items, defining calculation rules, and executing the project.

- The digital maturity model defines various phases in the digital transformation journey and each phase has a defined set of features, challenges, and digital elements.

- The various stages of the digital maturity model are basic, consolidated platform, personalized platform, omni-channel platform, and engagement platform.

- A quantitative risk management plan helps project managers make the informed decisions in uncertain situations and enhances delivery predictability.

- Quantitative risk management process includes risk identification, risk quantification, risk mitigation, and risk tracking.

- The continuous execution model provides frequent and iterative releases through continuous builds, testing, integration, and deployment.

- The key capabilities of the continuous execution model are continuous build, continuous integration, continuous testing, continuous deployment, and continuous monitoring.

- The project management dashboard provides a holistic snapshot of the digital project at any given point.

- The project management dashboard provides various details related to risk, metrics, activities, deliverables, change requests, project burndown, and achievements.

CHAPTER 6

Digital Project Execution

The success of project execution decides the success of the overall project. Project execution involves its own set of challenges, such as selection of the right execution model, monitoring the key project metrics, proactively looking for anti-patterns, and more.

We start this chapter by briefly looking at various phases of a project and then we will look at key execution models used during software development. We briefly discuss various execution models such as the waterfall model, the v-model, and the prototype model. As iterative and Agile models are commonly used in digital projects, the chapter covers them in greater detail.

This chapter covers various concepts related to project execution, including execution models and best practices. Project managers, account managers, and program managers will find this chapter useful.

High-Level Phases of Digital Project Execution

This section briefly discusses the four phases of a software project. End to end project execution involves four key phases—planning, design and architecture, implementation/build, and maintenance—as depicted in Figure 6-1.

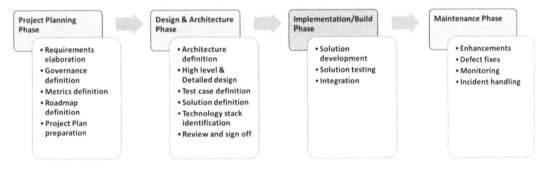

Figure 6-1. *Four key phases of software projects*

© Shailesh Kumar Shivakumar 2018
S. K. Shivakumar, *Complete Guide to Digital Project Management*,
https://doi.org/10.1007/978-1-4842-3417-4_6

During the project planning phase, the long-term vision and strategy of the overall program is used to define the main scope. Requirements are detailed and documented in the form of use cases or user stories. The key capabilities of the digital solution across various iterations are identified through a detailed project plan. The overall project governance structure and related processes (such as release management, deployment, and quality processes) are defined. The project performance metrics (related to schedule, cost, and effort) are defined. Any project specific requirements such as user experience, migration, integration, and security are also defined.

In the next phase, the application architecture and design activities are developed. The architecture document presents various views, such as solution architecture, security architecture, integration architecture, and data architecture. During this phase, the core technology components and technology stack are identified. The solution design principles are also defined during this phase. Test scripts are developed during this phase as well.

In the next phase, the application is developed iteratively and tested. All necessary integrations are done with the application. The developed application undergoes various levels of testing, such as unit testing, functional testing, regression testing, etc.

Once the application goes live, it enters the maintenance phase. The key activities during this phase are incident handling, enhancements, release management, system upgrades, patching, defect fixing, support, and application monitoring.

The governance process is followed during all phases and any risks are identified in all phases.

The digital project manager has to define the roadmap based on the key capabilities needed for the organization. A sample list of a future state enterprise vision that goes into the roadmap exercise is shown in Table 6-1.

Table 6-1. *Sample Future State in a Roadmap Exercise*

Category	Current State	Future State
User experience	Cluttered, inconsistent	Immersive, responsive, lightweight, self-service
Content management	Manual, no workflow	Automated, workflow-driven
Integration	Passive	Active, services based
Time to market	6-8 months	6-8 weeks
Total cost of ownership	High	Low

The next section looks at various execution models.

Traditional Project Execution Models

We discuss the traditional software development models, including the waterfall and v-models, in this section. In subsequent sections, we elaborate on the modern execution models, such as the prototype, iterative, and Agile models.

Overview

This section provides salient features of various software execution models. It also explains the strengths and weakness of each model. As the iterative and Agile models are the most common in digital projects, we discuss them in-depth in later sections.

The Waterfall Model

In the waterfall model, the software project phases are executed sequentially. Each sequential step requires the previous step to be completed. All activities are well defined and structured as they need to be properly scheduled. The main phases of the waterfall model are requirements, design, development, testing, deployment, and maintenance.

The waterfall model is rigid in the sense that each step depends strictly on the previous step and has less tolerance for requirements changes and enhancements during execution. As you cannot go back to previous step, it is difficult to accommodate changes. This model can only be used when the complete project requirements are defined at the beginning of the project and hence it is rarely used with modern digital projects.

The risk is generally high with this model, as the working software is delivered in the final stages of the project and changes are difficult to accommodate. Customers and end users can only see the solution once it is fully developed and feedback and change requests are not easy to accommodate. Testing is done in the final stages, which further increases the risk. When major defects or complex issues such as performance problems are discovered during the final stages of the project, it becomes very difficult to address those, leading to slippage in schedules and timelines.

The V- Model

In the V-model, the phases move upward after the coding phase. Each phase (such as requirements and design) has a corresponding testing phase; requirements analysis is accompanied by acceptance testing, system design is accompanied by system testing, and development is accompanied by unit testing. The main stages are requirements, high-level design, detailed design, coding, unit testing, integration testing, and acceptance testing.

The model can be used for small projects with clearly defined requirements. The model provides better testing support. The V-model can be used with small to medium sized projects with well-defined requirements that need thorough testing at every stage.

The Prototype Model

In this model, a working prototype is developed incrementally. Every prototype is a visual depiction of the currently known requirements and communicates the user experience, navigation, and information architecture to the end user. End users can provide feedback about the prototype and the feedback will be incorporated into the subsequent iteration. When the final prototype is delivered and frozen, the requirements are said to be complete.

The prototype model is generally used with Internet-facing web applications to get feedback from end users that will create a more effective system. The risk of expectation mismatch is greatly reduced due to iterative prototype development and constant interaction. Any gaps and deviations are detected early, thereby further reducing the delivery risk.

Based on the nature of the project, the digital project manager has to choose the most appropriate execution model. Table 6-2 provides a mapping of project categories and the most appropriate execution models.

Table 6-2. *Execution Models Based on Project Types*

Project Type	Project Characteristics	Most suitable Execution Models	Applicable Pricing Models and Estimation Models
Established/ Mature	Well-defined functional specifications, proven technologies, availability of skill set in the market, minimal change in requirements, industrialized processes and tools	Waterfall	Linear pricing model (wherein the cost is directly dependent on the quantity of work such as unit of work) Function point/use case based/complexity based estimation
Mainstream	High-level requirements known, mature technology stack, availability of technology packages	Iterative (incremental releases), Waterfall	Linear pricing model Function point/use case based/complexity based estimation
Digital Transformation Projects	Legacy modernization, Experience re-design, technology revamp, service enablement, niche technologies, frequently changing requirements, frequent releases, user-centered approach	Iterative, Agile (uses time boxed sprints explained in a subsequent section)	Non-linear pricing model (such as outcome or transaction based model) Function point based/user story based estimation model
Experimental	Unproven/emerging technologies, exploratory, research nature, frequently changing requirements, need for collaboration	Agile	Non-linear pricing model (such as outcome or transaction based model) User story based/story point estimation model

The next sections discuss the iterative and Agile execution models in detail.

The Iterative Execution Model

The iterative model incrementally develops the capabilities through time-sliced iteration. Each iteration targets a specific set of modules and functionality. Iterations are mainly defined for requirements, design, implementation, testing, and deployment. The model enables early development of a working module. Iterative models can be used to deliver early value to the client.

One version of software module is developed in each iteration and functionality is incrementally added to the module in each iteration. The model minimizes error due to early detection of gaps in the software module and due to iterative testing. Iterative delivery is flexible in absorbing just in-time requirements and enhancement requests.

Key Features of the Iterative Model

Here are the key features of the iterative execution model:

- The project is split into smaller work chunks called iterations that deliver the project goals incrementally.

- Suitable to high-risk projects with lots of uncertainty.

- Initial iterations can focus on business-critical or high-risk items.

- Reduced risk due to early and iterative testing and integration.

- End user feedback and change requests can be accommodated in subsequent iterations.

Details of the Iterative Model

Once the project vision is finalized, the project manager identifies the capabilities needed by the system. All business requirements and capabilities are prioritized based on business value. The project manager plans various iterations to cover all the project requirements and solutions. Each iteration consists of elaborating on the requirements to detail the iteration-specific needs, including design, build, integration, testing, and deployment requirements. Each iteration undergoes production deployment and user acceptance testing (UAT) before production go-live. The detailed steps of an typical iterative delivery are depicted in Figure 6-2.

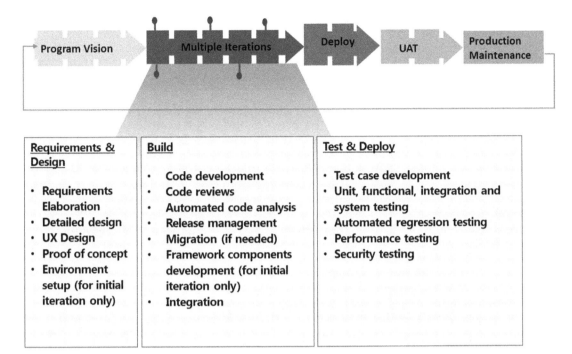

Figure 6-2. *Sample iterative delivery*

The project vision and high-level requirements are identified before the beginning of the first iteration. Based on the criticality and the complexity of the requirements, the iterations can be planned. For instance, if the project needs a complex environment, the project manager can plan the initial iteration of 3-4 weeks to set up the infrastructure and size it before other iterations.

Best Practices of the Iterative Model

Here are the key best practices of the iterative execution model:

- The project manager has to create a logical grouping of requirements that can become an iteration.

- The priority of each iteration has to be reviewed with business to get their buy-in.

- Initial iterations should develop the framework and common modules so that they can be reused in subsequent iterations.

The Agile Execution Model

The Agile model suits today's business scenarios that need to be responsive to changes and rapidly and continuously develop capabilities. Agile provides business value in incremental and time-boxed iterative deliverables. The user story forms the unit of requirement in the Agile model. In the Agile model, delivery is done in time-boxed sprints, with each sprint consisting of requirements, development, testing, and delivery of user stories defined for the sprint. In a few Agile projects, requirements are defined before the start of the sprint. Organizations are increasingly using the Agile execution model for faster time to market, increased productivity and quality, and better success rates.

Scrum is a popular Agile framework that we discuss in this section. Other Agile frameworks are extreme programming (XP and Feature Driven Development—FDD), wherein the unit of requirement is a feature, Agile Unified Process (AUP) is an incremental and iterative development framework. XP uses test driven development (TDD) and pairs programming with other key Agile features.

The Agile methodology is most appropriate if the project's requirements meets the following criteria:

- Requirements are not well understood or keep evolving or undergoing minor changes during the course of project execution.

- Requirements elaboration needs close coordination with various stakeholders and needs frequent prototype-based validation with stakeholders.

- If the project manager foresees high risk due to niche or unproven technologies or due to complex integrations.

- If the solution has to be delivered quickly to the market or if the solution has to evolve by absorbing the end user feedback.

One of the variants of Agile is "distributed Agile," wherein the teams are distributed across various locations.

Main Business Drivers for Agile Adoption

Agile is one of the most popular execution models used with the modern digital projects. Here are the main business motivations to adopt the Agile model:

- *Quick response to market dynamics*: Enterprises want to adapt to changing customer demands and market dynamics through reduced time-to-market and early/iterative realization of business value. Agile delivery enables quicker time to market and iterative delivery.

- *Business agility*: Enterprises need to quickly respond to changes from end users and stakeholders.

- *Cost optimization*: Enterprises like to realize the business value early and increase productivity with optimum cost. Iterative delivery and automated processes in Agile provide optimal program cost.

- *Risk reduction*: Usage of niche and evolving technology stack carries high risk and hence enterprises want to reduce the risk through the fail-fast and fail-cheap philosophy and iterative deliveries.

- *Delivery quality*: High quality and speed drives customer satisfaction. Hence, organizations need continuous quality improvement measures in the execution model.

Key Features of the Agile Model

Here are the key features of the Agile execution model:

- *Cross-functional and autonomous team structure*: Smaller self-directed teams with greater autonomy and greater decision-making authority. The autonomy enables teams to accept risks/changes and provides quicker decision making capabilities. The team consists of team members with all the skill sets needed for the project.

- *Customer-focused approach*: All aspects of the project keep the customer at the center of their focus. Customer inputs are given priority in requirement prioritization, user experience design, iteration planning, testing, change requests, and feedback analysis.

- *Agility*: Enables business agility to respond quickly to change and market dynamics.

- *Preference for working prototypes over documentation*: Agile projects use prototypes (small portion of working software) that are incrementally enhanced based on user feedback.

- *Short and iterative delivery*: Enables quicker time to market with early validation, leading to reduced risk.

- *Great collaboration*: Continuous collaboration among all the team members and close collaboration with end users and customers.

- *Responsive to change*: By incorporating changes and feedback into iterative releases, changes can be introduced at any stage of the iterative delivery.

- *Continuous integration*: Enables continuous automated builds, deployment, and improvement with every iteration.

- *High focus on automation*: Various automation measures are adopted for testing and release management activities.

- *Adoption of Agile culture*: Accept changes and risks, fail fast, and take the sprint ownership.

Details of the Scrum Model

The Agile execution model consists of sprints that usually span from 2-6 weeks. Each sprint has a well-defined backlog of work items and well-defined acceptance criteria. The Agile development methodology is depicted in Figure 6-3.

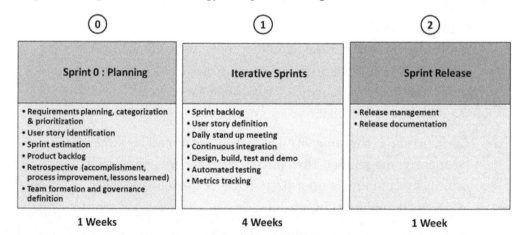

Figure 6-3. *Sample Agile model*

During sprint 0, the requirements are categorized and prioritized. The product backlog is planned based on the requirements. The product backlog consists of user stories and nonfunctional (such as security, performance, availability, scalability, etc.) requirements for the entire project. During this phase, the team reflects on previous iterations and formulates a plan to make the current iteration more effective; this is carried out as part of a "retrospective".

Iterative sprints are planned for 3-4 weeks and this phase consists of defining the user story. It includes designing, building, testing, and demoing the user stories. For instance, in Figure 6-3, you can execute a couple of sprints, each lasting two weeks. Prioritized user stories are selected from the product backlog and used as a sprint backlog applicable for the current sprint. User stories or story cards are units of requirements and units of scope in the Agile methodology that can be easily estimated and prioritized. A user story elaborates the requirements and flows from the end user standpoint. Each user story has a business owner, which is prioritized based on business value. All aspects of the user story design—such as user experience design, services design, and database design—are covered and clarified as part of the design activity. Sprint goals are defined and the team commits to deliver the planned sprint backlog. During development, developers closely collaborate with SMEs, architects, and testers to ensure that the user story is fully implemented. Daily standup meetings are used to discuss status, day-wise activities, dependencies, and risks. The system is iteratively built through these sprints. The continuous integration (CI) methodology is followed for continuously building, testing, and deploying the deliverables. Finally, the user story is tested based on the defined acceptance criteria.

During the Sprint release stage, the release steps are documented.

A sample user story related to user management for an admin user is given here:

User Story:

As an admin, I want to search for users so that I can find the exact user based on user attributes.

As an admin, I want to create new users and assign permissions so that I can set up the users.

As an admin, I want to update access permissions for the users so that I can control what users can do.

As an admin, I want to delete users so that I can remove unwanted users.

Acceptance Criteria:

User search box accepts username, user ID, and role.

Create User screen provides a list of user attributes such as username, e-mail, phone, role, and address and allows the admin to create the user.

Create/Update Permissions screen allows admin to map users to defined roles.

Delete User screen allows the admin to delete a user based on a user ID. The screen validates the admin permissions of the logged-in user.

Requirements:

12, 13, 14, 15

Note: Acceptance criteria is optional in a user story.

Table 6-3 provides details of various activities in sprint 0 and a regular sprint. All the one-time activities (such as team formation and metrics definition) are done as part of sprint 0. Non-functional requirements can be taken up in Sprint 0 or a separate user story can be defined for specifying non-functional requirements such as security, scalability, and availability with clearly defined acceptance criteria.

Table 6-3. *Sprint Activities*

Sprint	Activities
Sprint 0/Planning	• Definition of non-functional requirements related to security, performance, availability, etc.
	• Identification of tools for CI, accessibility, automated testing, and environment setup.
	• Metrics and KPI definition. Key metrics are percent of testing automation, response time, team velocity (story points delivered per person per sprint), percent of build automation, code coverage percentage
	• Definition of acceptance criteria
	• Formation of sprint teams
	• Setup of governance processes
Regular Sprint	Development Activities
	• Backlog planning done by business owner
	• Implementation of user stories based on sprint features
	Testing Activities
	• Development of test cases for user stories
	• Test data creation for functional and integration testing
	• Functional and integration testing
	• Performance testing for interfaces
	• Regression testing
	• Optional accessibility testing and compatibility testing

The roles and responsibilities of various team members of a sprint model are depicted in Table 6-4.

Table 6-4. *Roles and Responsibilities of a Sprint Delivery*

Role	Responsibility
Scrum Lead/Scrum Master	• Lead daily standup calls
	• Manage scrum meetings
	• Project progress monitoring
	• Quality assurance activities
Scrum Team Members (Development)	• Code, unit testing, and functional testing
	• Unit test case development
	• Collaborative development
Scrum Team Members (Validation)	• Test scenarios in the user story for each sprint
	• Regression testing
Project Manager/Product Owner	• Change management
	• Preparation and prioritization of product backlog
	• Planning and progress tracking
	• Schedule, cost, and effort management
	• Project support and coordination with scrum lead
	• Progress monitoring and risk management
Scrum Team Members (DevOps)	• Release management and deployment
	• Continuous integration setup

Typical activities of a five-week sprint are listed in Figure 6-4.

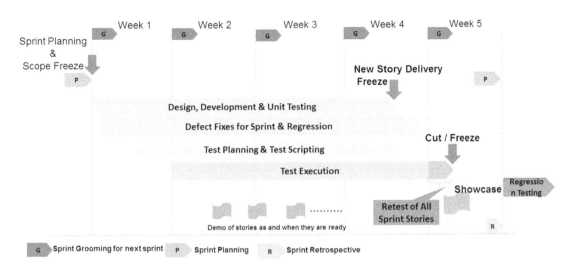

Figure 6-4. *Sample sprint activities*

Sprints can also be used during build phases. In this variation, each sprint is released to QA for early validation. A typical sprint-based build is depicted in Figure 6-5.

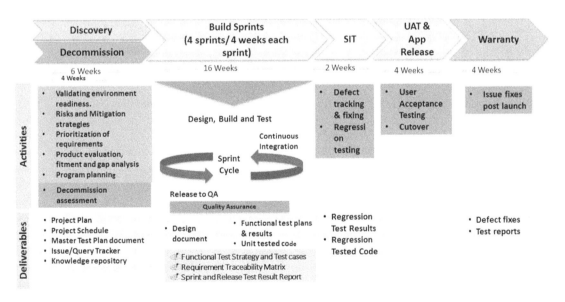

Figure 6-5. *Sprint based build*

As depicted in Figure 6-5, the phases are similar to the sequential waterfall model (except for the build phase). The build is planned in four sprints of four weeks each. Each sprint has its own design, build, and test activities with continuous integration. This model is used to minimize the risk caused by long development cycles.

A sprint is said to be "done" when it meets the following acceptance criteria:

- The deliverable meets all specified business and technical requirements.

- The deliverable is successfully tested by all applicable test cases (unit test cases, functional test cases, UI test cases, etc.).

- The product owner approves the product.

- The deliverable meets all specified non-functional quality criteria such as performance, scalability, modularity, extensibility, usability, and such.

- All key feedback comments from the user demo are addressed.

The key differences between the waterfall model and the Agile delivery model are listed in Table 6-5.

Table 6-5. *Waterfall vs. Agile Delivery Models*

Category	Waterfall Model	Agile Model
Execution process	Strictly sequential phase-wise approach.	Iterative sprints that incrementally build the system.
Documentation	Rich documentation of requirements, process, design, reports, etc. This includes creating various views of requirements, such as use cases views, process flow view, NRF views, and such.	Minimal documentation with high focus on working prototypes.
Time to market	Usually 6-8 months.	Usually 4-6 weeks.

(*Continued*)

Table 6-5. *(continued)*

Category	Waterfall Model	Agile Model
Risk	High due to the delayed testing process.	Low due to iterative and early testing.
Suitability	For mature technologies with well-defined business requirements.	For niche/unproven digital technologies with frequently changing requirements.
Change implementation and flexibility	Costly involving robust change management process. Less flexible as requirements, once finalized, cannot be changed.	Agile is highly responsive to change Changes to requirements can be absorbed in subsequent sprints.
Key processes	Traditional requirements elaboration process, development, and testing processes.	Daily build, daily standup, close collaboration, continuous integration.
End user involvement	Minimal. End user can view the solution after completion.	End user is involved in early stages. End user can provide feedback about iterative deliveries.

Table 6-6 lists the high-level guidelines for selecting the execution methodology among the waterfall, iterative, and Agile methods.

Table 6-6. *Applicability of Waterfall, Iterative, and Agile*

Category		Waterfall	Iterative	Agile
Project complexity	High complexity with multiple unknowns and high risk with ambiguous requirements Needs frequent and iterative validation	Not suitable	Suitable	Suitable
	Low-medium complexity with well-defined requirements Validation can be done after the completion of functionality	Suitable	Suitable	Not suitable
End user interaction	High, as customer is involved in all phases	Not suitable	Suitable	Suitable
	Low, as customer is involved only in final validation	Suitable	Suitable	Not Suitable
Requirements change rate	High, as requirements are ambiguous or change frequently	Not suitable	Suitable	suitable
	Stable, as requirements are well defined and rarely change	suitable	suitable	Suitable
Time to market	Fast	Not suitable	Suitable	Suitable

Best Practices of the Agile Model

Here are the key best practices of the Agile execution model:

- Use an automated continuous integration model.

- Develop automated unit test cases and functional test cases.

- Automate testing scenarios.

- Set up monitoring infrastructure for continuous monitoring of system availability and performance.

- Leverage checklists for coding guidelines and coding standards, security, and performance.

- Use leading metrics such as review effectiveness and sprint burndown rate as early indicators and proactively take course corrective measures to avoid potential issues. Lagging metrics such as defect rate, productivity, and schedule slippage can be used for reporting.

- For complex integrations and while using niche/unproven technologies, do a pilot release and proof-of-concept (PoC) to evaluate the feasibility. Based on the lessons of the pilot run, the methods can be scaled to larger projects.

As automation is one of the key features of Agile execution, there are various automation opportunities in a testing engagement:

- *SOA test automation*: The project manager can use a services testing tool such as SOAPUI to automate the service testing.

- *Automated sprint testing*: The digital project manager can use various tools like JUnit and Selenium to automate sprint testing. Security testing and mobile testing can be automated using tools such as ZAP (Zed Attack Proxy).

- *Automated regression testing*: For each sprint release, regression test cases can be automatically executed to identify any regression issues.

- *Automated business process validation*: Business process validation tools can be used to automate the validation of business process steps. Robotic Process Automation (RPA) based business process testing can be adopted.

- *AI-driven testing*: The digital project manager can employ Artificial Intelligence (AI) tools for testing. This includes automated test case design, test case optimization, and such. Machine learning techniques can be used with high-risk applications and to automatically trigger regression test cases during deployments.

The digital project manager should also actively pursue other testing optimization activities such as defect prevention activities (including historic test data analysis, predicting problem areas, and root cause analysis) and early validation (executing regression testing in early stages, iterative validation, and enhancing test coverage).

In addition to testing automation, the project manager can set up continuous integration (CI) and continuous deployment (CD) to automate various release management activities.

Project Level Metrics of the Agile Model

The digital project manager has to track the effectiveness of the project through metrics. Here are the key metrics used in the Agile model:

- *Time to market*: The average time taken for a feature to be released to production. As Agile projects need faster turnaround time, a quicker time to market is a better predictor.

- *Story point*: The complexity of the user story is expressed in a story point.

- *Sprint velocity*: Story points delivered per person, per sprint. The velocity helps the project manager track the completion date and forecast effort for future sprints.

- *Percent of test cases automated*: The ratio of automated test cases to the total number of test cases.

- *Effort burndown rate*: The effort spent over time. Usually a burndown chart represents the sprint completion time (in days) on the x-axis and the remaining effort (in story points or person hours) on the y-axis. The effort burndown chart helps the project manager efficiently track and predict/forecast the resource utilization and forecast the release date.

- *Customer satisfaction index (CSI)*: The customer satisfaction score obtained from the customer feedback survey. Usually the customer satisfaction ratings are obtained on a scale of 1-5 (1 being least satisfied and 5 being most satisfied). As Agile projects are user-centric, the project manager should aim for a higher customer satisfaction index.

- *Release cycle time/deployment frequency*: Average number of days for performing an end-to-end release. Fewer days are better.

- *Quality*: Quality metrics can be defined for code quality (for development projects), incident response quality (for production support projects), and such. Quality can be tracked using other metrics such as defect injection rate, production defect leakage, and defect reopen rate, and can be grouped under schedule (such as schedule variance and responsiveness), cost (such as cost variance), or productivity (such as average turnaround time). A few key metrics are defined here:

  - Schedule adherence: Actual date-planned date/Planned days

  - Production defect leakage: Production defects/Total number of defects.

  - Defect reopen rate: Number of reopened defects/Total number of defects

  - Test case automation: Number of test cases automated/Total number of test cases.

  - Defect injection rate: Average number of defects per user story/use case

- *Growth*: Business can monitor the growth percentage of key business drivers, such as online revenue, site traffic, etc.

Table 6-7 provides sample metrics for the waterfall and Agile models at various SDLC phases.

Table 6-7. *Sample Metrics for the Waterfall and Agile Models*

SDLC Phase	Business Goal	Sample KPIs for Waterfall Model	Sample KPIs for Agile Model
Development Phase	Code quality Time to market	Schedule variance Cost variance Effort variance Earned value Defect injection rate	Sprint velocity Sprint burndown rate Release cycle time/ deployment frequency Schedule adherence Defect injection rate
Testing phase	Code coverage Time to market Test automation	Requirement traceability Test case coverage Percent test case automation Defect density Defect removal efficiency Testing effectiveness	Defect reopen rate Test case automation Percent test cases automated Production defect leakage
Maintenance & Support phase	Application Availability Application scalability Customer satisfaction Application performance High-quality incident handling	Percent of application availability Average production outage duration Average incident resolution time Customer satisfaction index Average incident response time Root cause analysis metrics	

The Extreme Programming (XP) Model

XP is a type of Agile development practice that can be used with projects involving frequent requirement changes. Requirements are created as user stories through interaction with customers. The main features of XP are pair programming (two programmers working jointly, with one programmer doing the coding and the other doing an instant review of the code), continuous communication, and shorter release cycles (typically 14 days). The main deliverables of XP are story cards, code, and test cases. At all stages of the project, the team has direct and continuous access to the customer. The team takes collective ownership of the deliverable and all team members have equal knowledge of modules. The key stages in XP are as follows:

- *Planning stage:* The sponsors and stakeholders are identified and all requirements are defined.

- *Analysis stage:* Requirements are elaborated into user stories. User stories are prioritized and estimated. Iteration timelines are finalized.

- *Design stage:* Test cases are created for user stories.

- *Execution stage:* Code development, review, and testing is carried out during this stage. Demos are performed.

- *Closure stage:* The application is released.

The Test Driven Development (TDD) Model

In test-driven development, complete test cases are developed in the initial stages and functionality is built to "pass" the test cases. Test cases are written to test all the needed functionality providing 100% test coverage. Test cases minimize the requirements documentation and act as an early quality control criteria by ensuring robust regression validation.

High-Level Comparisons of Agile Methodologies

Table 6-8 shows a high-level comparison of various Agile execution methodologies and scenarios. Digital project managers can use this table to select the most appropriate Agile methodology.

Table 6-8. *Comparison of Various Agile Execution Methodologies*

Agile Methodology	Advantages	Drawbacks	Applicability Scenarios for the Agile Model
Scrum	Most used among all Agile methodologies. Iterative value addition, iterative and continuous validation, reduced risk, user-centric user story prioritization.	Only works well with technology experts and co-located teams and may be challenging for geographically distributed teams. Other drawbacks are minimal documentation.	Used when the scope changes need to be absorbed and when niche technologies are used to deliver solutions quicker to market.
Extreme Programming (XP)	High quality of code development and review. Easy to absorb volatile requirements. End user centric in prioritizing user stories. Provides strong technical best practices.	Needs heavy end user/customer involvement.	This methodology can be used when requirements are changing. The team needs technology experts.
Test Driven Development (TDD)	Provides 100% code coverage with high delivery quality and modular/reusable code.	Few features such as UI related functionality and usability. Test cases and test case execution will add to overhead.	Can be used with projects where functional requirements can be fully verified though test cases.

Summary

In this chapter we discussed various aspects of project execution:

- End-to-end project execution involves four key phases: planning, design and architecture, implementation/build, and maintenance.

- In the waterfall model, the software project phases are executed sequentially.

- In the V-model, the phases move upward after the coding phase. Each phase (such as requirements and design) has a corresponding testing phase.

- In the prototype model, a working prototype is developed incrementally. Every prototype is a visual depiction of the currently known requirements and communicates the user experience, navigation, and information architecture to the end user.

- The iterative model incrementally develops capabilities through time-sliced iteration.

- Agile provides business value in incremental and time-boxed iterative deliveries.

- The main Agile frameworks are extreme programming (XP) , Agile unified process (AUP) , Feature Driven Development—FDD (wherein the unit of requirement is a feature), and Agile Unified Process—AUP (an incremental and iterative development framework).

- The main business drivers for Agile are quick adoption to market dynamics, business agility, cost optimization, risk reduction, and quality.

- Extreme programming (XP) is a type of Agile development practice that can be used for projects involving frequent requirement changes.

- In test driven development (TDD) , the complete test cases are developed in the initial stages and functionality is built to "pass" the test cases.

CHAPTER 7

Achieving Quality in Digital Projects

Quality is of paramount importance in digital projects. Delivery quality positively reflects on user satisfaction, leading to the long-term success of the digital project. Managing expectations from various stakeholders and maintaining high quality is a challenging balance act that a digital project manager has to achieve. Achieving quality is an ongoing process and a digital project manager has to constantly look for innovative ways of improving quality. Achieving and maintaining high quality requires continuous application of new quality techniques and processes to meet the standards that all stakeholders expect.

We discuss various aspects of quality in this chapter. We discuss the quality strategy and framework and elaborate on the elements of the quality framework. A quality strategy defines the main elements such as goals and governance that are needed to achieve robust quality. A quality framework defines various elements such as knowledge management, standards, monitoring, and phase-wise quality measures.

Project managers, account managers, and lead developers will find this chapter useful.

Quality Strategy

During the requirements elaboration phase, the digital project manager has to define the quality strategy to cover all aspects of quality. A comprehensive quality strategy should satisfy the key tenets of a quality result, which are reliability (the ability of the system to maintain the SLAs under specified conditions), maintainability (the ability of the system to be easily extended and modified), portability (ease of transferring the solution from one environment to another), integrity (maintaining access control and preventing unauthorized data manipulation), correctness (degree of conformity of the system to its specifications), usability (ease of system learning and usage), and testability (ease of testing). The main aspects of a quality strategy are depicted in Figure 7-1.

© Shailesh Kumar Shivakumar 2018
S. K. Shivakumar, *Complete Guide to Digital Project Management*,
https://doi.org/10.1007/978-1-4842-3417-4_7

Figure 7-1. *Elements of a quality strategy*

The key aspects of a quality strategy are defined here:

- *Quality goals*: The digital project manager has to identify the key quality goals for the digital project. For greenfield implementation projects (involving development and integration), the quality goals would be to improve delivery quality, reduce deployment time, and reduce defects. For support/maintenance projects, the quality goals would be to improve the user satisfaction and average ticket resolution time. For each goal, the project manager has to define metrics that can be measured and monitored. The quality goals should be reviewed and signed off on by all key stakeholders.

- *Quality framework*: The quality framework essentially is a comprehensive quality measure to cover the quality of various project management functions involved in a project. The quality framework covers quality during project planning, estimation, resource planning, change management, communication planning, coding, testing, etc. The framework provides guidelines, checklists, and best practices for each key project management function. We define the quality framework in the next section.

- *Quality metrics*: Quality metrics define the quality goals in quantifiable terms. Quality metrics make it easy for a project manager to measure, monitor, and report quality goals. Sample quality metrics are defect rate, average customer rating, and average ticket resolution time.

- *Quality governance*: Governance involves quality processes that are defined to enforce the quality of all project lifecycle stages. The quality governance processes are designed to enforce quality goals. Governance includes code review processes, release management processes, estimation processes, etc.

- *Quality monitoring and compliance framework*: This framework elaborates the monitoring and setup for the defined quality metrics. For long-term effects, you need a robust quality monitoring and notification system. The monitoring and notification system should be able to monitor the digital application and its ecosystem and report any quality issues.

- *Continuous quality improvement*: The digital project manager has to constantly strive to improve the quality of the project management processes. The project manager has to leverage the latest digital technologies to improve the quality. The project manager should adopt recent trends in quality space, such as A/B testing and real user monitoring (RUM).

An example of a quality strategy is shown in Table 7-1.

Table 7-1. *Sample Quality Strategy*

Category	Focus Areas	Key Activities
Quality Goals	Achieving CMM Level 5 Compliance	• Current maturity level assessment • Identify gaps to achieve CMM Level 5 • Establish baseline numbers for productivity improvement, tools usage, reusability, schedule adherence, effort deviation, reduction in defects, increase in customer satisfaction

(continued)

Table 7-1. (*continued*)

Category	Focus Areas	Key Activities
	A comprehensive quality framework	• Develop comprehensive quality framework covering all project management functions. • Define standards, processes, checklists, best practices, and benchmark numbers for key project management functions. • Develop knowledge management framework to store the checklists and process artifacts.
Quality Metrics	Define quality metrics for the identified quality goals	• Identify and tracks compliance metrics. • Sample metrics for the quality goals are schedule slippage percentage, defect reduction percentage, and ticket reduction rate.
Quality Governance	Well defined processes for all project management functions	• Define processes for estimation, resource onboarding, defect prevention, reusability, change management, and such. • Define roles and responsibilities for all the identified processes.
Quality Monitoring and Compliance Framework	Develop a robust monitoring ecosystem	• Set up a monitoring infrastructure to monitor key metrics such as performance and quality metrics, and set up a real-time system health check monitoring systems to report resource usage metrics. • Define monitoring processes and related roles and responsibilities.
Continuous Quality Improvement	Improve the code quality, productivity and delivery quality on iterative basis.	• Establish center of excellence (CoE) to lead the innovation and thought leadership initiatives. • Identify and leverage open source tools and frameworks to gain productivity improvements. • Continuously benchmark system metrics and processes against global standards. • Monitor emerging trends in digital space and adopt the trends related to the functional domain.

Quality Framework

It is important for a digital project manager to establish a robust quality framework. Various elements of a quality framework are depicted in the Figure 7-2.

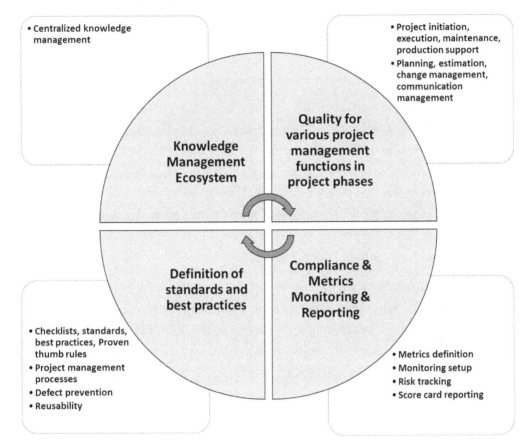

Figure 7-2. *Elements of a quality framework*

The key tenets of a comprehensive quality framework are detailed here:

- *Quality for various project management functions in project phases*: The project manager has to define and optimize the processes related to various project management functions, such as project planning, estimation, staffing, change management, stakeholder management, and communication management. The project manager has to define quality processes in various project lifecycle stages, such as project initiation, project execution, maintenance and support. We discuss these details in the next section.

- *Compliance and metrics monitoring and reporting*: The project manager has to define the key quality metrics for the project processes defined earlier. For instance, the main metrics for estimation are effort deviation, schedule deviation, etc., and for the change management, the key metrics are the number of change requests absorbed. For each of the defined metrics, the project manager has to develop a score card based on a continuous tracking mechanism to track the metrics. We discuss the details in coming sections.

- *Definition of standards and best practices*: As a part of this, the project manager has to define and compile the checklists, best practices, and rules that can be used at various stages of the project management. As a part of this, the project manager defines defect prevention best practices, reusability best practices, and configuration management best practices. The project manager also has to plan for continuous improvement for high effectiveness.

- *Knowledge management ecosystem*: One of the key components of a quality framework is the knowledge management ecosystem, wherein the project manager has to define the centralized knowledge base and processes to store and reuse the artifacts such as checklists, processes, project management templates, documentation of approved standards, reports, best practices, and such. As depicted in Figure 7-2, quality in various project lifecycle phases is one of the key tenants of a quality framework. The next section explains this in detail.

Quality in Various Digital Project Lifecycle Phases

Comprehensive quality in various project management functions at various project lifecycle stages is the key component of a quality framework discussed earlier. In this section, we explore the quality processes and initiatives that a digital project manager can undertake during the project lifecycle stages.

Quality in Project Initiation

During the project initiation stage, the main activities are requirements elaboration, architecture definition, resource on-boarding, and scope finalization. The main quality initiatives at this stage are covered in the following sections.

Induction Plan

The project manager has to create a resource on-boarding induction kit that can ease the resource on-boarding process. The induction kit includes an induction plan (onboarding plan, skills assessment plan, and background verification checks, software/hardware allocation, and access setup), learning materials (videos and reference materials), orientation materials (policies and regulations), forms (deposit forms, insurance forms, etc.), agreements (non-disclosure agreements), and any other needed skills training. The induction kit also includes the necessary tools and software for quick setup of project environment. The project manager also has to on-board functional and domain SMEs to define the functional requirements and model the business processes and flows. The project manager can also arrange for team introduction sessions for any new joiners and set up the necessary access controls.

Reusability Plan

The architecture team will be involved in creating the architecture views and the project manager has to work with the architecture team to identify the tools, requirements/business rules, and frameworks that can be reused in subsequent stages of development. Wherever needed, the project manager has to plan for automatable scripts and reusable components with the help of lead architects.

Compliance Plan

The project manager has to identify the compliance and regulation needs and has to come up with standards and governance policies to conform to the legal regulations.

Quality Governance Body

The project manager should establish a quality governance body to enforce the quality processes and set the direction related to quality matters of the project. The quality governance body periodically reviews the quality processes of the project and ensures compliance. Other responsibilities of the quality governance body are defining quality processes related to knowledge management, enhancing reusability, continuous improvement, preventing defects, and configuration management. The quality governance body has final decision making authority on all quality issues.

Quality in Project Execution

During the project execution stage, the main activities are development and testing. In this section, we discuss various quality initiatives that are part of the project execution stage.

Defect Prevention

One of the key quality initiatives during the execution stage is defect prevention. A project manager has to define a defect prevention framework that draws insights from the prior issues to proactively reduce defects in the future. A defect prevention methodology increases productivity and reduces testing effort. The main techniques for defect prevention are covered next.

Comprehensive Code Reviews

The project manager has to set up a multi-layered code review process. The developer has to use the checklist and coding best practices for reference. After code completion, the developer has to do a self-code review and perform unit testing. The second quality gating criteria is the peer review, wherein the module lead reviews the code against a predefined checklist. The third quality gating criteria is the automated code analysis on the integrated code using code analysis tools. The multi-tiered code review process ensures high-quality deliverables and minimizes the defects.

Checklists and Best Practices

During the project initiation stage, the project manager can define standards, best practices, and checklists that can be used by the team for reference purposes. Adhering to best practices improves the code quality at the source. Checklists contain the key quality items for each of the project tasks (such as development, release management, testing, deployment, etc.) Checklists are prepared based on past lessons and industry best practices and can enforce the quality governance at the source. In the digital project, a project manager can create checklists for code development, configuration management, knowledge management, release management, resource onboarding, and more. A checklist contains points that need to be verified by the owner of the task. Normally, the owner can provide a "yes" or "no" response for each point. A sample checklist for configuration management is shown in Table 7-2.

Table 7-2. *Sample Configuration Management Checklist*

No.	Checklist Question	Response (Yes/No)	Remarks
1	Has the configuration management (CM) plan been reviewed by all stakeholders?		
2	Does the configuration audit (audit to check the adherence to the configuration management plan) happen on a frequent basis?		
3	Is the team using the baseline version of the configuration management plan?		
4	Has the configuration audit report been shared with all stakeholders?		
5	Has the configuration management tool and source control structure been defined as per the CM plan?		
6	Has the access control to configuration items (code, test cases, and documents) been maintained as per the CM plan?		
7	Are the backup and archival processes defined as per the CM plan?		

A project manager can also use checklists at various project stages (see Table 7-3).

Table 7-3. *Checklist at Various Project Stages*

Project Stage	Sample Checklist Questions
Project initiation stage	Has a complete list of requirements been compiled and signed off?
	Have the governance and communication plans been fully defined?
	Has the estimation been done using an appropriate estimation method?
	Have risks and their mitigation plans been fully identified?
	Have all resources been appropriately trained?
	Has the project plan been fully prepared?
	Has the development environment been fully set up?
Project execution stage	Have the code reviews been planned on regular basis?
	Have checklists, coding standards, and best practices been defined and followed?
	Has the defect prevention framework been defined and used?
	Has the change management process been defined?
Project maintenance stage	Is SLA monitoring set up?
	Has the governance plan for maintenance been fully defined?

Historical Data Analysis

The project manager can analyze the historical defect data to understand the problem patterns. For each of the problem patterns, a root cause is identified and the corresponding solution is defined. Techniques such as pareto chart analysis (the analysis aims to find 20% of the causes that lead to 80% of issues), causal analysis diagrams (a technique wherein the causes for the problem are listed along with the potential solutions), and brain storming techniques (wherein major problems and possible causes are listed) are used to analyze the data. A sample analysis based on the defect type is shown in Figure 7-3.

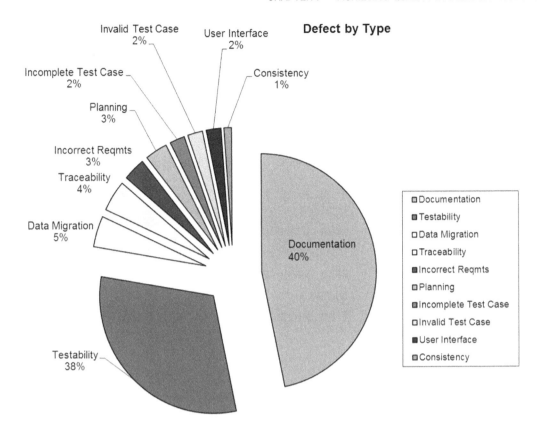

Figure 7-3. *Causal analysis based on defect type*

Note that the majority of the defects are caused due to lack of documentation and incomplete testing. The corrective action is to improve the code documentation and increase test case coverage. The project manager can draw insights through various cross-sections of the defect data; the project manager can categorize the defects based on the severity type, based on the stages where defects are detected, based on the identified root causes, and so on. Severity is also decided by the cost of the defect; for instance, documentation related defects are less costly and hence can be assigned a low severity, whereas requirement gap related defects are more costly to fix and hence get a high priority. These insights can further be used to take corrective actions.

A sample list of root causes compared to the corrective action that follows is shown in Table 7-4.

Table 7-4. *Sample Corrective Action for Identified Root Causes*

Root Cause of the Problem	Corrective Action Recommended	Severity
Absence of a centralized knowledge system	Develop a centralized knowledge base. Add the debugging steps, best practices, and checklists to it.	Medium
Interpersonal issues among team members leading to poor team coordination	Define role responsibility matrix. Assign mentors for the team members.	Medium
Poor collaboration	Establish open communication channels across all team members. Leverage various collaboration tools such as wikis, blogs, communities, forums, chats to improve collaboration. Conduct training on communication and soft skills.	High

Brainstorming Solutions

During brainstorming exercises, we repeatedly ask "why" questions followed by a "how" question. Here is a sample brainstorming set of questions related to a performance issue:

- Why is the web page response slow?
  - The backend code is slow.
- Why is the backend code slow?
  - The code was not tested for performance SLAs.
- Why was the backend code not tested for performance?
  - Iterative performance testing was not done.
- Why was the iterative performance testing not done?
  - Performance testing was planned only in the last stages.
- How do we fix the process issue related to performance?
  - The project manager has to plan for iterative performance testing.
  - The project manager has to use the performance best practices, coding guidelines, and checklists with each iteration.

A summary of outcome of this brainstorming exercise is given in Table 7-5.

Table 7-5. *Summary of Brainstorming Exercise*

Problem Root Cause	Possible Causes	Suggested Solution
30% of reported issues are due to performance	Absence of performance data and SLAs Absence of iterative performance testing	Get the complete performance data and SLAs during the requirements session. Follow an iterative performance testing model.

Process Improvement

With each iteration, the project manager can plan for optimization of key processes. For instance, the development processes can be optimized through reuse of framework components and reuse of open source frameworks and libraries. The testing process can be optimized by using automated test scripts.

Usage of Tools

A project manager can leverage various tools for efficient project management. Table 7-6 is a sample list of project management tools that can be used at various stages.

Table 7-6. *Sample Project Management Tools*

Project Lifecycle Stage	Key Activities	Tools That Can Be Used
Project initiation	Project planning	Microsoft Project
	Requirements elaboration	Requirement templates, use case documents, user story documents
Project execution	Development	Eclipse IDE
	Testing	Apache JUnit, Selenium, Apache JMeter
	Document repository	Microsoft SharePoint
	Issue management	Jira
Project closure	Reporting	Jira

Continuous and Iterative Testing

Testing should be done for each iteration for early detection of problems. A continuous integration (CI) setup can enforce and automate the iterative testing through automated tools.

Quality in Project Maintenance

Various quality initiatives in project maintenance stage are given in this section. We discuss the key activities in the maintenance phase, such as configuration management, knowledge management, and continuous improvement.

Configuration Management

Configuration management involves controlling changes to the project artifacts that allow the project manager to effectively trace, deploy, and roll back releases. Configuration management is needed to ensure that the correct version of the deliverables are released and delivered to the customers. A robust configuration management includes identifying the artifacts that can be tracked and controlled. Configuration control includes versioning, check in and check out, archiving, deleting, and auditing.

The configuration items that are managed by the configuration document are the source code, test cases, reports, code documents, libraries, and reports.

The project manager is responsible for defining the configuration management plan, identifying the tools needed for configuration management (such as a source control tool and a continuous integration tool), and performing regular audits to ensure conformance to the configuration management plan.

A typical configuration management plan document consists of the following sections:

- CM PLANNING
  - Lifecycle configuration items and their storage
  - Movement of configuration Items
  - Change control
  - Release
  - Backup
  - Archival procedure
- CM tools used
- CONFIGURATION AUDIT
  - Responsibilities of the configuration controller

- TERMS AND ABBREVIATIONS

- REFERENCES

- BASELINED FOLDER STRUCTURE IN SOURCE CONTROL

Knowledge Management

The knowledge management system can be used to store various documents such as the project plan, the defect prevention plan, the business requirements documents, test scripts, the configuration management plan, the knowledge management plan, and training resources.

The centralized knowledge management stores two types of knowledge artifacts: explicit knowledge and implicit knowledge. Comprehensive knowledge management consists of four dimensions, as depicted in Figure 7-4.

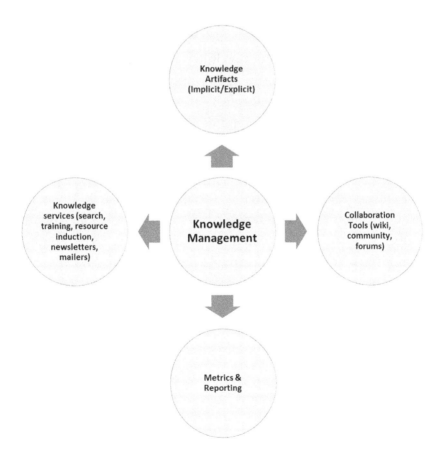

Figure 7-4. *Knowledge management dimensions*

Explicit knowledge artifacts include process documents, best practices, lessons, checklists, and reusable templates. Implicit knowledge artifacts store the documents that are created based on tacit knowledge from SMEs and domain experts. Implicit knowledge artifacts include process flows, business rules, and functional domain related expert material. Implicit knowledge artifacts reduce the dependency on individuals.

Besides these documents, the project manager should also create collaboration functionality on top of the knowledge management system. Collaboration tools include wikis, communities, forums, and question/answer functionality wherein end users can contribute and use the existing knowledge artifacts. Collaboration tools harness and add to the collective intelligence of the knowledge platform and can be used to share ideas. The third dimension of the knowledge system is the knowledge services. These services include training services leveraging knowledge artifacts, resource induction kit, and newsletters and mailers to periodically communicate the updates to the knowledge base. Search is the most important service that is built on top of a knowledge base. An effective search function is used with a self-service model and for incident prevention architecture. The last dimension is to use the metrics to track the use of the knowledge base. The metrics include number of articles created, number of documents downloaded, and so on.

The next section looks at details of continuous improvement.

Continuous Improvement

Continuous quality process improvement is an ongoing journey. The main goal is to improve the quality metrics and underlying business processes on a regular basis. Continuous improvement involves defect prevention strategies, leveraging reusable tools and frameworks, process optimization, automation, productivity improvement methods, and using metrics based insights to improve the processes. The project manager maintains a score card to track the improvement metrics for various quality goals and processes. A sample score card and its associated metrics are shown in Table 7-7.

Table 7-7. *Score Card for Quality Metrics*

Quality Processes	Quality Metrics To Be Tracked in the Score Card
Content management process	Content process completion time
	Content publish time
	Percent reduction in content errors
Risk management	Percent of risk mitigated through contingency plan
Change management process	Percent of successful changes
	Percent of effort deviation
	Percent of schedule deviation
Knowledge management	Percent reduction in incidents due to knowledge artifacts
	Number of knowledge artifacts reused

Metrics and Reporting

Metrics are quantitative values that assess the performance of the system against pre-defined quality goals. Project managers can set verifiable targets/success metrics, quantify the success, and accurately measure the ROI (return on investment) and can effectively track the progress using metrics. For each quality goal, the project manager has to define the metrics that can effectively measure the quality goals quantitatively. Sample quality metrics for testing are as follows:

- *Effectiveness of testing*: The metric is the ratio of the total number of defects identified by the validation team versus the total number of defects identified by validation team and end users.

- *Effort variance*: This metric is the ratio of difference between planned effort and actual effort.

- *Review effectiveness*: This metric is the ratio of the total defects found during review to the total defects. The metric indicates the defects that are prevented due to review.

- *Function point productivity*: This metric is the ratio of effort (in person months) to number of function points. For instance, if a project has 100 function points and if the team needs 10 months to complete the project the productivity factor is 0,1.

- *Defect rejection ratio*: This is the ratio of the rejected defects to the total number of defects.

- *Defect removal efficiency*: This is the ratio of the total number of defects identified before user acceptance testing (UAT) to the total number of defects identified. This is an indicator of test execution and review effectiveness.

Case Study: Achieving CMMI Level 5 in Digital Projects

Capability Maturity Model Integration (CMMI) is a set of processes that assess and benchmark existing software processes at an organization. CMMI can be used to identify the gaps in existing processes and can be used as a guide to reach a target level. CMMI Level 5 is the highest in the maturity of the processes. Other capability levels are capability Level 1 Initial (absence of standard processes, ad hoc and undefined processes), capability Level 2 repeatable (documented processes), capability Level 3 defined (standardized processes), capability Level 4 managed (strict usage of standards and specifications, informed and data based decision making processes) and capability Level 5 optimized (continuous improvement, tracked and monitored process metrics).

Background

An organization wants to assess current process maturity levels using CMMI and aims to reach the CMMI Level 5. This case study provides the list of quality processes followed to achieve this goal. The key objectives of targeting the CMMI level are as follows:

- Improve processes to meet the agreed-upon SLAs.

- Improve the overall quality, productivity, and time to market.

- Develop the matured governance processes for smoother maintenance.

Gap Assessment

One of the first tasks is to assess the maturity of existing processes and identify gaps with the defined business goals. Table 7-8 provides details of such gaps.

Table 7-8. *Sample Gaps with Addressing Steps*

Desired Business Goals	Current Gaps	Steps to Address Gaps	Measurement Metrics
Improve productivity	Absence of continuous improvement framework	Identify processes that can be automated	Time to market, size
Improve delivery quality	Absence of quality framework, absence of defect prevention process	Develop root cause analysis framework, adopt iterative delivery, adopt continuous integration	Review effectiveness, defect rate, defect reopen rate
Schedule adherence	Frequent slippage of agreed timelines	Real-time tracking of progress	Schedule SLAs

Quality Processes

The following sections explain the quality processes that are defined to help the organization meet desired maturity levels.

Project Metrics Tracking and Reporting

The project manager has to keenly track the key project metrics to ensure smooth development of the system. A project reporting dashboard is created to track the following metrics on a regular basis:

- *Effort metrics*: Deviation of the actual effort from the planned effort is tracked. The effort spent on change requests, defect reopens, and scope creep items are tracked separately to determine the impact of these items on the overall effort. Accordingly, the project manager has to revisit the change management and requirement prioritization processes to carefully absorb only needed changes.

- *Dashboard metrics*: The project manager tracks other key project metrics such as risks, defect fixes, and schedule deviations in the project management dashboard. Any deviations from the planned milestones are also tracked.

Defect Prevention Exercise

The previous section explained defect prevention. The project manager has to use various defect prevention activities such as brainstorming, root cause analysis, and causal analysis to proactively identify problem patterns and take corrective measures.

Continuous Process Improvement

The project manager has to maintain a process improvement tracker to identify various initiatives to improve the processes.

- Development of knowledge management plan to store the best practices, process documents, lessons, and checklists that the team can use during project execution and testing.

- Development of a configuration control plan for managing all project artifacts.

- Development of a requirements traceability matrix to trace the requirements, defects, and open items.

Summary

In this chapter we discussed various aspects of achieving quality:

- A comprehensive quality strategy should satisfy the key tenets of a quality result, which are reliability (the ability of the system to maintain the SLAs under specified conditions), maintainability (the ability of the system to be easily extended and modified), portability (ease of transferring the solution from one environment to another), integrity (maintaining access control and preventing unauthorized data manipulation), correctness (degree of conformity of the system to its specifications), usability (ease of system learning and usage), and testability (ease of testing).

- Key elements of a quality strategy are quality goals, quality framework, quality metrics, quality governance, quality monitoring and compliance framework, and continuous quality improvement.

- Elements of a quality framework are quality for various project management functions in project phases, compliance and metrics monitoring and reporting, definition of standards and best practices, and a knowledge management ecosystem.

- The main quality initiatives during the project initiation stage are an induction plan, a reusability plan, a compliance plan, and a quality governance body.

- The main quality initiatives during the project execution stage are defect prevention, using tools, and continuous and iterative testing.

- The main quality initiatives during the project execution stage are configuration management, knowledge management, and continuous improvement.

CHAPTER 8

Core Digital Project Management Functions

A digital project manager has to be aware of core project management functions such as requirements management, change request management, stakeholder management, and scope management. The project manager has to apply the proven methods and best practices in these core project management functions during appropriate phases of the project execution. The digital project managers need to be aware of the best practices and processes involved in the core project management functions in order to effectively handle contingencies.

This chapter discusses these core project management functions in detail.

Project managers, program managers, business analysts, and account managers will find this chapter useful.

Requirements Management

The project team needs to have a good understanding of the complete project requirements. A 360-degree view of requirements will play a key role in developing better design and test cases. This section looks at various aspects of the requirements management process. It first looks at the process to map the business drivers to the business requirements and then covers the requirements elaboration process in detail.

© Shailesh Kumar Shivakumar 2018
S. K. Shivakumar, *Complete Guide to Digital Project Management*,
https://doi.org/10.1007/978-1-4842-3417-4_8

Understanding and Mapping Business Drivers to Business Requirements

Understanding the overall program vision and the corresponding business goals and drivers are key to the overall success of the project. The business goals and drivers are mapped to elaborate the business requirements and the guiding principles, as depicted in Figure 8-1.

Key Business Drivers	Business Requirements Elaboration	Guiding Principles
• Seamless Omni-channel user experience • Personalized service • 24 x 7 online availability • Maximize reach through online channels.	• Business stakeholder interviews • Requirements elaboration workshop • Gap analysis • Design option brainstorming with business stakeholders	• Process standardization and optimization • Frequent, iterative delivery for faster time to market • Layered architecture with loose coupling using services based integration

Figure 8-1. *Business drivers to business requirements mapping*

Figure 8-1 depicts the most common business drivers in a typical digital project. The project manager and business analysts identify the key business drivers for the program as the seamless omni-channel user experience, personalized service, 24x7 availability and maximize reach. The business drivers can be obtained through explicitly stated BRD (business requirements document) and business stakeholder interviews, and by elaborating the program vision elements.

In order to deeply understand each of the business goals, the project manager has to arrange for a focused requirements elaboration session. The recommended business requirements activities include stakeholder interviews, requirements elaboration workshops, gap analysis, and painpoint analysis exercises. This includes brainstorming sessions with business stakeholders.

The project manager, along with the architects, should define the guiding principles for the digital solution. In this example, the guiding principles are process standardization and process optimization, using iterative delivery models for quicker time to market, and using a layered, services-based architecture for the application. The guiding principles provide an initial set of guidelines for application design.

We now look at the various elements of the requirements elaboration process.

Requirements Elaboration Process

The main steps in the requirements elaboration process are depicted in Figure 8-2. The requirements elaboration process mainly consists of four phases: requirements gathering, requirements elaboration, requirements validation, and requirements signoff.

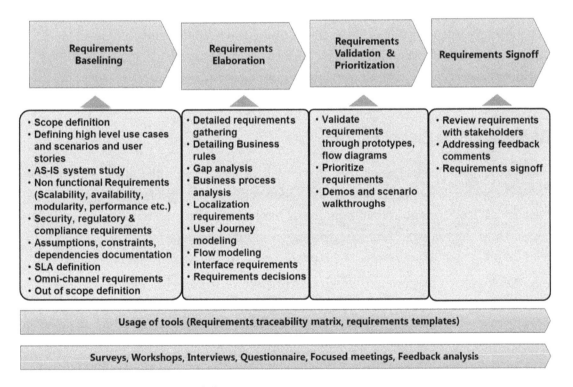

Figure 8-2. *Requirements elaboration process*

Requirements Gathering

As part of the requirements baselining process, the key requirement scope items are defined. The boundaries for the requirements are identified with well-defined in-scope and out-of-scope items. Business analysts and domain consultants document the requirements (through formats such as use cases, process flow diagrams, user stories, etc.) that need to be implemented in the solution. The team of business analysts and domain consultants also review the existing system and its documentation to understand the existing flows, scenarios, and painpoints. Nonfunctional requirements related to performance, scalability, availability, modularity, and extensibility, as well as the related service level agreements (SLAs), will be defined. Omni-channel requirements, such as any device-specific requirements, are identified. All related security requirements will be identified and defined with the help of security consultants. All applicable regulatory and compliance-related requirements (such as data sharing, privacy rules, data archival rules, data retention rules, etc.) will be defined. The identified items will be elaborated on in the next stage. All constraints (including technical constraints, organizational constraints, and process constraints) are documented.

Requirements Elaboration

Each of the identified use cases/user stories will be elaborated with details such as main flows, exception flows (for use cases based requirements gathering), and business rules. Because each of the requirements gathering has its own structure, it is recommended to capture and elaborate requirements through a couple of varieties (such as user stories with visual modeling or use cases with user stories) so that you cover all needed points.

Based on surveys and stakeholder/end user interviews and the existing system studies, business analysts identify the gaps and challenges with the existing systems. Process modeling and flow diagrams are created to model the business flows. Architects and business analysts create integration requirements to integrate the digital solution with the enterprise interfaces. All major requirements decisions are documented. The requirements document should detail (in the requirements specification document or in the requirements database) the exceptions flows and scenarios along with main flows. The requirements document should also call out the assumptions, constraints, and out-of-scope items (also known as boundary items) unambiguously.

Requirements elaboration activities are fine-tuned based on the nature of the digital engagement. For instance, for user experience (UX) related digital engagements, the user experience related requirements will be elaborated; the requirements are normally based on UX/UI standards and are technology independent. This includes activities such as user analysis (creating user groups based on their common needs, goals, and usage patterns), user journey modeling (tracing the user's journey across all touch points), competitive benchmarking (comparing the website with competitors), heuristic evaluation (application assessment against generic user experience standards), user experience analysis (usability assessment of the site), UX redesign approach assessment, usability analysis, and user touch point analysis.

Requirements Validation and Prioritization

Once the requirements are fully defined, they need to be validated by all concerned stakeholders. In order to cover the complex requirements from multiple dimensions, the following requirements should be used for validation. Business analysts should also schedule demos with all concerned stakeholders to get their feedback. Some of the demo types are as follows:

- User experience (UX) wireframes and prototypes/mockups to depict the end user experience, UI improvements, user journey improvements, information architecture, navigation model, and the omni-channel experience.

- For UX projects, persona definitions (categorization of users based on their interests, demographics, profile attributes, and purchase patterns), heuristic analysis, competitive benchmarking reports, usability reports, UX analysis reports, and mobile experience views will be shown.

- Use case documents and user story documents to elaborate the captured requirements.

- Process flow diagrams to depict the business processes, information flows, interacting systems, and business rules.

- For data intensive projects, you can design and demo the data model to depict the underlying database details.

- Various architecture views (such as solution view, infrastructure view, functional view, security view, integration view, process view, and data flow view) to explain the architecture viewpoint to architects and technology stakeholders.

These requirement artifacts should be presented to various stakeholders, seeking their feedback. In Internet-facing site scenarios, a small set of end users and application users will also participate in the review process to provide early feedback about the prototypes, user experience, and other aspects. These documents act as structured communication tools to depict the complex requirements. Each of the requirements should be verifiable through definitive validation steps and it should be possible to create executable test cases for the requirements. If any of the requirements are not verifiable, the business analysts should fill the gaps and define the requirement in more detail so that it can be verified.

Based on the business criticality, the requirements are prioritized for implementation. Prioritization is based on multiple factors, such as impact on business revenue, cost reduction, ease of implementation, degree of dependency (how much other components need the component), and effect on the program vision. MoSCow (must have, should have, and could have) principles are used to prioritize requirements.

Requirements Signoff

After the stakeholder review and prioritization, the project team addresses all the feedback and formally seeks sign off from all stakeholders. Signed-off requirements will be baselined and used as a reference for further design, development, and testing activities. Based on the execution methodology, the sign-off process and timelines can vary. In case of the Agile methodology, the user stories for the sprint will be finalized within two weeks, whereas in the iterative model, the requirements for the current iteration will be signed off at the beginning of the iteration.

Throughout the requirements elaboration process, the business analysts use various tools such as requirements capturing templates, traceability matrix, flow modeling tools, and prototype diagramming tools to effectively capture, articulate, communicate, present, and track the requirements. The requirements traceability matrix acts as a traceable repository for requirements that organizes and tracks every requirement, starting from the requirements definition through design, implementation, testing, and release. A sample entry in the requirements traceability matrix is shown in Table 8-1.

Table 8-1. *Sample Entry in the Requirements Traceability Matrix*

Requirement	Design Details	Code Details	Test Case Details
Users should be able to log in	Authentication design will be form-based	`Login_form.jsp` implements log-in functionality	`TestLoginScenarios` test case validates various login-related scenarios

The example in Table 8-1 depicts how a login requirement is translated into a design topic, a code module, and a test case. This ensures end-to-end traceability of all requirements and provides coverage for all requirements.

Change Request Management

Change requests (CR) or requests for change (RFC) are enhancement requests and are a deviation from the agreed-upon/baselined scope of work. CRs arise due to multiple factors, such as the following:

- End user feedback requesting additional features

- Change in regulations or compliance standards

- Change in business scenarios (such as business expansion, acquisition, merger, or market dynamics)

- Requirement of new features or need for competitive advantage

- Need for user experience enhancements based on feedback from stakeholder workshops

- Technical scenarios (system upgrade, patching, change in standards, quality issue, product release, or technology evolution)

- Other unforeseen changes (such as schedule changes, budget changes, etc.)

A well-defined change request management process is critical to the project's success without impacting the project schedule and cost.

The high-level steps of a sample change request management (CR) process are depicted in Figure 8-3.

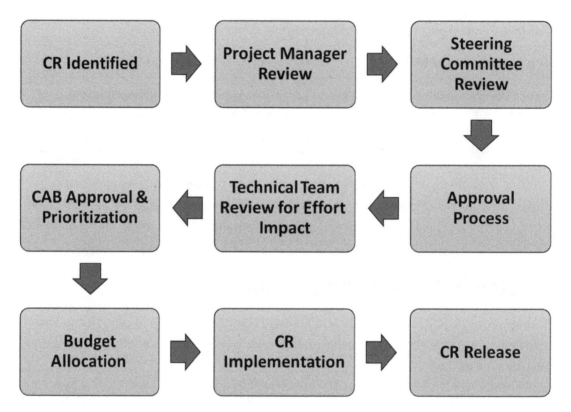

Figure 8-3. *Change request management process*

Once a change request is identified, the project manager reviews it. The project manager validates and confirms the change requests and assesses its importance and impact on the release. The CR will then be forwarded to the steering committee or configuration control board (CCB) for their review and approval. The steering committee mainly focuses on the business value of the CR before providing approval. Once the CR is approved by the steering committee, the technical team performs an impact analysis to assess the effort and schedule changes needed to implement the CR. If needed, all teams that are impacted by the CR should be involved in the impact analysis. The CR is maintained in a log file for easier tracking.

The CR is then forwarded to the change advisory board (CAB), a body that controls and tracks the change requests. The CAB is responsible for evaluating the impact of the CR, prioritizing CRs, detailing risk associated with the CR, stakeholder communication, go/no-go planning, and CR release planning. Post CAB approval, the budget is approved and the technical team implements and releases the CR after testing the CR. All the impacted parties are notified after the CR release.

The project manager has to maintain a log/registry of all the change requests and their details (such as priority, impact, execution status, release date, business value, implementation time, etc.). The change request log can be used to help improve the change request process by analyzing the implementation time and then continuously improving the implementation time.

Stakeholder Management

A project manager has to identify and should meet the expectations of all relevant stakeholders. Stakeholder skills, knowledge, support, and sponsorship contribute to the overall success and sustained adoption of the project. The main phases of stakeholder management are depicted in Figure 8-4.

Stakeholder Identification	Stakeholder Roles & Responsibilities	Continuous Stakeholder Engagement
• Identification of all types of stakeholders • Understand and analyze stakeholder goals • Business value articulation to identified stakeholders	• Governance model • Communication plan • Participation in Steering committee, PMO, CCB etc • Program level risks management • Drive program adoption • Definition of program vision, goals, metrics and program roadmap	• Communication management • Escalation management • Change request management • Project planning • Timely reports and notification • Project plan and status reviews • Project performance assessment reports • Project risk updates and reports

Figure 8-4. *Stakeholder management process*

The first step in stakeholder management is identifying all stakeholders. Any person who has a significant interest or who will be impacted by the project is considered a potential stakeholder. The project manager has to identify all the stakeholders early in the project phase through interviews, studying the organization structure, and through other formal meetings. The project manager has to analyze the needs/goals from each of the stakeholders and their expectations from the digital project. The project manager has to understand the main project goals from project sponsors to secure their continued support. The project manager has to articulate the business value (quantifying the stakeholder needs and expectations) of the digital program to the identified stakeholders. All conflicting goals from various stakeholders need to be identified and discussed to understand their impact and priority in order to reach an agreeable approach.

In the next phase, the project manager can define the stakeholders' roles based on their goals and interest in the project. The project manager can define the RACI matrix (explained in Chapter 5) to determine the ownership roles and communication plan for all stakeholders. Business stakeholders who are part of the steering committee look after the program vision, provide direction, and handle major contingencies. Other stakeholders can be part of the change advisory board (CAB) or project management office (PMO), based on their roles and responsibilities. Steering committee members are responsible for program level risk management, program roadmap definition, and driving digital program adoption. Steering committee members also define the program goals (such as operations optimization, revenue increments, etc.) and the associated KPIs/metrics.

During the continuous engagement phase, the project manager has to involve relevant stakeholders in various project activities, such as project planning, change request prioritization, and escalation management. The project manager has to regularly update the stakeholders through a well-defined communication plan. The project manager has to set up regular meetings with relevant stakeholders to address any concerns, answer any questions, and review the project status and other key deliverables. Stakeholders should also be kept informed of any changes to the cost and schedule of the project. The project manager has to regularly update the risk mitigation plan and provide project risk related updates to the stakeholders.

Stakeholder Communication

A well-defined and agreed-upon communication plan is necessary for continuous stakeholder engagement. A stakeholder communication plan should be defined during the project planning phase, with clearly defined objectives such as:

- Providing the current status of the project to all the concerned stakeholders at regular intervals.

- Providing an update of the progress against the defined milestones and quality attributes (cost, effort, and schedule).

- Enabling smooth communication channel between the project team and all stakeholders.

- Defining the communication processes and protocol that is agreed upon by all parties related to status updates, meeting setup, documentation, notification, and communication triggers.

- Identifying communication tools such as e-mails, real-time audio/video conferences, messengers, and online dashboard reports that can be used for stakeholder communication.

Handling Escalations

Any consistent deviation from the defined project SLAs (such as schedule, effort, cost, and quality) or non-adherence to defined project processes lead to an escalation. The stakeholders and system users try to fix the deviation and get the required results through escalation. For instance, a business sponsor raises an escalation if there is a consistent slippage in the release date.

Escalation indicates a project management issue and requires immediate course corrective measures. Mismanagement of escalation will likely lead to poor user satisfaction and greatly reduce user support and adoption. Consistent escalations that are left unattended could also lead to program failure. Here are the project manager's best practices for handling escalation:

- Clearly define and communicate the project processes such as the project management process, the communication process, the release management process, etc. to all the concerned stakeholders and get buy-in from all concerned stakeholders about the project processes.

- Constantly engage all the stakeholders and keep them updated on the project's status. The project manager has to understand the expectation from all key stakeholders and proactively address any stakeholder concerns before they snowball into larger issues.

- Proactively solicit feedback from all stakeholders and system users at regular intervals to predict early warning signs of any concerns.

- Constantly monitor the project risks and continuously update the risk mitigation plan to completely address the project risks. All stakeholders should be kept updated on the risk mitigation plan.

- Create a dedicated escalation management team consisting of subject matter experts (SMEs), an escalation manager, and a single point of contact (SPOC) for communicating the updates. The escalation management team also identifies the backup resource for each responsibility in case of emergencies. The escalation management team defines the action plan to address the escalation, assigns the roles and responsibilities for each of the team members, and uses efficient resources to handle the crisis. The escalation team has to commit to timelines and provide the needed resources to address the escalation.

- Conduct the root cause analysis of the problem that led to escalation and document the lessons to prevent such incidents from happening in the future. The project manager has to address any process gaps in the processes that led to the escalation.

Knowledge Transition Planning

Knowledge transition is planned during project planning and is executed during the final stages of the project, wherein the implementation vendor has to transition the application knowledge to the owning organization. The owning organization has to obtain licenses of all proprietary software and intellectual property as part of this transition. This section looks at the training plan, which is a key tool in knowledge transition planning.

Training Plan

Training is included as part of business continuity process (BCP) to ensure a smooth transition from the software implementation vendor to the organization.

Some digital projects will require formal training to maintain the system and to provide end user training. The project manager has to list training documents as formal deliverables in such scenarios and plan activities accordingly. Based on the scope of the training, the digital project manager has to plan for training documents, such as training documentation, videos, classroom sessions, e-learning materials, knowledge management systems, etc. Table 8-2 lists the key training deliverables and the scenarios in which they can be used.

Table 8-2. *Training Deliverables*

Training Type	Training Deliverables	Scenarios Where They Can Be Used
Application and solution documentation	User guide, how-to guide, solution documentation, solution manuals	For end user training and administrator training
	Troubleshooting tips, checklists, job aids	To train the system administrators and system users
Live training	Interactive instructor-led classroom training	To train developers and administrators on new skills and technologies
	Scenario walkthroughs	To explain the changes in business flows and scenarios
	Application demo	To provide an overview of the new application and its key features to the end user
e-learning	Recorded sessions	To facilitate self-paced learning
	Training web pages	To facilitate on-demand learning

The project manager has to understand the training expectations of each stakeholder and work with the training team to develop the relevant training and deliver it in the most appropriate mode. Each training delivery should also contain assessment exercises, such as quizzes and feedback, to gauge the effectiveness of the training. The high-level steps of a training delivery plan are explained here:

- *Training need analysis*: Understand the target audience for the training, their training expectations, and their preferred learning methods. All concerned stakeholders should sign off on the training delivery format.

- *Training content development*: Based on the training expectations, training content will be designed. For instance, scenarios and flows can be explained by step-by-step examples, along with screenshots or videos. Debugging and troubleshooting steps are best documented in a question-and-answer format.

- *Training content delivery*: The training team can schedule training workshops to deliver interactive classroom-based training. For online training modules, relevant training content can be published to a centralized repository and the training manager can communicate the details to all stakeholders. The training team can also conduct assessments to understand the effectiveness of training content and delivery mode.

Project Tracking and Success Quantification

The project manager has to constantly monitor the project's performance. Metrics and key performance indicators (KPIs) quantify the performance of the project. This section briefly looks at these tracking tools.

Goals, Objectives, KPIs, and Success Criteria

Digital program goals are long-term targets defined by the business and are outcomes of the business strategy. Objectives are tangible, measurable, and granular representations of goals. The project's objectives are derived from the program goals. Key performance indicators (KPIs) are mapped to these objectives and are used to evaluate the performance of the digital solution. A sample mapping of goal, objectives, and KPIs is given in Table 8-3.

Table 8-3. *Mapping Goals to KPIs*

Goal	Objectives	KPIs
Increase online revenue of the retail site	Increase revenue per user	Percent increase in average order value
	Increase site visitors	Percent increase in site traffic
	Increase cross-sell and up-sell	Percent increase in sale of product bundles/packages

Success criteria is based on the overall goals of the digital program and measure the related objectives, such as effort, schedule, quality, and others. Success criteria often use the KPIs to quantify the performance of the digital program.

Digital Project Governance

Project governance plays a key role in effective project management. We discuss various aspects of digital product governance in Chapter 12. This section looks at the governance aspects such as digital project governance model, PMO, proactive quality governance, and project auditing.

Overall Project Governance Model

Every digital project should define the governance model for the entire project. A sample governance model is depicted in Figure 8-5. It depicts a three-tier pyramid structure of a project management hierarchy with communication frequency, activities, and ownership at each of the levels. The roles, activities, and responsibilities are clearly defined at each level.

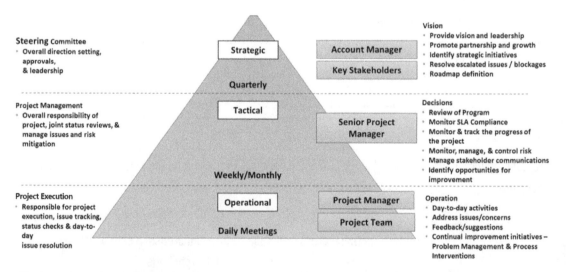

Figure 8-5. *Sample project governance model*

The top of the hierarchy shows the strategic initiatives, which consist of a steering committee made up of of account managers, engagement managers, and other key stakeholders. The steering committee is a leadership team consisting of senior stakeholders. They advise the team and provide overall guidance, manage escalation, and make critical decisions. The steering committee defines and monitors strategic initiatives, formulates the program's vision and goals, and defines the program's roadmap. Normally, the steering committee communicates on a quarterly basis. The frequency of communication can be adjusted based on the program's needs.

The next level in the hierarchy is for achieving tactical goals. It consists of senior project management team and senior managers who are responsible for managing the overall digital projects. The senior project managers monitor and track critical project deliverables and resolve any critical issues. They are also responsible for stakeholder communication and timely risk management. Senior project managers also define the continuous improvement and productivity improvement processes that are aligned with the overall project vision and long-term objectives. The communication frequency is weekly or monthly, based on the project's needs.

At the bottom of the pyramid are the project managers and the project team, who look after day-to-day operations. The team communicates daily for a smooth project execution. Project managers are responsible for managing day-to-day activities, such as incident management, problem management, and addressing any related issues. Project managers implement the continuous improvement processes defined by senior managers. Project managers track the project at a granular level based on the defined KPIs and communicate the status to senior project managers. The status reports mainly track the project quality attributes, such as cost, effort, schedule, variance, performance indicators, and other forecasting values.

Project Management Office (PMO)

The PMO is established to govern and monitor the project and is also responsible for the smooth execution of the project. The main responsibilities of the PMO are as follows:

- Defines the key project management processes such as change management, escalation management, and other controls.

- Defines the compliance standards from a project management standpoint.

- Guides the project managers in effective management of risk, escalations, change requests, and scope creep.

- Regularly controls and monitors the project status to ensure smooth project execution.

- Establishes communication channels with all key stakeholders for effective communication management and manages dependency across stakeholders.

Table 8-4 lists various activities performed by the PMO members.

Table 8-4. *Sample Activities of PMO*

Meeting Category	PMO Activities
Project review meeting	• Project progress review
	• Risk monitoring and mitigation measures
	• Contingency planning
	• Project performance assessment (cost, quality, effort, and schedule)
	• Provide any needed support in securing resources
	• High-level design and architecture review
Steering committee meeting	• Review program direction and roadmap progress
	• Assess program performance with respect to defined goals and metrics
	• Release planning and securing approvals from all stakeholders
	• Define governance structure
	• Manage change requests.
Ad hoc meetings	• Emergency risk management (production outage related meetings or business continuity meetings)
	• Change requests and scope change management

Proactive Quality Governance

The digital project manager has to proactively plan for quality improvements and measures like automation, productivity improvements, and such. We discussed the quality aspects in detail in Chapter 7. The digital project manager has to define the quality plan, covering all the aspects. Table 8-5 provides a sample mapping of challenges, mitigation strategies, and tools that can be used in various project phases.

Table 8-5. *Common Challenges and Mitigation Measures at Various Project Phases*

Category\Project Phase	Project Planning	Project Execution	Project Maintenance
Challenges	Incomplete requirements, incorrect priorities, incorrect estimation, lack of governance processes	Lack of automation, absence of quality control measures,	Absence of tracking and performance assessment metrics
Mitigation strategies	Requirements elaboration workshops and such tools can be used to prioritize requirements, business value articulation can be used to quantify project performance, usage of appropriate estimation models	Iterative delivery, automated quality control processes	Governance processes for release management, maintenance, and incident management, SLA based monitoring, automation, and continuous improvement process
Tools	Requirements traceability matrix tools Stakeholder management plan, risk management plan, scope management plan, and capability roadmap definition	Change request management process, coding guidelines/checklists	Monitoring framework, centralized knowledge management system, usage of best known methods (BKM) and best practices

We explain other key mitigation strategies in the following section.

Using the Appropriate Execution Models

Project managers can select the appropriate execution model based on the stability of the requirements and risk potential of the project. For high-risk projects, it is better to choose the Agile execution model or an iterative model to minimize risk.

The project manager has to constantly think about improving existing processes and project SLAs. Here is a sample list of continuous improvement measures that can be achieved in digital projects:

- Process improvements/optimization/automation

- Preventive maintenance activities, such as performance tuning, patching, and upgrades

- Automation of activities such as report generation, notification, access management, and account management (unlock and creation)

- Knowledge management setup to store the best practices and documentation

- Proactive monitoring in real time

- Self-service enablement for business and end users

Project Auditing

Auditing is the process of collecting, examining, and verifying the evidence against the agreed upon standards and references. Auditing plays a crucial role in ensuring that the project adheres to the best practices, industry standards, and agreed-upon specifications. A project auditor can use the standards, checklists, and best practices as references for auditing. Auditing helps projects achieve the desired performance and maturity levels/standards (such as CMMI levels) and reduces overall project risk.

Auditing normally happens throughout the project's lifecycle. Auditing checks for standards related to various aspects of the project, such as project management processes (such as release management, estimation and staffing, deployment, risk management, resource onboarding, and training processes), code quality standards, documentation standards, and security standards.

The key objectives of project auditing are as follows:

- To check for compliance to defined standards/guidelines.

- To assess the maturity level.

- To mitigate project-related risks.

- To check adherence to best practices, lessons, and checklists.

- To ensure quality and timely project deliverables.

The main steps in the project auditing process are described in the following sections.

Audit Planning

During this step, the project auditor defines the scope and boundary of the audit. The auditor has to identify the in-scope audit topics, such as the project management processes and deliverables that need to be audited. As part of the planning process, the auditor also compiles and prepares checklists, questionnaires, and surveys. Many functional domains require regulatory compliance (related to data storage/transmission restrictions, data exchange format standards, etc.) and all those compliance requirements are validated during auditing.

Evidence Gathering

During this phase, the auditor collects the needed information for all the in-scope audit topics. The evidence is collected through holding staff/stakeholder interviews, observing project practices, and examining the project repository. All the audit instruments are identified and created during this phase. For accurate results, an auditor has to define multi-dimensional evidence gathering mechanisms (for instance, interview the project team members about the check-in process and verify the check-in process in the release management document).

Evidence Analysis

During this phase, the gathered evidence is analyzed and compared against the predefined standards and best practices. The processes are analyzed to identify any gaps. If the auditor needs more information based on the first level of analysis, the auditor reaches out to the team again until all the evidence is obtained.

Audit Reporting

In this final step, the auditor presents the findings, suggestions, observations, and gaps from the audit exercise. The report is shared with all concerned stakeholders and, whenever needed, the auditor follows up to close/verify any gaps. If auditing is part of a maturity assessment or certification process, the auditor assesses the maturity level or certifies the project based on this audit exercise.

Summary

In this chapter we discussed various aspects of project management:

- Business goals and drivers are mapped to elaborate the business requirements and solutions.

- The business drivers can be obtained through an explicitly stated BRD (business requirements document) and business stakeholder interviews and by elaborating the program's vision.

- The requirements elaboration process consists mainly of four phases: requirements gathering, requirements elaboration, requirements validation, and requirements signoff.

- During the requirements gathering phase, the key requirement scope items and scope boundaries are defined.

- During the requirements elaboration phase, each of the identified use cases/user stories are elaborated on, with details such as main flows, exception flows, and business rules.

- During the requirements validation phase, the captured requirements are validated and prioritized by all concerned stakeholders.

- During the requirements sign-off stage, the project team addresses all the feedback and formally seeks sign-off from all stakeholders.

- Change requests (CR) are enhancement requests that deviate from the agreed scope of work.

- The CR process consists of steps such as identification, PM review, steering committee review (also known as configuration control board—CCB), approval, technical review, CAB approval, budget allocation, implementation, and release.

- A project manager has to identify and manage all relevant stakeholders for the overall success of the project.

- The stakeholder management process consists of stakeholder identification, assignment of stakeholder roles, and continuous stakeholder engagement.

- Any consistent deviation from the project SLAs (such as schedule, effort, cost, or quality) or lack of adherence to define project processes can lead to escalation.

- Training is included as part of the business continuity process (BCP) to ensure a smooth transition.

- Digital program goals are long-term targets defined by the business and are outcomes of the business strategy. Objectives are tangible, measurable, and granular representations of goals. Project objectives are derived from the program's goals.

- The PMO is established to govern and monitor the project and is responsible for the smooth execution of the project.

- Auditing is the process of collecting, examining, and verifying the evidence through project artifacts and processes against the agreed-upon standards and references.

CHAPTER 9

People Management in Digital Projects

People management is one of the key activities of a project manager. Successful implementation of any project requires a well-coordinated team effort. People management is more of an art than a science. A good manager should be genuinely interested in people. A digital program normally needs people with varied skillsets. In these cases, team coordination and people management assume a higher importance. Many digital projects need close collaboration across various teams and often test the limits of one's knowledge and traits. A fully motivated team is bigger than the sum of its parts. Hence, a good manager should understand the key motivations of all the team members, enable them to fulfill their aspirations, and align them to the program goals. An efficient people manager helps the team perform at its maximum potential. Achieving this task is easier said than done. This chapter discusses the various hats a project manager has to wear during people management.

Program managers, project managers, account managers, business executives, and enterprise architects will find the content in this chapter useful. We start with the key attributes of a people manager and then dive deep into the concepts related to coaching. We then look at various aspects of feedback management and team motivation. We also cover the main points related to team motivation, crisis management, and competency development.

Key Traits of People Management

Every individual is different and hence the motivations of each individual vary. In this section we look at the key qualities that managers and leaders need.

© Shailesh Kumar Shivakumar 2018
S. K. Shivakumar, *Complete Guide to Digital Project Management*,
https://doi.org/10.1007/978-1-4842-3417-4_9

Key Attributes of a People Manager

Here are the main attributes of an effective people manager:

- Active listening to the team member's problems and understanding body language. Active listening is listening with undivided attention and empathy.

- Create a positive atmosphere that encourages the team to fulfill the end goals with minimal obstacles.

- Recognize and reward top achievers and celebrate the success of the team. A project manager should use every opportunity to recognize the success and contributions of each team member.

- Inspire confidence in the team by leading all the way. The manager should earn the trust of the team and set high standards in quality and integrity. During difficult times, the team is more likely to help a project manager who is trustworthy.

- Celebrate the team's successes, such as milestone completion, client appreciation, and major release parties to create a positive atmosphere.

Leadership Qualities Needed for People Management

A leader inspires the confidence of the team and supports the team to achieve their maximum potential. Here are the main attributes of a leader:

- *Lead by example*: Every team member has a distinct responsibility and this rule is applicable to a project manager as well. A project manager should set the example in delivery quality, time management, and interpersonal communication.

- *Integrity*: A project manager has to make realistic promises and be able to keep commitments. The team is more likely to trust a leader with integrity and this helps the leader motivate the team during challenging times.

- *Positive worldview*: A leader should be able to see the opportunities in every challenge. The leader should be able to inspire the team even in difficult times. The leader should create a positive environment.

- *Proactive attitude*: The leader should be proactive in planning, risk handling, and in quality control measures. A leader should seek to constantly improve the productivity and quality of the deliverables.

- *Innovative*: A leader should foster innovation by creating a supportive environment. A leader should constantly strive to improve the outcomes and quality of the digital project through constant innovation. This could involve the exploration of open source tools, cloud deployment, and development of reusable frameworks and solutions, for example.

The Project Manager as a Coach

People coaching involves guiding and enabling people to achieve their fullest potential and aligning them to the defined goals. In the context of digital project management, the team coach should enable every team member to meet the needed challenges. More often than not, being a coach is one of the many hats a digital project manager has to wear.

Each person has a different social, educational, and economic background and hence his aspirations, motivations, and limitations also differ. A fully synergized team is greater than the sum of its parts and the coach plays a key role in helping the team reach those heights. The coach is responsible for creating the right team chemistry by acting as a catalyst for the team's overall success. An effective coach enables each individual to perform to his/her fullest potential.

Coaching is needed in various scenarios. Coaching can be used as a trust-building exercise as well. A people-centric manager is always approachable. As a part of coaching, the manager should identify gaps in expectations and articulate a clear path to fill any gaps.

Leveraging her experience, a project manager can coach the team members to handle difficult situations and meet the program expectations. A good coach is a good listener and explores the task from various dimensions. The coach has genuine interest in improving the outcome of the situation. Here are some of the best practices and tools that can be used when coaching:

- *Resource scorecard*: Maintain a scorecard/dashboard view for all the team members. The scorecard should depict the strengths and gaps of each of the team members and should reflect the performance (timeliness, quality of the deliverable, complexity of the work handled, consistency, helping peers, outstanding contribution, flexibility etc.) of the team members. The scorecard should be used to provide timely feedback to team members. The scorecard should be updated after each deliverable and can be used during performance appraisals.

- *Expectation setting*: Each member should know the expected outcome of the entire program (the big picture view) and their role in the program. The project manager should clearly and unambiguously articulate these roles to each team member. Each team member should know the deliverable for which he/she is accountable, including the ownership activities, timelines, and dependencies. The coach should periodically monitor the team member's performance regarding the set expectations and provide feedback wherever needed.

- *Actionable performance improvement plan (PIP)*: A course corrective measure is needed if any team member deviates from the set program goal. During such times, a coach needs to come up with an actionable and time-bound performance improvement plan, which typically consists of activities such as skill upgrade training, shadowing another resource, pair programming, and technology assessments.

Once the people with the right skillsets are on the team, the coach has to articulate the goals and purpose of the project and identify the development plan based on roles and responsibilities.

Here are the situations that need coaching:

- Addressing any skillset gaps among team members. In this case, the coach would determine a training plan based on individual strengths and interests. If an organization does not have a dedicated training team, the team can use e-learning material and online documentation as a starting point. Senior team members and experts in the functional domain should train others to address any skill gaps.

- Coaching is essential to get team members back on track when they are demotivated, lose focus, develop trust issues, have attitude issues, or develop commitment issues.

- Coaching is also sometimes needed to resolve hierarchical issues, inter-personal conflicts, project crises, and to resolve negative environments created within the team.

- Coaching can also be used as a performance enhancement tool that can be used to boost overall team performance.

Key responsibilities of a coach are as follows:

- Observe the performance of the team and listen to their issues with utmost care. Give timely and honest feedback and constructive criticism, with an actionable improvement plan when needed.

- Develop rapport with each of the team members through continuous engagements. This will help the project manager understand the emotional traits and build trust.

- Build confidence among the team members to influence outcomes.

- Improve the effectiveness of the team by optimizing the processes and removing any constraints or redundancies.

- Use the experience and subject matter knowledge to provide feedback and tips to troubleshoot issues.

- Understand the strengths and weakness of each team member and bring about behavior changes wherever necessary.

- Come up with the right training and learning plans for the team members.

- Provide all the tools and resources that help the team perform its defined duties.

- Maintain team focus and interest through job rotation, delegation, enablement, guiding, and facilitating team members.

- Foster innovation and creativity among the team members by creating healthy competition and challenges. Rekindle interest and create a sense of ownership to the deliverables.

- Align the team with priority activities and clearly define the responsibilities and expectations.

- Create direction, vision, and a positive atmosphere to motivate each team member to perform at her fullest potential.

- Take participative and inclusive steps in resolving issues and improving productivity.

- Celebrate team successes and give a vote of confidence when the team performs well. Value team members' contribution and reward the high-performance individuals.

- Set realistic targets for team members and assign stretch goals to high potential team members to challenge them with new ideas. The coach should discuss the targets and goals by collaborating with the team members to get buy-in.

- Motivate the team toward achieving the project's overall cause.

- In case of repetitive or mundane jobs, it is important to rotate the responsibilities to keep the team members motivated.

Coaching Process

The key steps of coaching are further explained in Figure 9-1.

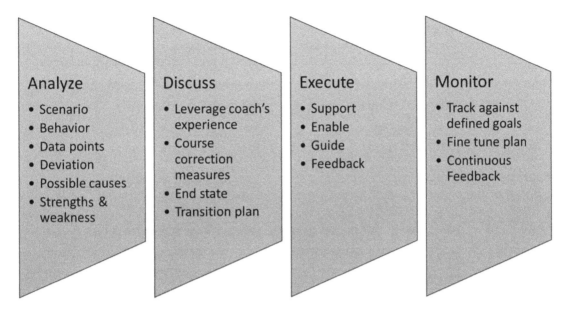

Figure 9-1. Steps in coaching

In the analysis phase, the coach gets a thorough understanding of the situation. The coach analyzes the context and behavior of the individual team members in those scenarios. The coach also compiles the necessary data points and specific examples that can be used for an objective feedback. The coach must also take note of any deviations from the defined path and analyze possible causes.

During the discussion phase, the coach conducts one-on-one discussions with each of the team members to discuss the deviations and data points. Based on his experience, the coach must come up with a transition plan and any course corrective measures to fix the gaps and reach the desired end state. The course corrective measures could be learning plans, training, behavioral tips, best practices, or other known solutions for a given problem. The coach should discuss the plan with the team member and get a commitment to change.

Execution is a joint effort between the team and the coach. While each team member should use the course corrective steps discussed earlier, the coach needs to support the team through tools and resources. The coach would also give continuous feedback about progress.

During the monitoring phase, the coach tracks the course correction plan against the goals and fine tunes the plan if needed.

Coaching Style

The coaching style should differ based on the potential and behavioral attitudes of each team member. Coaches can adopt their coaching styles accordingly. Table 9-1 provides a few coaching styles and includes scenarios where they can be applied.

Table 9-1. *Coaching Styles*

Coaching Style	Key Tenets	Applicable Scenarios
Direct coaching	• Clearly understand the low motivation levels and design course corrective measures accordingly. • Give highly structured, unambiguous instructions to team members. • Closely monitor progress. • Provide continuous nurturing and hand holding. • Identify motivational needs of the individuals. • Provide exact set of tools, solutions an, products, and methodologies to the team to achieve the goal.	• Applicable when coaching team members who have consistently deviated from the defined path and who lack intrinsic motivation. • Can be used for a major course corrective measure. • Can be used when there is strict deadline nearing or when there is a huge project risk or during crisis.
Guided coaching	• Provide tips on maximizing their potential. • Define the end goals and quality metrics for the task. • Understand and analyze the situation through active questioning. • Analyze the outcomes of each of the tasks and give iterative feedback. • Encourage people to develop the needed skills and knowledge for the job.	• Can be used for coaching motivated individual who are not performing to their fullest extent. • Applicable to people who have potential but are sometimes lazy in executing the tasks.

(continued)

Table 9-1. (*continued*)

Coaching Style	Key Tenets	Applicable Scenarios
Delegated coaching	• Provide little intervention. • Delegate most of the high-risk tasks. • Provide complex and challenging tasks. • Enable the individual with the necessary tools and resources and remove the obstacles. • Provide freedom and flexibility to improvise. • Lay out career plan and development roadmap and actively supporting career growth by providing all possible opportunities.	• Applicable to highly motivated individuals and high potential individuals and self-starters.

Coaching Tools

Table 9-2 shows a simple questionnaire-based tool to assess the skill level and behavioral level of each team member. The questions are organized into two categories: technical skills and behavioral skills. Coaches can use the responses from this questionnaire to select the most suitable coaching style and training needs for each team member.

Table 9-2. *Skill Questionnaire*

Question	Rating on scale of 1-5 (5 strongly agree, 4 moderately agree, 3 neutral, 2 disagree, 1 strongly disagree)
Technical Skills	
Does the team member possess the technical skills needed to perform the job?	
Does the team member possess relevant experience in the related technical domain?	

(*continued*)

Table 9-2. (*continued*)

Does the team member possess a broad range of technical skills that can be applied to a varied set of problems outside his/her core expertise?

Does the team member needs constant technical guidance and mentoring?

Does the technical team member deliver technical deliverables with consistent high quality?

Does the team member apply the industry standard best practices to all problems?

Behavioral Skills

Is the team member self-driven and motivated?

Does the team member take full ownership for the task assigned to him/her?

Does the team member collaborate well with his/her peers to achieve the common project goal?

Does the team member exhibit a positive attitude toward work?

Does the team member take on additional responsibilities when the team needs this?

Does the team member proactively mentor his/her peers to help the team cause?

Based on the overall scoring, you can determine the appropriate coaching style as follows:

- *Overall score between 48 and 60*: Team members in this category are generally self-motivated with little to no supervision needed. You can adopt the delegated coaching style for them. Project managers can challenge them with complex tasks.

- *Overall score between 36 and 48*: The team members in this category are generally self-motivated, with little to no supervision needed. You can adopt the guided coaching style for them. Project managers can challenge them with complex tasks.

- *Overall score below 36*: These team members need tighter supervision and project managers need to give provide defined task structure. Project managers need to adopt a direct coaching style for them.

Feedback Management

Timely and actionable feedback goes a long way to helping team members take course corrective measures. A project manager should use an effective feedback management mechanism to fix any gaps.

Feedback management channels should establish continuous multi-way communication across team members. It is always advisable to provide continuous feedback to team members. In many scenarios, managers hold on to their feedback until the completion of a project or a major milestone. However, the more you delay the feedback, the more you deny the person an opportunity to take course corrective measures. Feedback should be continuous and iterative.

Feedback should be a two-way street. A team should also be able to give feedback about its manager through a 360-degree feedback mechanism so that project managers can reflect on their effectiveness as well. If the organization lacks a formal 360-degree feedback process, project managers should use available processes and tools such as e-mails, performance meetings, and one-on-one discussions to solicit feedback from their subordinates.

Providing Feedback

Effective project management involves giving actionable feedback to team members. A project manager should be trusted by this team members; otherwise, the feedback will have little impact. Key attributes of feedback are:

- Feedback should be given about each deliverable/output. It is recommended to give iterative and continuous feedback rather than provide it once every six months, for example. This helps team members work on improving areas of weakness. Focus the feedback only to the specific job or output. The main intent of the feedback should be to improve the overall situation and this intent should be clearly articulated. A good feedback discussion should include the strengths and improvement areas against the set goals and the individual's career aspirations.

- Use the right channel for feedback. Written feedback through e-mail is good enough for generic/common issues, but for detailed feedback that needs to have a high impact, it is essential to have a one-on-one meeting.

- The feedback loop should form the culture of the organization. At every logical end point, each person should seek 360-degree feedback from all the stakeholders he/she interacted with.

- Feedback should be honest and should unambiguously call out the actionable items, such as improvements areas, skill gaps, and such. The feedback points should be nonjudgmental and objective in nature and they should be benchmarked with mutually agreed upon goals. Each action item should be backed by a detailed action plan.

- Conclusions should be objectively based on facts rather than on opinions. Cite specific scenarios and examples wherever needed rather than providing vague/generic comments.

- Coaches should watch out for biases—such as attribution bias, the anchor effect, and the halo effect—when giving feedback. Attribution bias causes judgment error while assessing people's behavior. The halo effect is caused when we judge a person in one subject based on his/her expertize in a completely unrelated topic. With the anchor effect, people come to a judgment based on recent point of discussion. All these biases can be overcome through an objective analysis of the context and finding the real root cause.

- Feedback should also include attitude and behavior issues, if any.

- Keep the feedback as two-way communication. Listen with empathy to understand the issue in its entirety.

- Ensure that the feedback and response is compatible with the person's emotional traits.

- A project manager should keep a log of key achievements so that it can be used to provide data-driven objective feedback during the feedback discussion. A simple feedback template is shown in Table 9-3.

Table 9-3. *Feedback Template*

Date	Team Member	Key Achievement	Areas for Improvement	Key Impact/Outcome of the Achievement

The Project Manager as a Team Motivator

The team can achieve more than the sum of the parts if all its team members are inspired toward the end goal. The project manager has to constantly motivate the team to realize its full potential. The first step in this regard is establishing trust. The project manager has to earn the trust of the team members. Trust always works two ways and has to be earned over a period of time. A project manager has to enable her team members with all the necessary skills and training to perform the job. In crisis situations, it is important to focus on the problem at hand and not on the people. Once the team trusts the project manager, it's easier for the project manager to motivate the team toward the greater goals.

Key points in team motivation are as follows:

- Always challenge the team to take up new initiatives and set the bar high. The challenges could be a reduction in defect volume, productivity improvements, and so on.

- Encourage the team members to question the status quo. Enable the team to improve quality, productivity, time to market, and automation, for example. Many times we have seen businesses optimize by questioning the status quo. Teams can cross-pollinate ideas from different contexts to optimize business processes.

- Enable team members to constantly innovate upon existing processes. This involves automating the process steps, reducing process steps, enhancing user experience, and so on.

- Keep changing roles and rotate responsibilities. This inspires team members who are performing repetitive tasks such as maintenance and support. A project manager can rotate the people performing jobs such as production support, L2 support, and customer support so that they get exposure to various tasks. This not only enhances their skillsets, but it also enhances their skill breadth so that they can be deployed to a wide variety of jobs when the need arises.

- Encourage constant learning among team members so they can constantly upgrade their skills. Continuing to learn is key to surviving in a fast-changing digital world. Many organizations formally set appraisal targets that are linked to technical certifications.

- Create open communication channels and collaboration platforms so the entire team can communicate and share knowledge. Likewise, the project manager should be approachable.

- Regularly conduct team building exercises where team members get a chance to interact with each other outside of their work environment. Team bonding exercises serve as a great tool to maintain harmony.

The Project Manager as a Crisis Handler

Conflicts arise on a team for a variety of reasons. Regardless of their source, they have a detrimental effect on the team's goals. The main sources of conflicts are inter-personal issues, misunderstanding project goals, individual work styles, and deadline pressures.

Here are some of the best practices for project managers to handle such conflicts:

- Establish well-defined roles and responsibilities for each team member.

- Regularly monitor for potential crisis or inter-personal conflicts and address them early and often.

- Define the ground rules. Clearly define the behavioral-related ground rules. Make sure that the team is aware of the organization-related rules as well.

- Create a common code of conduct that the entire team has to adhere to. A common code of conduct should cover the topics related to general behavior, integrity, and communication. This should complement general company policies.

- Seek out a 360-degree view of the conflict. Critically analyze the scenario from various perspectives and viewpoints to get a full understanding.

- During the time of conflict, focus on the issue and not on the people. This helps you fix the problem at hand quickly. Once the issue is fully resolved, the team can jointly conduct a post-mortem of the issue and document the lessons from the incident.

- Monitor behavioral changes regularly and identify problems in the early stages. Take course corrective measures to prevent a larger problem.

- Document the lessons from the conflict resolution and adopt any necessary policy changes.

- Regularly conduct team building activities to build rapport among team members and to build team culture.

- Adopt best practices of collaborative development.

- Actively engage team members through all communication channels. Listen to, understand, and address their concerns in a timely manner.

Competency Development

Continuous learning and competency development are key essentials of any software project. This is even more relevant in the context of digital projects, where technologies are continually evolving. More often than not, it's hard to find the right skilled people for a digital project. Some of the best practices in competency development are as follows:

- Identify the requirements, technologies, and product challenges ahead of time. Plan accordingly for the resources.

- Provide a competency development plan as part of the regular feedback and appraisals.

- Regularly shuffle key resources across various technologies to improve their breadth of knowledge.

- Create a central knowledge repository and provide self-paced e-learning channels. The centralized knowledge base should contain self-learning materials such as wikis, tutorials, user guides, how-to articles, and product documentation.

- Factor in the learning curve for digital projects involving niche skills.

- Constantly look out for emerging trends in the digital space and support the team so they can learn and acquire those skills and apply them to the current context.

Maintaining a Work-Life Balance for the Team

Some projects are long-term and therefore require a long-term commitment from the team. Besides this, the team might also have to log extended hours during production releases. An occasional late night stay is a reasonable ask, but the project should not demand sustained extra hours from the team. When this happens, you get loss in productivity, loss of morale, and eventually attrition. Sustained extra hours impact the personal life of your team members. The next section looks at some common causes of a team having to work extra hours on a continuous basis.

Common Causes of Continued Stretching of the Team

Here are some of the common causes that result in effort overrun:

- *Incorrect estimation model used on the project.* Under estimating a project's scope leads to a team putting in extra hours to make up for an overly aggressive estimation.

- *Improper handling of scope creep.* A project manager has to manage the scope with a well-defined scope document. The project manager has to use a baseline version of the requirements document to accept any new requests. While minor/cosmetic changes can be absorbed without much effort, big changes should qualify for a change request.

- *Mismatch in skillset.* If the team members lack the required skills for a project and if they are not sufficiently trained, they will end up spending many hours implementing the requirements.

- *Uneven workload distribution among team members.* This leads to a selected few consistently clocking overtime, leading to loss of productivity and morale.

- *Absence of change management process.* If a change request (CR) is not identified and handled properly, it will impact the development and testing processes.

Best Practices to Maintain a Good Work-Life Balance for the Team

Almost all organizations and HR managers aim to provide a healthy work-life balance for the employees. A good work-life balance is necessary for long-term sustained productivity and high motivation levels. Here are a few rules of thumb that you can use to achieve a work-life balance.

- Initiate a robust requirements process. Have a complete requirements document reviewed and signed off by all stakeholders. Freeze the requirements/user stories for a given release. All subsequent changes and requests after that should be prioritized for the next iteration.

- Initiate an effective change management process. The project manager has to establish the change management process, which provides the impact, effort, and cost estimate of the change. A high priority ad hoc request that's not in the scope of the release is an ideal candidate for a change request.

- Involve team members in some of the key project planning activities, such as estimation, schedule planning, and such. This collaborative planning will normalize the estimates and bring accountability/ responsibility to the team members.

- Create the work breakdown structure (WBS) to ensure skill-based even load distribution. Project managers can spend approximately 10-20% of their effort on planning activities.

Summary

In this chapter we discussed various aspects of people management:

- The key attributes of a good people manager are active listening, recognizing and rewarding top talent, building team confidence, celebrating team success, and creating a positive team atmosphere.

- A leader should possess these qualities: lead by example, integrity, positive worldview, proactivity, and innovation.

- The main tools used when coaching are the resource scorecard, expectation setting, and an actionable performance improvement plan (PIP).

- The key steps involved in coaching are analyze, discuss, execute, and monitor. During the analysis phase, the coach seeks to understands the situation and all the needed data points. The coach discusses the action plan with the team members during the discussion phase. The coach and the team members jointly execute the discussed and agreed upon plan during the execute phase. The coach closely monitors the outcomes of the execution plan during the monitor phase.

- The three main coaching styles are direct coaching, guided coaching, and delegated coaching. In direct coaching, the coach closely monitors the team member and provides well defined tasks. In guided coaching, the coach enables the team member to achieve the set goals. In delegated coaching, the coach does minimal monitoring.

- The key qualities of effective feedback are timeliness, objectivity, and data-based justification.

- Some of the team motivational factors include setting realistic challenges, encouraging the team to question the status quo, encouraging innovation, rotating job duties, encouraging continuous learning, providing open communication channels, and conducting team building exercises.

- The best practices of crisis handling are defining a common code of conduct, regular monitoring, defining the ground rules, and documenting the lessons.

- Common reasons for effort overrun are incorrect estimation, improper handling of scope creep, uneven load distribution, skill mismatch.

- The best practices to handle the effort overrun is to have a well-defined requirement process, a change management process, collaborative planning, and a WBS (work breakdown structure) structure.

PART III

Monitoring and Maintenance of Digital Projects

CHAPTER 10

Why Digital Projects Fail?

Digital projects, just like many software projects, generally have moderate success rates. In addition to the issues pertaining to any software project, digital projects carry additional risk factors related to the use of niche technologies, unproven products, lack of availability of skillsets, and complex integrations. We discussed the unique challenges of digital projects in Chapter 1. Identifying the risk factors and known issues early during the digital project lifecycle helps project managers take course corrective measures to improve the success rate. There are a few recurring and common themes that typically lead to project failures.

This chapter looks at various anti-patterns, failure scenarios, leading indicators of failure, and common challenges encountered when building digital solutions. We elaborate risk mitigation measures and best practices to address the failures and challenges. Although the focus is on digital projects, the topics we discuss hold true for any software project.

This chapter will help project managers and program managers understand the common failure scenarios so they can tackle these issues early and effectively.

Brief Analysis of Failure Factors

Digital programs are unique in their business goals and have their own unique set of inherent challenges.

Here are some of the common challenges seen across large-scale engagements and the most common causes for digital management failure.

- Scope underestimation or scope creep
- Undefined/ambiguous requirements
- Communication and coordination issues

© Shailesh Kumar Shivakumar 2018
S. K. Shivakumar, *Complete Guide to Digital Project Management*,
https://doi.org/10.1007/978-1-4842-3417-4_10

- Incomplete design

- Incomplete project planning (cost, effort, schedule), tracking, and reporting

- Inexperience or lack of training

- Lack of end user focus

- Poor expectation management

- Poor requirement tracking

- Inappropriate execution methodology

- Misalignment between project team and business goals

- Absence of well-defined metrics for tracking effort, cost, and schedule

- No comprehensive mechanism to track defect, effort, cost, and schedule

- Lack of proactive risk-mitigation measures

- Selection of inappropriate execution method, tool, or technique

- Lack of stakeholder management

The most common technology-related factors leading to failures in digital projects are:

- Inefficient enterprise integrations. This category includes integration methodologies that use numerous synchronous invocations leading to performance issues.

- Incomplete validation process that does not provide adequate code coverage and absence of coverage of comprehensive functional and non-functional test scenarios.

- Application scalability issues due to improper application design and suboptimal infrastructure sizing.

- Performance issues due to improper application design leading to lower adoption rate and higher application abandonment rate.

- Lack of monitoring/notification infrastructure.

Challenges Due to Digital Technologies and Evolving Requirements

Modern digital projects comprise of multiple niche technologies and engage users from different geographies. The world of digital technologies is constantly evolving and hence their project management and technical teams need to adopt due diligence processes in product and technology selection. Niche technologies and a multitude of technologies will further lead to staffing challenges, as well as to training and learning issues, leading to increased complexity of the overall program. As digital projects need people with varied niche skillsets, the digital project managers would typically face challenges in finding the right set of candidates leading to increased lead time in on-boarding the resources. Digital programs should also balance various stakeholders and the solutions should meet highly demanding end users. All these factors bring in a unique set of challenges for digital projects.

In many cases, project managers receive many change requests during the testing phase from end users and concerned stakeholders. For greenfield digital projects (that need new ground up development), requirements are less structured and have a higher degree of ambiguity.

Best practices to address these challenges are:

- As a project manager, identify the skillset needed for the project and come up with a training plan for retraining team members.

- Use a proof-of-concept (PoC) approach to validate complex and unknown technologies and integrations. A good PoC approach would mitigate the risk involved in the actual project. For instance, security implementation and legacy integration normally involve lots of unknowns and hence are ideal candidates for PoCs.

- Create a comprehensive risk-management process to address various aspects of the project.

- Baseline the requirements document and freeze the scope at the end of the requirements phase for a given iteration.

- Establish a change management process to anticipate and manage change. Perform the impact analysis, prioritize the change requests, and communicate the change request implementation plan to all stakeholders.

Challenges in Project Management

Modern digital projects rarely use the waterfall model; iterative delivery and Agile models are assuming the de facto delivery model due to constantly changing requirements and to bring the solution faster to market. The delivery teams and stakeholders need to be aligned to the chosen delivery model. All related aspects of project management, such as scheduling, planning, milestone planning, and testing cycles, should be aligned with the chosen delivery models. For instance, an Agile delivery model needs iterative testing and hence you need to align the developers and testers accordingly to each sprint (as opposed to aligning the testing team at the end of the development).

Continuous process improvements, usage and development of productivity improvement tools, stricter SLAs, continuous real-time monitoring, metrics based tracking, and automation are other ways to tackle the challenges of modern digital projects.

Best practices to address these challenges are:

- The lessons from previous projects, project planning tools, case studies, and estimation templates should be stored in a central repository that can be used by other project managers.

- Use the appropriate execution model that is relevant to the digital project. Normally, the Agile and iterative delivery model is best suited to a greenfield project or complex digital projects. To minimize risk and support/maintenance, projects can adopt steady-state execution models.

Managing Expectations from End Users and Stakeholders

When using Internet facing digital solutions, end users expect highly responsive and immersive experiences. Users expect interactive UI, self-service tools (such as search, product comparators, and page configurators), single views of data, optimized processes, high performance, collaboration, and co-creation (involving end user participation in development of a feature) features. Digital applications should be designed to meet and exceed these expectations.

Best practices to address these challenges are:

- Set realistic expectations with all stakeholders and articulate the risks, goals, challenges, tangible benefits, and assumptions with clearly defined ownership.

- Establish a robust communication management process and set the roles and responsibilities of all the team members during the project initiation stage. Communicate the deliverables from each project phase to all concerned stakeholders. Use appropriate communication channels to engage each stakeholder.

- Define measurable and quantifiable goals and objectives and assign the owners accountability for each goal.

- Identify the key stakeholders for business, technology, operations, and other related aspects. Create a focused communication and management plan for stakeholders based on their importance. Send a focused communication to each stakeholder on a regular basis.

Challenges in Team Management

Sometimes project teams are distributed across various locations. In this case, project managers often face challenges during collaboration, planning, monitoring, and enforcing quality standards. Project managers need to constantly plan for competency development and training to meet the demands of the digital projects. Team motivation and achieving work-life balance are other key challenges in team management.

Best practices to address these challenges are:

- Project managers should provide the big picture to all team members so that they understand their role in the overall project. A big picture view also helps digital project managers align all team members to a common goal.

- Project managers should identify skillset gaps and domain expertise and then equip the team with needed resources. This exercise helps the project manager plan for skillset trainings, resource deployment, and proper resource selection.

- Engage the team members in all phases of the project that would bring in more accountability, including estimation and milestone planning. Collaborative planning helps accurately plan and identify risk. It also helps you get commitment from your team.

- Practice employee motivation exercises such as performance-based rewards, recognition, job rotation, and other such incentives.

Issues at Various Project Lifecycle Stages

So far, the chapter has listed some common challenges in digital projects in the initial stages. Figure 10-1 provides the list of key issues you might face at various project lifecycle phases.

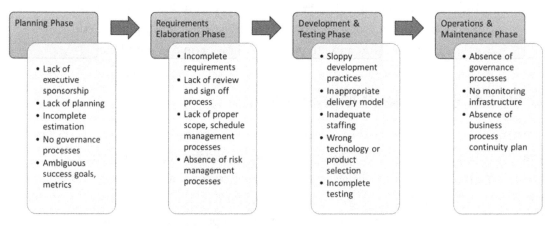

Figure 10-1. *Common challenges in project lifecycle phases*

During the planning phases, if the digital programs fail to secure executive sponsorship from the business stakeholders, this would later lead to budget issues and adoption challenges. Project planning and estimation are two key activities that should be handled properly in the planning phase. Poor planning and estimation can later lead to schedule slippage and cost/effort overrun. Defining robust governance processes is another important activity in the project planning phase. Lack of defined governance processes can later lead to quality issues. If the success criteria, metrics, and KPIs are not well defined, it is challenging to understand the business benefits.

In the requirements elaboration phase, absence of robust requirements management process is one of the key issues. Failure to elaborate detailed functional requirements and non-functional requirements and associated business rules impacts the subsequent phases and leads to a higher defect rate during the validation phase. All requirements documents should be reviewed and signed off by all stakeholders to freeze and baseline these requirements. Failure to define processes related to scope management, change request management, and risk management processes can later lead to effort and schedule overrun.

During the development and testing phases, adopting sloppy development and testing practices can lead to poor quality deliverables. Not staffing the right skilled resources and the right number of resources (based on accurate effort estimation and staffing) can later lead to deliver slippages. Due diligence and product evaluation should be done to select the appropriate technology and product. As the digital software ecosystem is continuously evolving with niche technologies, it is important to select the right products and technologies.

During the operations and governance phase, absence of a monitoring infrastructure can impact the performance and availability SLAs. Without a real-time monitoring and notification infrastructure, the operations team cannot respond quickly to production incidents. Absence of a business continuity plan (BCP) (using a disaster recovery setup) will severely impact availability during natural/unexpected emergencies.

Common Best Practices to Address Challenges in Digital Programs

The common best practices to address challenges in digital programs are as follows:

- Clearly articulate the business values and goals and define traceable success metrics and KPIs. Align the program goals, team, and stakeholders to realize the business value.

- Use the right tools and models for estimating time, cost, and schedule.

- Capture all the requirements and business rules with specific details and get them reviewed by all concerned stakeholders to get their buy-in.

- Test the solution modules thoroughly through unit testing, functional testing, integration testing, performance testing, security testing, and any other applicable forms of testing.

- Establish development guidelines, checklists, standards, tools, open source frameworks, guidelines, and libraries during the design phase. Adhere to the defined principles and standards during the development and testing phases.

- Set the right expectations with all stakeholders through proper communication planning.

- Develop well-defined requirements and scope management processes to handle any change requests and scope creep items.

- Have the right sized infrastructure to meet the nonfunctional SLAs related to scalability, performance, and availability. Plan for the disaster recovery (DR) environment as part of the business continuity process.

- Establish comprehensive quality processes for defect prevention, early defect identification, and code reviews/walkthroughs.

- As digital projects tend to be complex in terms of technologies, it is always recommended to use iterative releases involving iterative development and testing.

- Develop UI prototypes and demos to solicit frequent feedback from all stakeholders. Involve the business in all major decisions and get their buy-in. Get buy-in from all stakeholders through established acceptance criteria.

- Establish a governance process to manage changes, scope creep, releases, role-responsibility matrix, requirement traceability, and tracking and monitoring KPIs.

- Develop a comprehensive requirements management plan. Capture functional and non-functional requirements from various angles. Apart from the regular use case modeling and business rules documentation, project managers can also plan for capturing requirements through workflow modeling, business process modeling, and prototype modeling. Plan for a traceability matrix to trace the requirements from the requirements phase to the release phase.

- Engage stakeholders from the beginning of the project. Seek their approval and articulate the business benefits of the program. A properly engaged stakeholder will become an advocate of the program to the wider community.

- Plan to achieve "quality at the source" through automated code reviews, peer reviews, code coverage reports, unit testing, and other proactive quality initiatives.

- Develop a comprehensive risk management framework that scores the risk based on its likelihood of occurrence, its material impact, and its mitigation cost.

- Create a centralized knowledge management system to store the project lessons, best practices, proven methods, checklists, process/ policy documents, and domain knowledge.

As projects tend to grow, quality processes play a major role in their continued success. Quality processes related to code quality, deployment, testing, and change requests should be clearly defined. The majority of the software project failures are due to schedule overruns, cost overruns, and issues with requirements (such as incomplete, inaccurate, conflicting, unverified, or ambiguous requirements).

Challenges and Best Practices in Digital Transformation

Digital transformation is one of the most prominent scenarios for digital programs. Digital transformation enables the enterprise to leverage the latest digital and web technologies for their offerings. Digital transformation involves legacy modernization, converting a monolithic application into a layered architecture, service enabling legacy applications, experience redesign, centralizing integration, platform migration, and technology consolidation/standardization (see Table 10-1).

Table 10-1. *Challenges and Best Practices in Digital Transformation Projects*

Common Challenges	Best Practices
Absence of governance processes to manage change	• Conduct a thorough impact on all stakeholders; explain processes that happen due to digital transformation. • Communicate the change to all stakeholders. • Identify the risks and come up with mitigation plans. • Manage the dependencies across various teams through clearly-defined collaboration and communication processes and dependency matrixes.
Ambiguous role-responsibility matrix and task ownership	• Create well-defined ownership, accountability, and role-responsibility matrixes among all the teams. • Track and monitor the progress of all teams involved in the digital transformation.
Poorly defined change management process	• Establish a robust scope management and change management process and get buy-in from all stakeholders.
No common standards for the applications, technology, and products	• During the design and architecture phase, consult all stakeholders to define common industry-accepted open standards for the technology. • Use digital transformation as an opportunity to standardize the disparate technologies, systems, and standards.
Business goals and success metrics not clearly defined	• Define traceable and measurable metrics to capture the success of the digital transformation. • Clearly articulate the critical success factors for the project and the tactical and strategic business benefits.
Lack of executive sponsorship	• Secure sponsorship from all key stakeholders at the beginning of the engagement. • Articulate the business value and benefits of the transformation program.

(continued)

Table 10-1. (*continued*)

Common Challenges	Best Practices
Failure to execute digital transformation	• Validate the unknowns and complex functionality in digital transformation through proof of concept (PoC). • Perform thorough validation steps at each transformation step. • Establish a traceability matrix from the requirements to test cases. • Capture nonfunctional requirements related to performance, security, and such and validate them during intermediate steps of transformation.
Failure of co-existence strategy	• Clearly define the data, content, and code synchronization processes between the new system and the old system. • Design the routing, transaction management, and data integrity processes between the new and old systems. • Use the new system to create new data and the legacy system to handle existing data.
Lack of user adoption	• Involve the target audience in the requirements definition, design, and testing processes. • Create awareness campaigns about the program.

Leading Indicators of Project Failures

Table 10-2 explains some of the lead indicators of potential future problems in digital projects. It includes sample root causes and best practices to address them.

Table 10-2. *Lead indicators and Best Practices for Digital Projects*

Lead Indicator	Common Root Cause	Best Practices to Address the Issue
• Team members consistently work beyond stipulated hours to meet deadlines • Team consistently delays deliverable	• Improper project planning • Scope creep • Suboptimal change request management • Incorrect cost/effort estimates	• Use proper project planning tools and use appropriate delivery method (Agile/iterative) • Establish robust scope management and change request processes • Deploy right skilled people for the project • Fill the skill gap with suitable training and enablement sessions • Automate mechanical jobs such as code deployment through tools and scripts • Involve team in planning
• Validation team detects too many defects during system integration phase • UAT team detects numerous defects during the user acceptance testing	• Quality processes not followed • Iterative testing not followed • Requirements not clearly defined	• Use manual code review and automated code analysis tool • Establish stricter quality gating criteria such as unit testing and code checklists • Target for good code coverage through unit testing • Ensure comprehensive requirements documentation and review
• Lower productivity of team • High amount of rework	• Process improvement practices not followed • Design and code review not followed	• Automate mundane activities • Optimize development and release management processes • Use productivity improvement tools

Common Pitfalls/Anti-Patterns in Digital Programs

This section lists the common pitfalls faced in digital programs. It also discusses the proven best practices to overcome these challenges.

Absence of End User Involvement

For B2C applications and Internet facing applications, active engagement of end users is very important. End users and other concerned stakeholders need to be actively involved from the beginning of the project. You can get sample representatives from the end user group to be actively involved in design, prototype validation, A/B testing, and beta testing to get feedback. This active engagement is key to the overall success of the program.

Absence of Incentives and Loyalty

Many of the consumer facing digital applications use Web 2.0 features, such as collaborative functionalities, that encourage participation from the end users. Web content will be co-created with active participation from end users through blogs, wikis, communities, and forums. In such a scenario, gamification principles (the principles that use game concepts such as points, loyalty, etc.) should be used to provide incentives to active participants. Badges and points are some of the ways to reward high-value contributors. Similarly, for e-commerce and shopping digital applications, frequent shoppers should be rewarded with loyalty coupons and personalized sales offers.

Incentives and loyalty are critical success factors and lead to sustained success of the Web 2.0 based digital programs.

Migration Challenges in Digital Programs

Digital transformation often involves migration of as-is legacy applications to a new digital technology stack. The key challenges faced in this scenario are incompatible interfaces and technologies, impacts on business continuity, and such. Here are the key best practices to adopt for migration projects:

- Adopt an iterative migration strategy
- Mitigate risk by validating proof-of-concept (PoC)

- Create a knowledge repository to document a migration approach

- Create reusable migration tools

- Leverage migration tools and automated components to improve productivity

Failure Analysis

Each organization needs to perform a "root cause analysis" at the program level and project levels. All lessons and best practices should be stored in an organization-wide repository. Similarly, the project statistics (program complexity, defect rate, resources, etc.), checklists, and best practices should be stored in the project repository, which can be used as benchmark data for future projects.

Requirements Mismanagement

Requirements management involves various aspects, such as correct, accurate, and complete descriptions of requirements, tracking and monitoring requirements, change request handling, traceability of requirements to design, code unit test cases, and such. Arbitrary and unplanned scope changes without impact analysis lead to scope creep and schedule slippages. Failure to properly manage the requirements is one of the key reasons for project failure.

Issues in Project Estimation

Inaccurate estimates of cost and effort have a ripple effect on project resources, timelines, and planning. Appropriate estimation models should be followed based on the project technology, delivery model, skillset, and timelines. A general rule of thumb is to adopt Agile and iterative models for complex digital projects or projects with multiple unknowns.

Inadequate Staffing

Staffing of the right number of people with the appropriate skillset is important for project success. Inadequate staffing leads to effort and schedule overrun. Staffing closely follows the effort estimation, which is discussed in chapter 4.

Risk Mismanagement

Project managers need to properly identify potential risks and plan for appropriate risk mitigation measures. Failure to manage risks leads to escalation in cost and schedule slippages. We defined the quantitative risk management model in chapter 5.

Expectation Mismatch

Setting appropriate expectations with all stakeholders and team members is important for the success of the overall project. A well-defined governance plan with a role-responsibility matrix can be used to set expectations with all team members.

Lack of Stakeholder Involvement

Insufficient understanding of the goals and needs of all involved stakeholders and failure to get review and sign-off and executive support/sponsorship from key stakeholders can often lead to delays.

Inadequate Quality Measures

Projects that don't adopt comprehensive quality measures such as iterative testing, defect techniques, and thorough review processes are likely to deliver substandard deliverables.

Absence of Change Management Processes

Lack of comprehensive change management processes lead to scope creep and cost/schedule overruns. Change management is applicable to all stakeholder and project groups.

Inadequate Development Practices

A project team that doesn't follow development best practices such as iterative development, code reviews, iterative testing, and iterative delivery can eventually lead to poor-quality deliverables.

Poor Communication Management

Lack of proper communication processes covering all stakeholders can lead to poor problem management.

Schedule Mismanagement

Integrated project analysis and critical path analysis are the key to properly managing the schedule.

Summary

In this chapter, we discussed:

- The main failure causes are scope creep, incomplete requirements, incomplete design, incomplete project planning, and lack of user focus.

- The key technology related factors are inefficient integration, incomplete validation, scalability/performance issues, and lack of monitoring.

- The main best practices for addressing challenges due to niche digital technologies and evolving requirements are right onboarding of resources, adopting proof-of-concept, risk management process, requirement baselining, and a change management process.

- The main best practices for addressing challenges due to complex delivery models and evolving requirements are creating a centralized learning repository and selecting an appropriate execution model.

- The main best practices for addressing challenges due to communication are right expectation setting, robust communication, goal definition, and establishing a good communication process.

- The main best practices for addressing challenges due to team issues are aligning the team with the big picture, skill-based training, and right engagement.

- Some of the key best practices of digital transformation are a right governance process, definition of the responsibility matrix, definition of common standards and metrics, and PoC based validation.

- Common pitfalls in digital programs are lack of end user involvement and absence of incentives.

- The key migration challenges in digital programs are lack of root cause analysis, requirements mismanagement, improper estimation, inadequate staffing, risk mismanagement, expectation mismatch, lack of stakeholder involvement, inadequate quality measures, absence of change management processes, inadequate development practices, poor communication management, and schedule mismanagement.

CHAPTER 11

Digital Project Management Best Practices

Project management best practices consist of practically proven methods that address some of the core recurring issues and proven best practices in the project management domain. This chapter also includes the lessons learned from large digital engagements. This chapter looks at some of the proven project management best practices for digital projects. While the best practices provided in this chapter addresses unique challenges in digital projects, many of them can be adapted to regular software projects as well.

We categorize the best practices into various phases of digital project management: initiation, execution, and monitoring and maintenance. We look at various project management best practices such as continuous integration, continuous improvement, stakeholder management, communication process, project metrics, and automation tools. Project managers can use these best practices as a reference while managing large-scale complex digital projects.

Project managers, program managers, account managers, business executives, and enterprise architects will find the content in this chapter useful.

Typical Challenges with Digital Projects

Typical challenges faced with large digital engagements include:

- Niche technologies in digital space lead to staffing issues
- Managing demanding stakeholder and customer expectations

© Shailesh Kumar Shivakumar 2018
S. K. Shivakumar, *Complete Guide to Digital Project Management*,
https://doi.org/10.1007/978-1-4842-3417-4_11

- Challenges related to delivery model in absorbing changes and releasing the solution quickly to the market

- Organization culture in adopting changes

- Lack of well-defined governance structure

- Siloed departments within organizations

- Multiple technology products and standards

- Lack of quality controls and lack of automation

The best practices should be designed to address these challenges at various phases.

Project Management Best Practices During the Project Initiation Phase

This section looks at some of the project management best practices that you should follow during the project initiation phase.

Awareness of Next Generation Digital Platform Trends

It is important for a project manager to be aware of the latest happenings and emerging trends in the digital space. This not only helps the project manager provide valuable inputs to the overall project, it also helps the project manager actively add value during the requirements elaboration phase.

To achieve this awareness, the project manager has to keep up-to-date on happenings in the digital space and closely track the trends and best practices. Sometimes project managers tend to ignore this crucial factor and focus heavily on the project management aspects. Knowing about digital trends only makes the project managers more effective. It helps them plan more efficiently, staff smartly, and select the most appropriate execution methodology.

Knowing and tracking digital trends of a given domain acts as a force multiplier for a project manager. Table 11-1 lists trends with the intranet digital platforms (such as employee digital portal) and maps them with essential digital capabilities. Awareness of these trends will help project managers in identifying critical components of the digital platform (see Table 11-1).

Table 11-1. *Next Generation Digital Platform Trends*

Intranet Digital Platform Trend	Required Digital Capability
Productivity and process improvements: Users need all essential tools with optimal processes to complete the tasks quickly and efficiently	Digital platform should provide productivity-enhancing tools (such as search tools, navigation tools, knowledge management tools, service requesting logging tools, etc.) with streamlined processes. Wherever possible, processes should be optimized and automated. The platform should provide self-service model (such as self approvals, automated workflows) to enable users to perform tasks independently and efficiently.
Collaboration: Internal users need to share knowledge and documents and harness collective intelligence to work more efficiently	Social and collaboration tools such as blogs, wiki, chat, communities, forums, connections, message boards, and web conferencing are primary enablers of collaboration in a digital platform.
Customer experience enhancement through better understanding of customer needs	Customer experience can be shaped by two approaches: Inside out approach includes analysis of current applications, integration, and business processes; gap analysis; obtaining inputs from internal stakeholders. Outside in approach includes external benchmarking, surveys, and interviews of external stakeholders and customers, compliance against industry standards and best practices.
User engagement: Long-term success of the platform requires long-term relationship enhancing features	Digital platforms should provide highly interactive and compelling user experiences, integrate with available social media platforms such as Facebook, and provide collaborative features such as blogs, wikis, etc. to actively engage users. Proactive communications (such as release mails and seasonal offer communications), notification feeds (such as outage communications), proactive feedback analysis (based on user's explicit feedback and through surveys), and analytics-driven user insight monitoring are some of the digital capabilities that fall into this category.

(continued)

Table 11-1 (*continued*)

Intranet Digital Platform Trend	Required Digital Capability
Anytime anywhere access: Next generation users need to access applications on the go	Digital platform should be mobile enabled and adopt responsive designs to cater to various mobile devices and browsers.
Agility: User community needs quicker bug fixes and instant updates	Agile development methodologies, continuous integration, and other best practices in dev ops are needed to achieve this.

Stakeholder Management

Stakeholder management is relevant to large digital projects with multiple tracks and corresponding stakeholders. Stakeholder management involves identifying the stakeholders and their backgrounds, assessing their influence on the project, managing the stakeholders, implementing the strategies, and establishing a robust communication plan. Stakeholder needs and expectations should be managed to ensure a successful project. Support from various stakeholders can be guaranteed only if they are involved in the right decision making process, communication processes, and various planning meetings. Project managers have to create a stakeholder matrix that identifies all the project stakeholders and devise a communication plan based on their levels of involvement and interest.

Quality Assurance Process

Quality assurance best practices for digital project management include the following:

- *Quality tracking metrics*: Define the project quality metrics. This includes metrics parameters like code coverage, test effectiveness, effort deviation, number of defects, review effectiveness, project schedule, and defect reopen rate.

- *Preventive measures*: Undertake defect preventive measures proactively. This includes root cause analysis, increased automated code reviews, increased code coverage, quality checklists, and quality control measures.

- *Testing automation*: Plan for continuous and iterative testing and automate testing through various tools.

- *Proactive quality measures*: Adopt various proactive measures like automated code reviews, leveraging coding checklists for development, integration, and testing.

Digital Readiness Assessment Checklist

Before embarking on a digital project, a project manager has to determine the readiness of the team for smooth execution of the project. Consider these high-level set of questions to assess readiness:

- Do you have the right set of resources skilled in the digital technologies?

    - This helps in assessing the right skilled people in the project. Project managers should on-board resources with matching skillsets to execute the project and guide the team.

- Do you have a training plan in place for cross-training the project team members?

    - Project managers can use this to come up with training plans for various needed technologies.

- Has the project team executed a project of similar complexity and duration in the past?

    - Prior experience is a big plus for digital projects that heavily use niche technologies. If the project managers identify that the current team has less or no prior experience in the chosen technology, they can on-board experienced consultants to help the team until the project is stabilized. Experienced consultants can bring in proven best practices, productivity improvement tips, applicable automated tools, and so on, to improve delivery quality.

- Have the schedule, cost, and effort been completely estimated?

    - If this is not already done, project managers should estimate the cost, effort, and schedule. This has a ripple effect on project planning, resource planning, and so on.

- Do you have commitment from all project sponsors?

    - Project managers should secure buy-in from all stakeholders and project sponsors. The scope, deliverables, and schedule of the project should be communicated to all involved stakeholders. This prevents expectation mismatch at later stages.

271

Communication Planning

A robust communication plan keeps all concerned stakeholders updated about the project status and updates. The communication plan is created during the planning stage to ensure that communication is streamlined and customized to the project and to the needs of the stakeholders. Once the communication plan is reviewed and signed off on by all stakeholders, the project manager uses it to communicate and notify stakeholders as needed. The communication methodology is defined by keeping the following points in mind:

- With whom to communicate

- What to communicate

- How to communicate

- Who will communicate

- How often to communicate

Based on the audience and the communication type, different tools are used. For instance, email can be used for simple communication and tools such as Excel or Word with a predefined structure can be used to communicate multiple items to stakeholders.

Best practices in communication strategy include:

- Create a stakeholder matrix during the project definition phase. Any scope changes should be immediately communicated to all stakeholders in the matrix.

- Establish issue resolution and escalation channels to remove any hurdles encountered.

Generic Rules During the Project Initiation Stage

During the project initiation stage, identify all participants and stakeholders needed for each of the meetings. Review the project scope documents (consisting of in-scope and out-of-scope items) and the requirements document (details the user stories, use cases, and flows) and get a buy-in from all concerned stakeholders. For complex digital projects, the requirements should be captured from multiple dimensions. The multi-dimensional requirements document includes requirement related artifacts, such as business requirement document (consisting of core functional and business rules), interface requirements (elaborating the integration requirements), and nonfunctional requirements (detailing non-functional requirements such as security, modularity, scalability, availability, and extensibility, along with their SLAs). Prioritize the requirements for each of the release iterations.

- Identify and get buy-in from all stakeholders about all the nonfunctional/quality attributes such as security, performance, availability, scalability, modularity, accessibility, and portability.

- Establish the change management process.

- Create a role-responsibility matrix as part of the governance process.

- Establish a communication plan and compliance standards (such as development standards, technology standards, and integration standards).

- Create a project scope document and get sign-off from all stakeholders (see the template in Appendix D).

Project Management Best Practices in the Project Execution Phase

This category looks at the key project management best practices that are needed during the project execution phase.

Knowledge Management

During the course of project execution, you develop a number of artifacts. While source control is the default repository for code artifacts, other knowledge artifacts (such as troubleshooting documents, support documents, configuration documents, project process documents, requirements documents, architecture documents, design documents, etc.) are stored in a centralized knowledge repository. Documents from the knowledge repository are accessed by authorized persons through an intuitive interface. Normally a knowledge platform is accessed by three main roles: the creator, reviewer, and accessor. The creator is authorized to create and update knowledge articles; the reviewer can review the validity of the content before it's published, and the accessor can read/access the articles but not make changes.

The main idea of the centralized knowledge repository is to facilitate knowledge sharing across various teams and interested stakeholders to foster collaboration. Knowledge assets not only improve the productivity of the project teams, but also act as structured storage modules for the organization. The support and maintenance teams can reuse the articles (such as how-to and troubleshooting articles), business process documents, which enable them to respond to production tickets and incidents quickly and effectively.

Various other personnel, such as business analysts (for storing and accessing business flow documents), developers (for storing and using design documents), and architects (for storing and accessing architecture artifacts), can use the knowledge repository. Project managers should track the contribution and usage of the knowledge base with the goal of making it more effective. Frequently accessed and most downloaded articles can be placed in easily accessible locations such as in a Popular Articles link on the home page. Project managers can examine the rarely accessed articles and explore ways to improve usage. Project managers can also apply gamification principles and incentives (such as badges, credit points, and gift vouchers) for people who contribute most to the knowledge repository.

Code Development Best Practices

The following are the best practices to guide you in developing code:

- Develop frameworks that can be used for development and extension.

- Create a repository of reference code, checklists and code snippets that can be reused.

- Use configuration-driven components such as configurable widgets and portlets to reduce development effort.

- Build scripts to automate routine activities.

- Reuse open source tools and frameworks for project needs.

- Use code generators, continuous integration frameworks, and static code analyzers to improve code quality.

Adoption of Open Source Tools and Frameworks

You have seen that open source adoption is one of the key trends in the digital space. Enterprises are increasingly embracing open source technologies to enable various digital capabilities. Some of the factors to be considered while evaluating open source technologies and commercial products are explained in Table 11-2.

Table 11-2. *Factors to Consider: Open Source Technologies and Commercial Products*

Factor	Open Source	Commercial Product
Functionality enablement	Most open source products provide full access to source code (based on license type). Enterprises can reuse, extend, or customize it to build desired functionality. It works well if the organization has a good skillset and experience in open source technologies.	Enterprises need to use the available functionality and provided extensions to extend features wherever required. If the architecture is not planned properly, it could result in vendor lock-in or in tight coupling to proprietary technologies.
Support model and maintenance	Most open source products offer good community support. With the subscription model, enterprises can also request for feature enhancement, patches, and defect fixes.	Commercial product vendors offer support licenses and normally provide good product documentation. Support processes are generally well-defined with strict SLAs based on incident severity. Product vendors also regularly release product updates, patches, and maintenance releases.
Overall project cost	Depends mainly on requirement fit. If the solution needs lots of customization, it can result in high development and maintenance costs.	Largely depends on licensing and maintenance costs.
Standards Adoption	Most open source products use open standards, which can help in future extension and interoperability.	Commercial products generally are closed systems and use proprietary standards. However, most systems provide standards based integration options (such as web service interfaces through SOAP/REST based interfaces).

Other factors, such as time to market, mainly depend on the out-of-box capabilities offered by the product (open source or commercial), solution fit, and the maturity of the governance processes. If the product offers a closer solution fit, it requires less customization and hence delivers a faster time to market. Conversely, the need for more customizations will delay release timelines.

Explore the open source and commercial tools that can be used for the project through proof of concept (PoC) before finalizing a product. During the PoC phase, you need to understand the requirement fit, feasibility, and implementation complexity. Organizations need to examine the skillset for implementation and long-term alignment of product roadmap with the organization's vision. Organizations also need to assess the technology readiness, process maturity, and experienced skillset needed for the project and plan for training accordingly.

Project Metrics

One of the key responsibilities of a Project manager is to manage the project metrics to ensure that the project is healthy. Project managers monitor these metrics through project dashboards or through scorecards. The key project metrics can be categorized into process metrics and product metrics, both of which are discussed next.

Process metrics:

- *Effort variance*: Provides the variance of the actual effort against planned effort (using person hours as the unit of effort).

   Effort variance = [(actual effort - planned effort)/planned effort] * 100

- *Schedule variance*: Measures the schedule variance of the project through cost.

   Schedule variance = Earned Value – Planned Value

- *Cost variance*: Measures the cost variance of the project.

   Cost variance = Earned Value – Actual Cost

Product metrics:

- *Test effectiveness*: Measures the ratio of the number of defects found through test cases to the total number of defects.

   Test effectiveness = (Defects detected through test cases)/(Total number of defects)

- *Requirement creep*: The rate at which new requirements are logged.

  Requirement creep = (Total number of new requirements)/Initial number of requirements

Testing metrics:

- *Defect detection rate*: The rate at which defects are detected as compared to total time spent.

  Defect detection rate = Total defects/Total testing effort (in person hours)

- *Defect removal rate*: The rate at which defects are removed.

  Defect removal rate = Total defects removed/Total effort spent in defect removal (in person hours)

- *Defect slippage rate*: The rate at which defects are identified in the production environment.

  Defect slippage rate = Total real defects reported in production/ Total number of defects

- *Test effectiveness*: The measure of testing team's effectiveness in identifying defects.

  Test effectiveness = (Total defects reported by testing team)/ (Total defects reported by testing team+ Total number of production defects)

- *Test coverage*: The total number of requirements covered by testing.

  Test coverage = (Total requirements covered by testing)/ (Total requirements)

- *Defect severity index*: Provides the defect count grouped by defect severity.

- *Defect age*: Provides the total age of the defect.

  Defect age = (defect resolved date – defect open date)

- *Defect density*: The ratio of the number of defects to the total number of requirements.

  Defect density = (Total number of defects)/(Total number of requirements)

The project metrics category includes the metrics used for measuring the health of the project, including:

- Risks metrics provide risk related data, such as the total number of open risks, closed risk count, etc.

- Customer complaints metrics provide the total number of customer complaints, service calls, and incidents.

- Issues metrics provide issue related metrics, such as the total number of issues, issue age, issue closure rate, etc.

- Requirement change metrics indicate the total change requests received.

- Customer feedback provides the total amount of customer feedback received.

The code metrics included in this category are used to measure various code attributes, as follows:

- Cyclomatic Complexity (CC) indicates the total number of independent paths through the source code. Code complexity is a measure of the number of independent paths in a code block. Code with higher complexity needs more testing. The higher the CC, the more complex the code.

- Code Coverage indicates the extent to which the source code is tested. This can be measured through test coverage.

- Coupling Between Objects (CBO) indicates the interdependency among classes and interfaces. Tight coupling impacts an application's modularity and reusability (indicates how easily the module can be independently reused).

- Code quality metrics indicate the improvements to code quality over a period of time. Tools such as CheckStyle, PMD, and SonarQube provide a high-level estimates of code quality.

Business metrics in this category measure the business objectives of a given project.

- Productivity improvements by continuously reducing the effort needed for each release. Effort optimization can be achieved by using automation, open source tools, process improvements, and reusable artifacts in subsequent iterations.

- Time to market indicates the overall time needed to bring a product/ enhancement to market. This metric reflects how nimble and responsive an organization is to the change.

- Schedule adherence indicates the compliance to the specified SLAs related to cost, quality, and timelines.

Automation Tools

During various phases of digital project management, you can use tools for task automation, productivity improvement, and quality improvement. Table 11-3 lists some of the popular tools (mostly open source) that can be used during various project lifecycle phases.

Table 11-3. *Automation Tools for Project Management*

Utility/Accelerator	Tools Used	Benefits
Code quality analyzer to determine maintainability and stability of code	• SonarQube (http://www.sonarqube.org/) • FindBugs (http://findbugs.sourceforge.net/) • CheckStyle (http://checkstyle.sourceforge.net/) • PMD (http://sourceforge.net/projects/pmd/)	• Automated static code analysis • Code complexity and maintainability index • Issue hot spots and quality heatmap • Comprehensive static code analysis
Code coverage	• Emma (http://emma.sourceforge.net/) • Cobertura (http://cobertura.github.io/cobertura/)	• Provides the percent of code covered by test cases. It helps you identify the least covered areas and devise test cases to improve coverage. Code coverage determines the gaps in test cases
Change impact analyzer to accelerate enhancements	• JRipples (http://jripples.sourceforge.net/) • Eclipse (https://eclipse.org/)	• Tracks and analyzes direct and indirect dependencies • Changes status tracking ensuring better traceability

(continued)

Table 11-3. (*continued*)

Utility/Accelerator	Tools Used	Benefits
Accessibility and usability analysis	• JSlint (`https://github.com/douglascrockford/JSLint`) • AChecker (`http://achecker.ca/checker/index.php`) • W3C Validator (`https://validator.w3.org/`)	• Site accessibility testing • HTML validation • Conformance checking
Security scanning and security testing tools	• Lapse+ (`https://www.owasp.org/index.php/OWASP_LAPSE_Project`) • Arachni (`http://www.arachni-scanner.com/`) • SQL Inject • Zed Attack Proxy (ZAP) • Browser Exploitation Framework (BeEF)	• Vulnerability detection for data injection attacks • Helps with penetration testing • Helps simulate and test injection attacks
Activity monitoring to improve business performance	• Jenkins (`https://jenkins-ci.org/`) • Cabot (`https://github.com/arachnys/cabot`)	• Aids application and performance monitoring • Monitoring of business transactions in real time • Bottleneck identification from user request
Web performance analysis	• Yslow (`http://yslow.org/`) • Google PageSpeed (`https://developers.google.com/speed/pagespeed/?hl=en`) • Sitespeed (`https://www.sitespeed.io/`)	• Analyzes web pages from a performance standpoint • Provides actionable suggestions for performance improvements
Continuous integration	• Jenkins (`https://jenkins-ci.org/`)	• Used for automating build and release activities • Used for continuous activities

(*continued*)

Table 11-3. (*continued*)

Utility/Accelerator	Tools Used	Benefits
Testing tools	• JUnit (http://junit.org/) • Selenium (http://www.seleniumhq.org/) • SOAPUI (https://www.soapui.org/) • JMeter (http://jmeter.apache.org/) • OpenSTA (http://opensta.org/)	• Unit testing (JUnit) and functional testing (Selenium) and API/services testing (SOAPUI) • Could be used for automating testing activity • Performance testing (JMeter)
Agile Project management	• JIRA Agile • RTC	• Can be used for Agile project management
Web analytics	• Piwik (http://piwik.org/) • Open Web Analytics (OWA) (http://www.openwebanalytics.com/)	• Web analytics tools can be used to monitor user activities and track user access, navigation, and downloads
Caching frameworks	• EhCache (www.ehcache.org/) • Memcached (memcached.org/) • Redis (redis.io)	• Caching frameworks can be used to cache frequently used data in the memory for optimal performance

Root Cause Analysis Framework

Root cause analysis (RCA) is the process of identifying the underlying root cause of any problem. While RCA can be adopted during any phase of the project, it is widely used during the support and maintenance phases for handling incidents and analyzing support tickets. The RCA framework is mainly used by technical support and operations/maintenance staff who have all the information such as defect rate, user load information, time patterns, etc. to do the root cause analysis.

The root cause analysis framework consists of three key steps:

- *Identify and define the problem*: You need to identify the main problem (not just the symptoms) and define the problem. You should collect all the facts of the problem such as recurrence patterns, time of occurrence, user load when the problem occurred, any repeatable sequence of steps leading to the problem, and any particular data pattern causing the problem. Here is an example of a performance problem definition: "The performance of the page decreases by two seconds when the user load increases to 50 concurrent users".

- *Analyze the root cause*: The next logical step is to identify all causes that led to this problem. There are many commonly used methods, such as layer-wise elimination (eliminate the root cause per each layer), visual analysis (pictorial analysis of cause and effect), five-why analysis (discussed shortly), fishbone analysis (a diagram depicting cause and effect), and Pareto analysis (a statistical decision-making technique that establishes a connection between a small set of tasks and the higher degree of impact). The identified root cause is tested against the problem pattern to determine the actual root cause.

- *Document and communicate*: Once the root cause is identified, it is fully documented with supporting evidence and communicated to concerned teams. The recommendation for the problem fix and the impact of the fix are also documented.

Here's an example of the five-why analysis and layer-wise elimination methods applied to the performance problem.

Definition of the performance problem: "The performance of the page decreases by 2 seconds when the user load increases to 50 concurrent users."

Layer-wise elimination method for root cause analysis:

- Eliminate all presentation components (such as widgets) to identify the problem-causing widget.

- Eliminate the widget code to identify the problem-causing integration code.

- Identify the service invoked by the widget's integration code.

- Identify the problem-causing section of the service leading to performance.

Five-why method for root cause analysis:

1. Why is the page slow?

   One of the widgets of the page is blocking the page.

2. Why is the widget blocking the page?

   The widget performs badly during heavy user load.

3. Why does the widget perform badly during heavy user load?

   The widget's integration component performs badly during heavy load.

4. Why does the integration component perform badly during heavy load?

   The underlying service call does not scale well.

5. Why doesn't the service call scale well?

   The service was not tested during heavy load.

Continuous Improvement Best Practices

Continuous improvement checklists consist of a few best practices that can be used during various phases of the project:

- After completing each milestone, identify the best practices that worked and lessons learned. Store all the best practices and lessons learned into a centralized knowledge repository. This can be used in subsequent phases of the project. Categorize the topics and make them easily searchable.

- Use the lessons learned to recommend future courses of action for the remaining phases of the project.

- Identify opportunities to automate well-defined and structured tasks. Backup jobs, deployment, build, and reporting are some of the repetitive and routine jobs that are ideal candidates for automation.

Visual Tools

Adoption of visual tools (such as Jira or the Jenkins dashboard tool) for project health check analysis and tracking/monitoring is one of the key best practices. Visual tools can be used to improve the efficiency of project execution and address any key opens. They help in understanding the overall project status more efficiently and controlling it better control. Some of the commonly used visual tools for project management include:

- *Project dashboard*: A project dashboard provides the main project parameters such as effort burn rate, team productivity, code quality, project metrics, resource utilization, and key opens such as long running defects, etc. It provides a holistic view of the project activities.

- *Build and release reports*: These reports are usually sent to the project managers after the code builds. The reports provide information about build failures, build time, and other build related statistics.

- *Code quality report*: The code quality reports depict the key code metrics such as code coverage, bugs injected, reopen bugs, code test reports, etc. The report reflects the health of the overall project.

- *Project risk dashboard*: This dashboard view provides the status of key risks, risk types, risk probability, and the impact of the risk mitigation measures.

Project Management Best Practices During the Monitoring And Maintenance Phase

DevOps is an essential part of the Agile delivery model, wherein the code development, build, and deployment happens iteratively and continuously. Successful DevOps facilitate early and iterative testing, automated release management and deployment, and frequent deployment. An effective DevOps process results in reduced cost, quicker delivery, reduced risk, and increased team productivity. Continuous integration (CI) is an integral part of the modern DevOps setup. The next section discusses CI in detail.

DevOps Metrics in Project Management

From a project manager perspective, you will look at the main DevOps metrics that can be used for tracking and efficiently managing various processes in DevOps.

The metrics indicated in Table 11-4 must be continuously tested in iterations. Hence a robust DevOps setup should implement these best practices:

- *Continuous integration*: Build, test, and release continuously in iterations. As this is critical aspect of DevOps, it's discussed in detail in the next section.

- *Automation*: Automate activities such as static code analysis, build, testing, and deployment.

- *Develop processes*: Develop well-defined source processes for code checkin, checkout, parallel development, branching, and other source control activities.

- *Early and iterative testing*: Test code artifacts early and in iterations. This process uncovers the defects early.

- *Knowledge repository*: Develop an integrated and centralized knowledge repository to share the documents, content, and training material. Use the knowledge repository to eliminate silos and to foster cross-functional collaboration.

- *Key Performance Indicators (KPIs)*: Define KPIs and use them to track the effectiveness of the processes.

- *Focus on agility*: Adopt the Agile model for development, testing, and deployment. Develop flexible and standardized processes.

Table 11-4. Key DevOps Metrics

Focus Area	Key Tracking Metrics	Metric Calculation Method	Significance
Time to market (TTM)	Overall feature release time	Total time required for the production deployment of a feature (user story definition time + implementation time + testing time + release and deployment time)	The metric indicates the agility and responsiveness of the DevOps processes. In many business functions (such as business to customer—B2C—domains and retail domains), TTM plays a vital role in providing a competitive edge.
	Average change implementation time	Average total time to implement a change request (change request impact analysis + change request implementation + change request testing + change request deployment)	The metric indicates the responsiveness and effectiveness of the DevOps processes.
Delivery quality	Code coverage	Total amount of code covered through test cases (includes statement coverage, branch coverage, and path coverage)	Higher code coverage increases the confidence in code quality and reduces testing and maintenance effort. It also indicates testing effectiveness.
	UAT defect rate	Number of new defects in UAT/total number of defects in UAT	UAT defect rate reflects compliance and fulfillment of user requirement. It also indicates the quality of delivery and usability.
	Production defects	Number of production defects detected in production environment post deployment	The metric determines the robustness of the application. It signifies the application quality in terms of scalability, performance, and availability.
	Release rate	Number of successful production releases/total number of releases	The metric indicates the effectiveness of the DevOps setup and continuous delivery processes.

Focus Area	Key Tracking Metrics	Metric Calculation Method	Significance
Application Performance	Availability	Percent of application uptime per year Recovery time objective (RTO), Recovery Point Objective (RPO)	Application availability impacts the business revenue and user experience. Recovery time objective (RTO) indicates the required time to recover from outage and recovery point objective (RPO) indicates maximum permissible time period that could lead to data loss.
	Response time	Average application response time	The response time directly influences user experience, site traffic, and user loyalty.
Reliability	Mean time to recovery (MTTR)	Average time required to recover from outage	The metric indicates the robustness of the application.

Continuous Integration (CI)

Continuous integration (CI) is a development practice wherein you build and deploy the code from source control on a continuous basis using automated code review, build, test, and deployment tools. The main advantages of CI processes are earlier and faster discovery of potential issues, tracking build failures, and enhanced build quality resulting in improved delivery quality. An ideal CI process aims to achieve high-quality, error-free code in source control at any given time through the "fail fast" concept (a design in which the error is immediately reported and notified). CI also reduces integration defects, deployment issues, and overall project risk. This can be achieved through a robust set of processes in continuous integration which ensure a high-quality build and reduce dependency on individual people. The team practicing CI integrates their work frequently; usually each person integrates at least daily. This leads to multiple integrations per day. Automated builds and tests run on the top of this to verify the integration. This practice leads to significantly reduced integration problems and allows teams to develop cohesive software more rapidly and in shorter cycles.

CI adds tremendous value in all lifecycle phases of the project. A high-level overview of CI activities and advantages at various project activities is shown in Table 11-5.

Table 11-5. *CI Activities and Advantages*

Project Activities	CI Activities	Advantages of CI
Code development	Continuous integration Efficient change traceability Code quality control through automated static code analysis	Provides well-defined processes for efficient source control Early defect detection Enforcement of coding standards Provides automated code analysis reports
Code build and release	Build automation Build health check reporting	Reports and notifies developers about build failures to take corrective action Provides dashboard view for viewing build logs, build status, and change history

(continued)

Table 11-5. (*continued*)

Project Activities	CI Activities	Advantages of CI
Code test	Automated test case execution Automated unit testing, functional testing Continuous validation Automated code coverage reports	Helps with early validation and ensures code quality in each release Reports code coverage and helps testers develop comprehensive test cases
Code deployment	Automated deployment to various environments	Provides robust, Agile, and on-demand deployment features to a specific environment Manages environment-specific standards and manages dependency through configurations

Challenges with Traditional the Build Process

In order to understand the significance of CI, this section explains the main challenges with traditional build processes in the context of a globally distributed development team:

- *Multiple checkin instances by distributed teams*: When a distributed teams work on the same code base, handling multiple checkin instances (multiple branches, code merges, and conflicts) is a challenge. Sometimes, checkin limitations (such as locking or simultaneous checkins) pose challenges and cause overhead for the build process.

- *Maintenance of multiple source code files*: Each development activity comprises not only source code creation, but also build-related resources such as configuration files, library files, DB schema, SQL files/patches, automation test scripts, etc. It is essential to maintain these critical resources in the respective code repositories (sometimes files are stored in multiple code repositories). Missing any of these resources may lead to compilation or build errors.

- *Long build times*: Traditionally, it takes many hours for a build to complete, which makes it more difficult to run builds more frequently. Another limitation is that a large amount of manual effort is required to complete the build process.

- *Identifying and fixing checkin and build failures*: Many times, checkin issues and build failures go unnoticed during the build creation process, which leads to integration issues and defects. The errors are only detected during integration testing.

- *Lead time to integrate and prepare deployable software*: One of the major challenges faced by the team is the amount of time required to integrate the changes and prepare packages that can be deployed to the target system. The more complex the system, the longer the release and deployment time. This severely impacts the time to market.

The Value of CI

The main objective of practicing continuous integration (CI) is to optimize the development capabilities of the team. The scope of implementing CI is beyond the installation and configuration of the build and integration tools. The key purpose is to produce feedback on an integrated build and make improvements on continuous basis. You fix the problems quickly and at the early stages of the release.

The key drivers for CI are:

- Automating build and release activities
- Productivity improvement
- Increased delivery quality
- Improved time to market
- Early identification of integration and functional issues
- Efficient integration of code base

Continuous integration practices enable project delivery teams to implement frequent integration builds, so that it becomes a regular activity that includes:

- Compilation
- Code testing (unit, functional, and web testing)
- Static code analysis
- Executing automated tests and inspections
- Deploying software
- Reporting and notification

CI Best Practices

The following CI best practices make CI most effective:

- Always use a centralized source control system to manage the code and other project artifacts. Build robust control mechanisms for code versioning, branching, locking, and committing. Provide appropriate access controls for source control operations to authorized users.

- Use Agile development models such as test driven development to leverage CI setup for frequent build, test, and deployment. Commit code frequently and integrate code early and frequently to detect issues early in the project lifecycle.

- Automate activities such as static code analysis, build, unit testing, and deployment using build scripts and the CI server.

- In addition to the code inspection at the CI server level, it is recommended to also use the IDE plugins (such as CheckStyle, FindBugs, PMD, and others) to inspect and analyze code and check for code coverage on individual developer machines. This prevents code quality issues at the source and acts as additional code quality gating criteria.

- Use the CI setup to create a comprehensive dashboard to provide the overall health of the project. The dashboard should provide code coverage report and build failure reports, and create deployment reports, code quality reports, and testing reports. All code quality reports and build failure reports should be automatically sent to developers and project managers so they can take corrective action.

- Establish quality thresholds/metrics as the gating criteria for code promotion to subsequent environments. For instance, you could specify that there should be 95 percent code coverage, 100 percent test success, and 90 percent code quality as gating criteria to promote code from the development environment to the test environment.

- Establish and track metrics for various CI activities. You could define appropriate metrics such as percent of build failures, average build time, percent of code coverage, percent of code compliance, and percent of build automation.

A sample continuous integration setup with Jenkins CI is depicted in Figure 11-1.

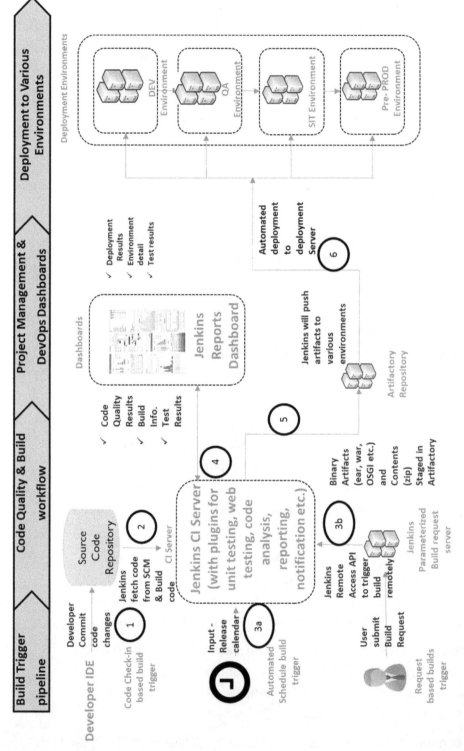

Figure 11-1. Sample continuous integration setup using Jenkins CI

In a continuous integration process, you can configure the CI server (such as Jenkins) to trigger the build based on various conditions from source control management (SCM). Figure 11-1 shows three conditions that would trigger a build in Jenkins CI: Firstly, code checkin from a developer through an Integrated Development Environment (IDE), secondly, scheduled builds and Jenkins API to trigger build, and thirdly remote triggering of builds. These triggers execute the configured steps (such as code analysis, unit testing, etc.) and build the deployment packages (such as JAR, WAR, EAR, or OSGI bundles).

You can configure a number of plugins for unit testing (through the JUnit plugin), web testing (through the Selenium plugin), static code analysis (through the PMD, CheckStyle, FindBugs, and SonarQube plugins), deployment (through deployment plugins), reporting, and notification activities. These plugins can be used to automate many of the release management activities, such as code review, unit testing, web testing, reporting, etc. To support simultaneous development, you can leverage the features such as locked and checkout, which is supported by the SCM system. When a developer tries to check in code that does not contain the latest copy, the system will flag it and the developer has to merge the changes with the latest code base before checking in.

You can view the results of the code review and testing activities along with build reports in the Jenkins dashboard. The project manager can assess the overall health of the project and get an overview all its quality issues.

After a successful build, the CI server will push the binary artifacts to the artifact repository and, from there, the artifacts are deployed to each of the environments.

Note   We depicted Jenkins CI in the diagram for educational purposes. You can use any alternative CI server to implement this model.

Content Continuous Integration Process

This section looks at adoption of the continuous integration process for a CMS project. Many of the CMS release and deployment activities can be automated using a continuous integration process. A sample continuous integration process is shown in Figure 11-2.

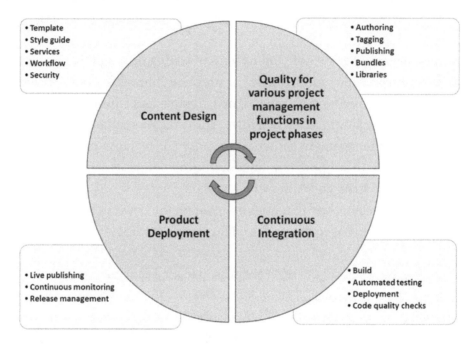

Figure 11-2. *Content continuous integration process*

Content development artifacts (such as templates, omni-channel content, workflows, CMS components, bundles, and libraries) are developed on the developer's machine and tested on the development server. Once they are checked into the source control system, a continuous integration engine (such as Jenkins) could be configured to automate the packaging and deploy and run the code review activities. Content packages can be built using ANT or Maven and deployed to the integration server, followed by SIT, pre-production, and then production. In each phase, you can perform validation. Continuous integration setup can also be used to automate code review (using open source tools such as CheckStyle, PMD, and FindBugs), unit testing (using the JUnit plugin), web testing (using the Selenium plugin), and other release management activities.

During continuous integration, you build, test, and deploy continuously in iterations. This process catches the errors in early stages.

Continuous Improvement Framework

Project managers should develop a continuous improvement framework using lessons and best practices from initial releases. A continuous improvement framework includes the following:

- Iterative improvement in team productivity by using automation tools and processes

- Iterative improvement in delivery quality by using continuous integration and automation measures

- Proactive problem identification based on root cause analysis of the logged defects

- Iterative improvement in incident resolution time by using knowledge base and self-service features

- Robust monitoring framework to identify production issues and take course-corrective measures

- Continuous improvement of user satisfaction and user experience through intuitive user interfaces and enabling self-service features

- Reduction of support calls and incidents through self-service tools

- Continuous improvement framework adds incremental value to optimize key project metrics (related to cost, effort, and schedule) with each iteration

The project manager has to devise tracking metrics and KPIs for these continuous improvement initiatives and track them through the project management dashboard. A sample continuous improvement framework for digital projects is depicted in Figure 11-3.

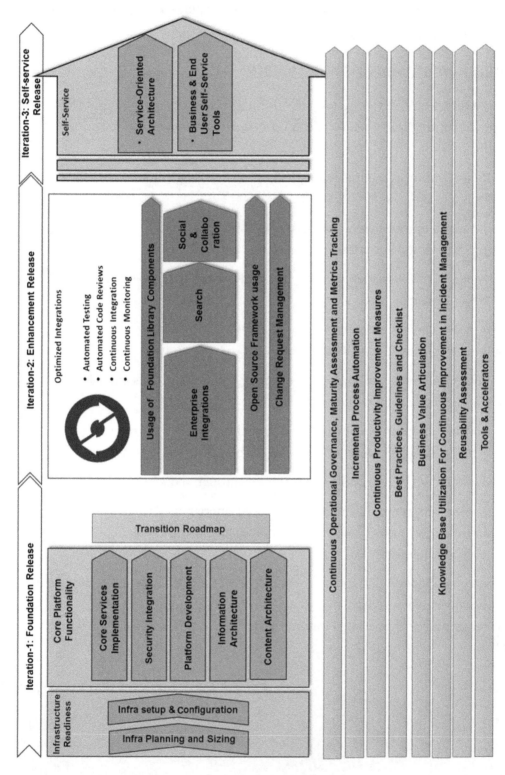

Figure 11-3. *Continuous Improvement framework for digital projects*

The digital continuous framework consists of iterative releases aligned with the business transition and rollout plans. With each release, you add business capabilities incrementally. The first release provides the foundational components (such as infrastructure setup, core services, security setup, information architecture, content governance, and content strategy). In the second iteration, you enhance the platform through enterprise integrations and develop search and social collaboration capabilities. To improve quality and productivity you adopt various measures such as continuous integration, automated testing, automated code reviews, continuous monitoring, open source tools usage, etc. The final release enables self-service capabilities for both business stakeholders and end users.

Continuous improvement enablers are adopted across all releases. This includes operational governance, metrics tracking, process automation, business value articulation, usage of knowledge repository, reusability assessment, and usage of tools and accelerators.

Proactive Problem Identification and Avoidance

Problem avoidance methodologies involve various techniques to anticipate future problems and take measures to address them before issues occur. In support and maintenance projects, you can analyze defects to understand common patterns and do root cause analysis to reduce ticket volume. You can also trace the defects to the corresponding code modules and improve the quality of those code modules.

Project Management Checklists at Various Phases

The following checklists are provided for your convenience.

Initiation and planning phase:

- Create a business case document with opportunity details and business justification.

- Carry out detailed requirements and document them in the requirements document.

- Ensure that all relevant requirements documents and business case documents are signed off by relevant stakeholders. In the Agile methodology, the sprint requirement is reviewed and signed off on by relevant stakeholders.

- Ensure that risks, assumptions, and constraints are reviewed and approved by all stakeholders.

- Be sure that SLAs and success metrics are reviewed and approved by all stakeholders.

- Finalize the risk mitigation and communication plans.

- Define, review, and sign-off on all nonfunctional requirements (such as requirements related to security, performance, scalability, availability, etc.).

- Ensure that the release plan and milestones are defined and signed off on by business stakeholders.

- Have a plan and the metrics to improve the business effectiveness through:

  - Achieving customer-centric design. The user experience should be centered on the relevant user personas (such as the customer persona) and include features such as personalized and contextual content delivery. It should provide the business value relevant to each of the user personas and engage the user through all channels. A user-centric design includes a user experience catering to the users' wants and needs, targeted to user personas. It includes providing accessible features and services across all channels and providing mechanisms and metrics to understand customer interaction throughout the journey.

  - Innovation and continuous process improvement.

Execution phase:

- The requirements traceability matrix is developed and all use cases/ user stories and requirements are mapped to their test cases.

- The risk mitigation plan is updated on a periodic basis, with risk prevention and contingency plan details.

- Test results per SLAs and compliance testing on all support platforms and standards.

Monitoring and maintenance phase:

- Existence of monitoring and SLA tracking infrastructure.

- Creation of knowledge repository for storing knowledge and solution artifacts.

- Development of continuous improvement plan.

Generic Project Management Best Practices

This section looks at common best practices that can be applied to all phases of a project.

Center of Excellence (CoE)

The Center of Excellence (CoE) involves technology and domain experts who engage in highly specialized research-oriented activities. Many organizations use a CoE as a strategic tool and invest in building these specialized units. CoE acts as a leadership unit to provide differentiated value across various projects. Here are the key activities carried out by a CoE:

- *Solutions and accelerators development*: Technology experts of the CoE team develop various solutions, plugins, custom adaptors, Intellectual Property (IP) and accelerators that can be reused across various projects.

- *Framework development and architecture principles definition*: The CoE team develops the framework and defines the architecture/ design principles and various standards (such as development standards, integration standards, code review standards, etc.) and checklists for the organization. This brings consistency to the technology implementation, which makes it more portable and easier to integrate and reuse across projects. The framework also standardizes the technology stack.

- *Product and technology evaluation*: The CoE team evaluates candidate products and technologies and recommends the most suitable products and technologies for the project.

- *Open source usage*: The CoE team evaluates and identifies open source technology stacks that are suitable for the projects.

- *Reusability analysis*: The CoE team has greater visibility across projects in an organization and hence can identify reusable candidates during the requirements phase.

- *Thought leadership*: The CoE team publishes point of views (PoV) and whitepapers and creates other intellectual property (IP) for the organization. The CoE team is also involved in benchmarking technology components on an as-needed basis.

- *On-demand consultancy*: Due to their specialized expertise, the CoE team members provide on-demand consultancy in execution, troubleshooting, and other areas to various projects. They are involved in complex technical troubleshooting activities such as memory leak analysis, performance optimization, etc.

- *Industry trend tracking*: The CoE team tracks emerging trends in technology and functional domains and provides input to the strategy teams and senior management teams. Enterprises can frame the technology-related policies based on these assessments.

As you can see, the CoE can impact projects in multiple ways. Hence, it is important for project managers to build these units during the course of project execution.

Risk Reduction Best Practices

Consider the following risk reduction best practices:

- Clearly define the scope and have the scope reviewed by all stakeholders. Get the scope for various non-functional requirements (NFRs) along with their SLAs.

- Perform appropriate infrastructure planning and hardware sizing based on the user load.

- Use iterative releases and continuous testing and build a comprehensive testing plan to cover all functional and nonfunctional scenarios.

- Involve clients in various phases of project management, such as planning, design, reviews, and testing. Seek early feedback.

- Develop prototypes of the visual design and get sign-off from all stakeholders.

- Use the correct estimation model to arrive at accurate estimates.

- Develop a robust communication plan and communicate the status regularly to all concerned stakeholders.

- Monitor the risk mitigation measures on a regular basis.

- Enhance reusability of code artifacts through a centralized code repository.

- Increase automation through open source and reusable tools and frameworks.

- Continuously track and meticulously plan all project activities.

Case Study: Lessons from a Large Digital Project

An enterprise that sells apparel planned to increase the traffic to its online platform by 40 percent. The enterprise has more than 500 million USD annual revenue. The digital transformation plan was designed to increase the conversion rate by 3.5 percent and increase the range of product choices in the marketplace. Other goals of the digital transformation project include:

- Increase basket value through cross-sell (sell different categories of the same product) and upsell (sell higher version of the same product).

- Develop a robust e-commerce platform and develop the marketplace.

- Extend the business to newer geographies.

- Create a new omni-channel user experience (accessibility across various mobile devices and browsers), loyalty feature, enhanced and consistent brand identity, and enhanced distribution network.

The digital transformation needed more than 50 million USD of investment and more than 200,000 person hours of effort. It was spread across two years.

Key Lessons from Various Project Lifecycle Phases

The solution was developed using an e-commerce product along with other systems such as a CMS platform, an Enterprise Service Bus (ESB), campaign management, reporting tools, web analytics, and document/asset management systems.

The next sections discuss the various project management best practices followed during the various lifecycle stages of the project.

Lessons from the Requirements Elaboration Phase

During the requirements elaboration phase, the associated business processes and architecture were defined. Key lessons from this phase are listed here. These lessons helped the project managers create a comprehensive requirements document and close all open requirements:

- Develop and review a comprehensive requirements document covering the functional and nonfunctional requirements and the business processes.

- Perform detailed product fit and evaluation to shortlist the right set of products.

- Conduct detailed fit-gap analysis for the product selection and baseline all business processes.

- Baseline architecture and close all key architecture opens.

- Involve the development team in the early phases to get their input on product selection and proof-of-concept and to ensure continuity.

Lessons from the Design Phase

- Functional and domain experts should review the technical design and architecture to ensure that all key features are addressed.

- You need to have a dedicated integration team to manage the enterprise integrations, data mapping, and compliance and to manage cross-team collaboration.

- SMEs and representatives from various third-party systems should be part of the development team.

- Performance engineering team should be established to look after the performance for all systems and flows. The performance engineering team is responsible in benchmarking internal and third-party applications and integrations.

- All nonfunctional and quality attributes such as scalability, availability, accessibility, usability, internationalization, multi-tenancy, security, and compatibility, should be factored into the design. Appropriate test plans should be created.

Lessons of the Build Phase

- Progressive development involving phased development and iterative and early integration and testing is required.

- Continuous integration should be used to ensure early detection of defects.

- Plan for a dedicated release and deployment team for a robust code release process.

- Automate various activities such as static code reviews, build, deployment, unit testing, and web testing using open source plugins and a CI tool.

- Plan for a dedicated data migration team to work in parallel during the development phase.

Generic Lessons for Project Management

- With large projects, you need to have a project management office (PMO) that manages the risks, dependencies, and escalations and provides the project vision and direction.

- With large projects, teams can be spread across locations with different skillsets. You need to create a "one team" philosophy with common goals for the overall success.

- The project hierarchy should be properly defined. The hierarchy should consist of module leads, program managers, and project managers with well-defined responsibilities.

- Team morale should be maintained through incentives and performance-linked rewards and recognition.

- You need to have robust governance covering scope management, contract management, and change management.

Summary

This chapter discussed digital project management best practices, including:

- Project management best practices include continuous integration, knowledge management, and center of excellence, continuous improvement, stakeholder management, quality assurance process, communication process, project metrics, and automation tools.

- CI is a release management activity wherein you build and integrate the code on a frequent basis. CI automates build and release activities, improves productivity, enhances delivery quality, and efficiently integrates the code base.

- A centralized knowledge repository facilitates information sharing among various project teams.

- CoE are units that involve technology and domain experts who engage in highly specialized research-oriented activities.

- The continuous improvement framework aims to continuously add value to execution through automation, process improvement, productivity improvement, reusability, tools, and accelerators.

- Stakeholder management involves identifying the stakeholders and their background and using an appropriate communication plan.

- The communication plan includes the target audience, communication frequency, communication owners, communication structure, etc.

- Project metrics include process metrics, product metrics, testing metrics, project metrics, and code metrics.

CHAPTER 12

Product Evaluation, Product Migration, and Governance in Digital Projects

A digital technology portfolio consists of various technologies. The key digital technologies are experience platforms/portals, content management systems, enterprise search systems, and business process management systems. Evaluating the right set of products and finalizing the most suitable product is an important exercise during the requirements elaboration phase of your digital project. This chapter proposes a sample product evaluation methodology for a digital product. While the exact set of evaluation criteria varies across products and technologies, the evaluation methodology can be reused. Digital project managers can reuse the methodology proposed in this chapter for product evaluation. We look at the details of comparing the enterprise search products.

The second topic of this chapter is migration. Digital transformation largely deals with migration of product, technology, data, and content. This chapter proposes the migration approach of a search product. Digital project managers can learn from the design considerations and approach used in this chapter.

Robust operations and governance are essential to the long-term success of the program. You should establish a robust governance process and define KPIs and search metrics to monitor the impact. Other operations aspects of digital projects are product evaluation, technology/product migration, and defining KPIs for monitoring.

© Shailesh Kumar Shivakumar 2018
S. K. Shivakumar, *Complete Guide to Digital Project Management*,
https://doi.org/10.1007/978-1-4842-3417-4_12

Key governance aspects of digital projects include product administration, tracking and monitoring, handling product updates, roadmap definition, and using best practices. This chapter mainly looks at the operational and governance elements of the enterprise search product. The enterprise search product forms a good reference/indicative product for digital product portfolio. The templates and processes we follow for enterprise search works for other digital products such as portals and content management systems.

Digital project managers can reuse the product evaluation framework discussed in this chapter. Though the migration approach, KPIs and governance aspects are discussed in the context of the enterprise search product, but these concepts can be extended to any digital product. A deeper understanding of digital products will help project managers effectively plan, staff, schedule, and monitor them.

Digital Product Evaluation Framework

Due to the availability of numerous digital products and technologies, it is important for project managers to thoroughly evaluate digital products and choose the most appropriate digital product.

This section discusses the various aspects and dimensions involved in evaluating digital products. As an enterprise search product is used with all the topics in this chapter, we provide the evaluation framework for an enterprise search product. However, the evaluation framework can be used with other digital products as well.

Digital Product Evaluation Approach

The high-level steps involved in evaluating and selecting digital products are listed in Figure 12-1.

Requirement Analysis
- Interviews, workshop, demo, metrics & SLAs, requirement analysis
- Gaps & Pain point analysis
- Evaluation criteria and needed capabilities

Assessment
- Shortlisting candidate products
- Score card based product evaluation
- Configuration vs customization analysis
- Fit gap analysis

Recommendation
- Validate ratings
- Final product selection
- Plan for PoCs & Quick wins
- Best practices recommendations
- Roadmap definition & Metrics definition
- Maturity model definition

Figure 12-1. *Digital product evaluation approach*

During the Requirement Analysis phase, the digital project manager has to understand the requirements through demos, interviews, and joint workshops and has to define the requirements, business processes, and application portfolio. Through these interactions, you will come to understand the key business drivers, goals, and core requirements of the program. You must also list the core capabilities needed for the future digital platform at this phase. A sample list of core capabilities is shown in Figure 12-2.

Experience Management		Content Management & Key Functionality			Robust & Scalable Platform	
User Experience	**Security**	**User / Profile Management**	**Features**	**Reports**	**Architecture**	**Integration**
Integrated, Consistent	Authentication	User roles / Customize Profile	Secure File Sharing	Search / Analytics	Ease of Customization / Performance	Standard Integration (REST, SOAP, API)
Ease of Use	Support for OpenID, Oauth, SAML	User profile administration / Notification Settings	Document Generation	Client Surveys / Custom reports	Scalability / Caching	AI & Machine Learning
Multi-device Rendering	Two factor authentication	Custom Attributes / Profile based Personalization	Self Service Modules	Reporting	Multi-lingual / Extensibility	Video Meeting
Cross browser support	Single Sign On (SSO)	Authorization Settings / Customer Registration	Insights	Document Sharing	Open Architecture	External Systems
Personalization	Authorization		Web Content Development	Administration	Modularity	Workflow Integration
Pages/Templates/Widgets	Information Protection		Audit & Logging		Maintainability	Bill Payment System
Collaboration	Multiple site support					Service Catalogue & Pricing
	Security Trimming					Cloud Auth Providers

Figure 12-2. *Sample list of core capabilities of a digital platform*

You must also analyze any painpoints and gaps in the existing ecosystem. You compile the applicable industry standards, best practices, and lessons relevant to the functional domain. At the end of this phase, you have a comprehensive list of evaluation criteria that can be used to shortlist and evaluate products. During this phase, you also compile enterprise integrations, existing tools, products, and the areas impacted by the new product.

During the Assessment phase, you use the evaluation criteria identified in the previous step to shortlist the top three to five products that need to be further evaluated. You do the fit-gap analysis (which reveals how much of a requirement can be satisfied with out-of-box product features) and configuration vs. customization analysis (which reveals the amount of product configuration and customization needed). Configuration vs. customization maps the amount of configuration effort (effort needed to configure a product to implement the specified requirement) and customization effort (development effort to implement the specified requirement). Less customization is better. A sample configuration vs. customization analysis is depicted in Figure 12-3.

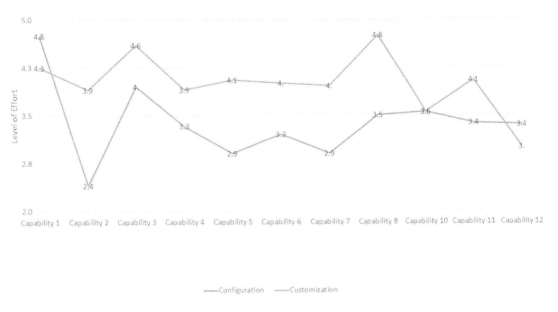

Figure 12-3. Configuration vs. customization

You then create detailed scorecards of the shortlisted products. These scorecards usually consist of key categories with functionality listed under each category and each category having a weight based on its importance. You provide a score for implementing the functionality for each of the candidate products (normally, a high score indicates ease of implementing the functionality). A weighted sum of scores is used to rank the products. You can see a sample scorecard for the enterprise search products in the next section.

During the Recommendation phase, you validate the scores with all the stakeholders and recommend the final product. You also identify the proof-of-concept (PoC) and quick wins that can be planned during initial project sprints. Based on your needs, you use the PoC outcome to do a SWOT (Strength-Weakness-Opportunities-Threat) analysis for the highest scored products to select the final product. In some engagements, you might also place the top products in the quadrant, having key business goals as its dimensions. A sample ranking quadrant with total cost of ownership (TOC) and solution strategy as the key business goals is depicted in Figure 12-4 as an example.

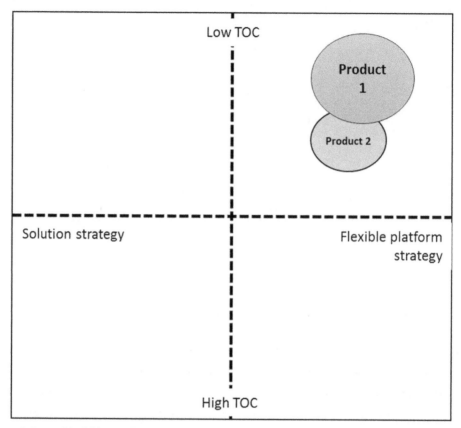

* Size of bubbles indicate degree of support each product provides to business requirements

Figure 12-4. *Sample product ranking quadrant*

The digital project manager works with product SMEs and architects to define the implementation roadmap and the maturity model of the selected product. The roadmap consists of time-bound milestones and the capabilities that will be implemented in each of the milestones. This chapter defines a sample roadmap for enterprise search. It also defines the success metrics and the key industry-standard best practices.

Evaluation of Enterprise Search Products

This section applies the digital product evaluation approach discussed in the previous section to select the best enterprise search product. Enterprise search product is taken as a representative of digital product and hence the evaluation approach can be applied to other digital products as well.

Comprehensive evaluation of the search platforms is required to properly implement a search strategy. This section discusses the framework for evaluation and selection of search tool.

During the Requirements Gathering phase, you perform following activities related to search capability:

- *Search requirements gathering*: Elaborate functional and non-functional requirements for enterprise search needs.

- *Analysis of existing search design*: Analyze and identify gaps in the existing information retrieval process.

- *Creating search goals and metrics*: Define search goals and metrics that could be used for measuring and quantifying search effectiveness.

- *Preparing search environment*: Cleanse (remove duplicate content), structure, and tag the enterprise content for enhancing content relevancy.

- *Search governance*: Define structured processes for search operations, maintenance, and administration.

Once you have completed these activities, you'll be left with various assessment parameters for evaluating the search product. Based on this approach, this example provides a sample evaluation framework in Figure 12-5 for search, wherein we identified "Business" and "Technology" as broad categories under which we have listed various evaluation criteria.

Product Evaluation Framework			
58%			**42%**
Business		**Technical**	
Security	10%	Pluggable/Modular Architecture	5%
Personalized Search	5%	Integration	6%
Support for full and partial indexing	6%	TCO	3%
User Experience	5%	Nonfunctional capabilities	5%
Social Search	5%	Future Readiness	4%
Semantic Search	5%	Flexibility	4%
Multi lingual support	5%	Accelerator and Plugins	3%
relevancy rank adjustment for business promotion	4%	Federated Search	2%
eMail Notification	4%	Analyst Rankings	2%
business-specific synonyms, stop words, black list	3%	Crawl & Index Flexibility	2%
Cloud support	3%	Artificial rank boosting	3%
Ease of Release & Deployment	3%	Ease of search administration	3%

Figure 12-5. *Sample search product evaluation framework*

If you apply the weighted scoring methodology for the shortlisted products, you get something like Figure 12-6.

Business Capability	Weight	Search Product 1	Search Product 2	Technical Capability	Weight	Search Product 1	Search Product 2
Security	10%			Pluggable/Modular Architecture	5%		
Personalized Search	5%			Integration	6%		
Support for full and partial indexing	6%			TCO	3%		
User Experience	5%			Nonfunctional capabilities	5%		
Social Search	5%			Future Readiness	4%		
Semantic Search	5%			Flexibility	4%		
Multi lingual support	5%			Accelerator and Plugins	3%		
relevancy rank adjustment for business promotion	4%			Federated Search	2%		
eMail Notification	4%			Analyst Rankings	2%		
business-specific synonyms, stop words, black list	3%			Crawl & Index Flexibility	2%		
Cloud support	3%			Artificial rank boosting	3%		
Ease of Release & Deployment	3%			Ease of search administration	3%		
Total				Total			

Figure 12-6. *Sample product evaluation scorecard*

The product with the highest scoring is naturally recommended for further validation.

Migrating from one Digital Product to Another

During digital transformation, you need to migrate from one digital product to another. Digital transformation also involves migration of relational data, web content, digital assets, web pages, documents, configuration, code and such. This section looks at the steps involved in switching digital products.

The high-level steps involved in product migration are depicted in Figure 12-7.

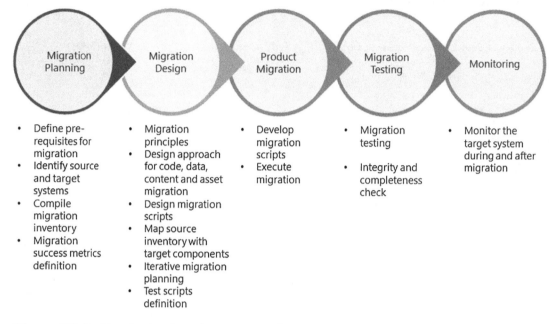

Figure 12-7. Product migration approach

During the Migration Planning phase, you lay out the groundwork for migration. You need to fulfill all the prerequisites for the migration. The prerequisites could include identification of source systems, cleaning source data, removing duplicates in the source content, and such activities. During this phase, you also compile the inventory of the source components (such as code, libraries, content, database, files, images, assets, etc.) that need to be migrated. You also define the success metrics for the migration. The success metrics are related to cycle time of migration, degree of migration automation, and such.

During the Migration Design phase, you lay out the migration principles and design the migration approach for migrating code, data, content, and other artifacts. You map the source inventory components to the target system components and design the migration approach for each of those components. For instance, you could design an automated migration approach for migrating the data, whereas you may need manual migration for migrating pages. You also design the migration test scripts and the migration frequency. Very few scenarios need a one-time big-bang migration; most digital projects need iterative or delta migration.

During the Product Migration phase, you develop the necessary migration scripts and perform the migration based on the designed migration approach. Migration happens in batches and if you decide to maintain both systems in production, you should design the synchronization jobs to synchronized data, content, code and configuration as well.

During the Migration Testing phase, you test the completeness and integrity of the migrated data. During the Monitoring stage, you continuously monitor the performance of the target system and check for any unwanted side effects.

The next section describes a case study of applying a product migration approach to the enterprise search product.

Product Migration Case Study for an Enterprise Search Product

If enterprises need to switch search products, they should be able to achieve this with minimal impact on other systems, such as enterprise web applications, consumer services, and dependent web systems. Coming sections cover the detailed steps of product migration.

Migration Planning

Broadly, you need the following steps to migrate from one enterprise search product to another.

Source Data Readiness

If the current search engine is using a data repository that consists of data in a particular structure, that data should be transformed into a format that's compatible with the new search engine. Alternatively, you could also use this migration opportunity to consolidate enterprise content into a new repository with search-friendly data. ETL (Extract, Transform, Load) tools can be leveraged to acquire and transform data into a format compatible with your new search engine.

Table 12-1. *Input for Search Schema*

Field Name	Data Type	Primary Key	Searchable Field	Enable Facets	Join	Multi Valued	Indexed	Mandatory	Comments
ID	Number		Yes	Yes	NA	No	Yes	Yes	ID for the record

For example, while migrating to the Apache Solr search engine, the Solr schema defines the input data structure for proper indexing. You could specify the input for the search schema in the format shown in Table 12-1.

You could use the Schema Generator plugin to generate the `Schema.xml` file by configuring the properties in the Solr interface. The Solr interface provides options to add, modify, and delete fields and generate the `schema.xml` file on the fly, which enables the schema to be generated and deployed to the modified index dynamically.

At the end of this phase, your new search engine should be able to crawl all the source content using the defined schema.

Migration Design

Here are some of the key design considerations:

- *Expose search only through services*: As a best practice, you need to create a services abstraction layer that hides the search engine details from external systems. Consuming applications could use the service facades in the services layer. The service façade would internally invoke required search APIs/services and provide SOAP/REST-based interfaces. This approach would enable easy switching of underlying search engines without impacting the external consumer.

- *Standard-based intermediate repository*: Wherever possible, you should migrate the enterprise data into an intermediate repository that the search engine can crawl and index. During the migration process, you could standardize data structure and tag it with semantic metadata. This standardization and metadata tagging process improves the content discovery and the overall relevancy of the search results.

Search Migration

Each search engine has a different way of achieving its search functionality. Document processing (reading and indexing document content) and query processing (parsing and extracting keywords from a query string) pipeline activities can vary across search engines. You need to map all the features of the source search engine to their corresponding features of the target search engine and do the necessary migrations. This requires changes to search engine configuration settings, configuration files, search database changes, and so on. Key focus areas of this phase are:

- *Indexing strategy*: Partial and full indexing features in the source system should be migrated to equivalent features in the target system.

- *Merchandising feature migration*: Merchandising and promotion features (such as products that the business wants to promote or products that have sales offers) that are configured in the source system should be migrated to the target system.

- *Relevancy rank configuration*: All relevancy ranking parameters (content IDs, paths, URLs, metadata, etc.) should be properly migrated and tested.

- *Business term configuration*: In some scenarios, there are domain specific business terms and domain specific word synonyms, as well as blacklisted terms (that should not be shown in the search results). For such cases, you need a plan to maintain such business constraints.

API and Services Migration

In the search services layer, the search façades (frontend services) should be updated to invoke the APIs/services of the new search engine. During this process, the signature of façade should not be modified for backward compatibility. However, you need to provide new methods in the same façade.

Fresh Index Creation and Validation

Once all the migration steps are completed, you need to run the new search engine to crawl all the content sources and repositories so that the engine can build the new index. Search engine logs should be monitored for any errors during crawling.

Migration Testing

For validation, you need to execute searches of popular keywords and ensure that the results are consistent with the expected baselines.

Performance Indicators (KPIs) for Digital Products

KPIs are needed to effectively track the success of the digital product. This section defines the KPIs used for search products. While technical KPIs are specific to each search product, business KPIs are applicable to other digital products as well.

Tracking search effectiveness is important to fine tune searching on a continuous basis. KPIs provide an efficient means to understand and quantify the success of search implementation. KPIs provide quantitative measures to signal the search effectiveness and measure ROI. Hence, it is an important aspect of search governance. This section looks at various KPIs from technology and business standpoints.

Technical KPIs

Table 12-2 lists some of the main KPIs related to an enterprise search technology.

Table 12-2. *Technical KPIs Related to Search Product*

KPI	Details
Search exit rate	Depicts the rate at which the users are abandoning search or when users are not finding the right information. This can be used to root cause an issue.
Search performance	Provides the response time of the search function in all geographies and in all supported languages. It is measured as time taken to present the search results in the presentation layer.
Zero-result query	Identifies the keywords and queries that are returning empty search results. For all terms returning zero results, you can use synonyms and related terms to include them in the search results so that the query keyword provides non-zero results.
Query metrics (queries per day, queries per session, query performance, top queries, usage of query facets, queries that returned error, time on result set page, result pages viewed per query)	These are some of the core metrics for measuring the performance of a search query. Based on these metrics, the query performance is analyzed and optimized. Many enterprise search engines provide explain plans (providing the details of the internal query) that could be used to troubleshoot performance issues.
Successful search rate	The metric measures the rate of users who ended up clicking on search results.
Top pages in search results	This would indicate the most popular and important pages that are featured in many search results. We could further optimize these pages.
Keywords metrics (most used keywords, conversion per keyword, keywords driving traffic)	This indicates the main keywords used in search and driving traffic and conversions for the site. We could optimize the search results for these keywords to further enhance traffic and conversion rate.
Content metrics (most used content, most popular document, content/document not reached by search)	Content metrics shed light on usage of particular content and documents. If the search engine cannot reach certain content, you need to analyze its metadata, path, and content formats to root cause the issue and take appropriate corrective measures.

Business KPIs

Table 12-3 provides the main enterprise search KPIs from a business standpoint.

Table 12-3. *Business KPIs Related to Search*

KPI	Details
Customer satisfaction index	As many websites use a search-centered experience, the overall user satisfaction of the website depends largely on crucial functions such as search. The index provides insights into users' search experience and the search effectiveness.
Conversion rate	Rate of increase in conversion (the ratio of number of people who purchased something to number of visitors) due to a search function. Other related metrics in this domain are percent increase in average order value, percent increase in revenue per customer, and percent increase in average transaction amount.
Most popular keywords	Be sure to know which keywords are popular so that you can enhance users experiences and return quality results to them.
Percent reduction in support calls	Rate of reduction in support calls due to search-based self-service.
Percent improvement in issue resolution time	In self-service applications, search success can be measured based on its effectiveness in improving the issue resolution time through relevant results and enabling service representatives.
Page-related metrics (popular pages, pages with high exit rate)	These metrics can be used to identify the root cause of success or failure of the pages. You can analyze the content, navigation model, and information architecture and take appropriate corrective measures for poorly performing pages. Since search is a key information discovery tool, it can be used to improve page metrics.
Click-through rate from search results of every page	These metrics indicate that users are finding the search results useful.
Query metrics (queries that satisfy a large set of users, queries that satisfy least set of users, etc.)	These metrics indicate query usage among the user population. You can fine tune the performance of the most frequently used queries.

Digital Product Governance

Governance of digital products involves regular maintenance, updates, administration, fine tuning, and other such activities that keep products running at their optimal performance. This section covers various governance-related activities for an enterprise search product.

Governance of Enterprise Search Product

Enterprise searching usually spans multiple technology and business domains, as the search aims to organize the information across a wide spectrum of enterprise content. Managing search therefore involves various business functions. The following sections discuss the key processes and activities that make up search governance.

Search Administration Process

You have seen various options available for business and technical administrators. Technical administrators can configure search sources (database, file system, and CMS), collections (set of data and configuration), whitelist and blacklist values, plugins and connectors, integrations, performance parameters, cache configurations, index frequency (the frequency with which search engine indexes), and other core search parameters. Business administrators can configure relevancy parameters, synonyms/alternative terms/related terms, rank boosting configurations, stop words, and blacklisted terms, which can all be used to promote the business.

Most search engines provide a built-in administration interface that can be used for these administration activities. You can assign distinct roles for managing technical and business administration processes and reuse the built-in administration features.

On-Boarding Process of the New Information Source

You need to define a clear set of requirements and processes for on-boarding new information sources. The following information needs to be provided by the owner of the information source as part of the on-boarding process:

- *Starting point for the information source*: In the case of web applications, this could be a home page URL or a start URL that has links to all pages. In the case of dynamic pages, it could be a link to a seed list page (the start page consisting of links to further pages) or it could be the service endpoint of the information source. The starting point should be provided for all environments (development, User acceptance Testing, pre-production, and production). A search crawler uses this information for crawling and indexing the content.

- *Indexing frequency/search freshness*: The owner of the information source can specify the content update frequency for the information source and the freshness expectation from the search results. A separate business domain manages each information source and they have different content freshness expectations. Hence, the crawling frequency (and the caching strategy) varies across various information sources based on the content update frequency and the expected content freshness.

- *Security policy*: In the case of secured resources, the information security owner should configure the access credentials in the search engine. As a best practice, you can create separate user credentials for the search crawler so that it is easy to audit and track the activities.

- *Source connectivity*: The information source owner can also provide any available connectors or adaptors that can be used to connect to the information source. If there are no available connectors, a new connector should be custom-built using the search plugin architecture.

- *Requirements for the search user interface*: Each application has its own requirements for the user interface. In some scenarios, it is possible to modify the built-in search portal UI (which contains the search box and the search results page) to meet those requirements. In other cases, the owning application can use search APIs or search services to build its own user interface as per its requirements. If the requirements and the user interface can be implemented through the search engine's built-in feature, you fully reuse the functionality; otherwise, you can integrate through API or services.

Based on these inputs, the search administrator creates a separate search collection and configures the start URL, indexing frequency, security policies, and caching frequency.

Search Tracking and Monitoring

Search performance and KPIs should be regularly monitored on a continuous basis. We discussed the technical and business KPIs in earlier sections. Search monitoring dashboards and reports provide insights into the queries that are performing badly or queries that consistently return zero results. Search administrators should do a root cause analysis of these deviations and address them.

In addition to these, you should also collect feedback from end users to gauge their search experiences.

Search Maintenance and Operations

Search administrators should apply product patches for product defect fixes, security fixes, and updates on a regular basis. In addition to this, administrators should carry out search infrastructure maintenance activities, such as resource monitoring and index server optimization.

Process for Handling Emergency Updates

During production releases, the enterprise search engine is expected to index all production content. When the page goes live, end users should be able to see the live links in their search results instantly. This can happen only when you have a process to "force" the search engine to crawl the entire production content before it goes live. As a best practice, the production release checklist should include a step to manually trigger the search to crawl for production content as soon as pages are live.

For subsequent production updates, this process should also include search cache invalidation (clearing the cached search results) and an incremental indexing process. For instance, if it is known that only a given set of pages or only a particular site section has been updated as part of a new release, you can invalidate the search cache related only to those pages and crawl/index only those pages. Another candidate for an emergency update could be artificial rank boosting for a business promotion.

Search Governance Best Practices

Here are some of the best practices related to search governance:

- The search process should be plugged into activities that the audience uses in day-to-day activities. For instance, collaboration, approval process, information discovery, and self-service knowledge bases are some of the key opportunities where you can adopt search. Searches should make these features more effective through improved information discovery.

- Always map search KPIs to business goals and closely track them. KPIs serve as quantifiable metrics for search success and can also be used as a feedback loop to continuously improve the search process.

- Involve business stakeholders throughout the search design process. Provide easy-to-use administration interfaces for business stakeholders to configure business-related search settings, such as rank boosting, relevancy adjustment, and search-based promotions.

- Search can be very effectively used to enable a self-service model. Efficient searching can be used to reduce incidents and call-center calls.

- Actively seek the feedback from end users about the search experience. A user satisfaction index is an important search tracking metric.

- Define structured processes with a role/responsibility matrix for search operations and maintenance. This includes incident management processes, support processes, emergency update processes, etc.

- Create a reporting framework to periodically monitor the query trends, popular keywords, and zero result queries and then take the appropriate action.

Defining a Roadmap for Digital Projects

A digital enterprise embarking on digital transformation journey to create a compelling next generation user experience must have a clear strategy for all its digital technologies. The roadmap defines phase-wise (capabilities for each milestone phase) and prioritized capabilities that an enterprise needs in its digital transformation journey. It lays out the blueprint for enabling the technology planning the project. This section looks at the roadmap for adding a search capability.

As search is one of the main technology enablers, we look at an enterprise search roadmap for digital enterprises. A search roadmap provides a blueprint for enterprises to iteratively enable search capabilities on their digital platform.

A sample enterprise search roadmap is depicted in Figure 12-8. The roadmap can be fine tuned based on required business capabilities.

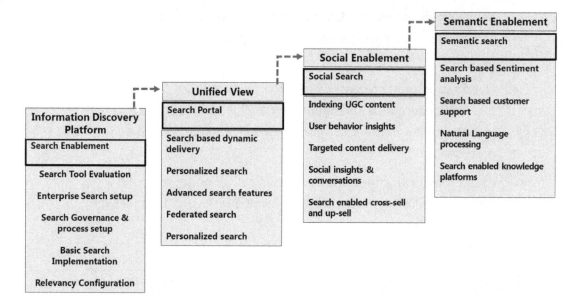

Figure 12-8. *Enterprise search roadmap*

Information Discovery Platform

The initial release should enable core search capabilities required for the enterprise, such as:

- *Enabling search*: Evaluating and finalizing the enterprise search tool that has the optimal fit for the enterprise's needs and identifying the opportunities for creating a differentiated user experience through search. This includes search based navigation, information discovery, recommendation, promotion, and advertisement, which are all driven by searching.

- *Search setup*: Configure and fine tune search relevancy ranking parameters to suit the business needs. Identify all the enterprise content sources that need to be crawled and indexed and configure those content sources in search engine.

- *Search process setup*: Establish an end-to-end search process, including crawling, indexing, content transformation, content cleansing, uniform content tagging, and categorization.

- *Search implementation*: Develop a robust search infrastructure for indexing a large amount of data with a high performance.

- *Search governance*: Establish a search governance process to manage search operations.

Unified View

Creating a unified view through a search portal involves search based dynamic delivery and information consolidation:

- Leverage search features to position search as a solution platform for aggregating data from enterprise sources.

- Provide complete dynamic delivery through the search technology.

- Offer personalized and context-sensitive relevant content through search-powered recommendations, location-based search results, localized search results, saved search results, top/trending search terms, etc.

- Implement advanced search features that provide unique search experience, such as faceted navigation, synonym support, linguistics support, search based data mining, sentiment analysis, etc.

- Implement federated searches to aggregate search results from multiple sources.

- Streamline the search operations.

- Provide search-based applications such as search-based portals, search-based business intelligence platform, search-based analytics, and search-powered knowledge management.

- Enable search on all channels.

Social Searching

Enable search-based user engagement features through user collaboration and engagement to aim toward long-term customer loyalty and relationship. Additionally increase monetization features using your search technology:

- Pro-active cross-sell (sell product across different categories) and up-sell (selling the high-end version of the product) offers through search-powered recommendations.

- Index user generated content (UGC) from social platforms through big data search to provide personalized search results.

- Establish usage of content and monitor user behavior to gain insights into user actions and improve personalized delivery.

- Provide targeted content and ads powered by search to increase business outcomes.

Semantic Searching

Enable linguistic processing capabilities to make the search more user friendly. Search engine aims to understand the actual meaning of the term in a given context instead of just doing a keyword match.

- Search-based sentiment analysis

- Search-based automated customer support

- Search-enabled voice of customer functionality

- Search-enabled knowledge platforms

Search Best Practices

This section looks at the most effective best practices while implementing an enterprise search. This section can be used as a checklist while implementing your enterprise search strategy.

Search User Experience

Best practices include the following points:

- The search component should be prominently placed on the page and it should be available to all pages and all users. This increases the visibility of the search function, leading to its increased use for information discovery.

- The search tool should provide intuitive features, such as type-ahead, synonym support, auto-complete, spell check, related search terms, and wildcard search. These features enhance the user search experience, leading to increased effectiveness in information discovery.

- Dynamic navigation should be supported through search facets and users should be able to refine or narrow the search using filters.

- Users should be able to use facets to filter the search results to reach the needed information quickly.

- The performance of search functions should be optimized for all geographies, languages, and channels. Increased search performance brings the relevant results quickly to users.

Personalized Search

Best practices include the following points:

- The search should include user context (location, preferences, interests, browsing history, profile attributes, and roles) and provide a personal ranking of search results. Personalized search results provide highly relevant content to users.

- Role- or interest-based search results should be provided for users based on user roles and expressed preferences. Administrators could configure personalized searches based on groups or roles. Role-based search results enforce security policies.

- The search interface should provide a Saved Search feature for quick access to the search results. Features like Saved Search and Top Search Keywords save users lots of time.

Content Search

Best practices include the following points:

- Content should be broken down into modular and logical chunks to enhance the effectiveness of the content search. Modular content chunks not only enhance content reusability but also increase search effectiveness.

- Content should be tagged with the right metadata so that search engines can better index and use it to return relevant results. Content metadata plays a crucial role in enhancing the relevancy in search results, as the search engine matches query terms with tagged metadata values.

- Content systems should provide a structured content model that's relevant to the business domain.

- An organization-wide metadata strategy should be defined. The value of enterprise information and its relevancy and discoverability can be enhanced through the right metadata tagging.

Search Monitoring

Best practices include the following points:

- Analytics software should be used to monitor the search performance, search accuracy, popular query terms, and such to collect insights into search effectiveness. Active monitoring enables administrators to respond to any production outages quickly.

- Search KPIs need to be identified based on business goals and should be closely monitored. KPIs and metrics provide quantifiable values to measure search effectiveness.

- Explicitly collect user feedback through surveys and feedback forms to understand users' search experiences.

- Monitor the search logs to analyze any search-related exceptions or security incidents. This helps identify system related issues.

Search Performance

Best practices include the following points:

- Do a comprehensive capacity planning for the search index server to handle the content volume. The right capacity planning and infrastructure sizing is required to handle large content volumes.

- Enable search results caching at various layers based on the expected content freshness frequency. Provide a cache invalidation API and service to invalidate the cache on demand. Search results caching enhances the performance of popular search queries.

- Test the search query performance for various load scenarios and for various keywords. Ensure that popular search terms have optimal performance.

- Keep the search user interface design simple by avoiding unnecessary images or server calls.

- Use asynchronous requests to fetch query results and provide the search results in a paginated form to optimize initial page load times.

Summary

This chapter discussed operational and governance aspects of enterprise search and the following topics:

- Enterprise search evaluation includes technology criteria, functional criteria, and operational criteria.

- The main technology criteria are support for basic search, advanced search, index formats, performance, and scalability. The main functional criteria are support for analytics, federated search, social search, semantic search, personalization, and SEO. The main operations criteria are to crawl large content volume, support relevancy configuration, and include partial indexing.

- The main technical search KPIs are the search exit rate, the search performance, zero-result queries, query metrics, and the successful search rate.

- The main business search KPIs are the customer satisfaction index, the conversion rate, the most popular keywords, the percent reduction in support calls, and the percent improvement in issue resolution time.

- The SEO strategy includes content SEO, web page SEO, SEO governance, and SEO validation.

- Search governance includes search administration processes, on-boarding processes for new information sources, search tracking and monitoring, search maintenance and operations, and processes for handling emergency updates.

- The main phases of the search roadmap are an information discovery platform, a unified view, enabling social searching, and enabling semantic searching.

CHAPTER 13

Trends and Innovation in Modern Digital Solutions

Many recent changes and developments in digital technologies (along with customer expectations) are shaping digital project management aspects. Digital project managers have to be educated about the latest developments in the digital space in order to effectively manage digital projects. Being aware of the latest advancements in the digital world enables digital project managers to use the right set of tools, techniques, and best practices effectively. Innovation provides a competitive edge.

This chapter looks at some of the main trends seen in the digital project management space. It discusses Agile execution, the software as service model, the mobile first strategy, and techno-functional roles (a technical subject matter expert performing a functional role) in detail. The chapter also covers innovations in the digital world such as design thinking, continuous improvement, automation, and Artificial Intelligence (AI). Digital project managers can use the techniques discussed in this chapter to execute digital engagements more effectively.

Trends in the Digital Solution Space

This section looks at the emerging trends in the digital solution space.

© Shailesh Kumar Shivakumar 2018
S. K. Shivakumar, *Complete Guide to Digital Project Management*,
https://doi.org/10.1007/978-1-4842-3417-4_13

Customer-First Vision to Digital Solution Development

Traditional project management always relied on the three-fold optimization of cost, effort, and schedule. Digital solutions require a customer-first mindset to anticipate the needs and wants of the end users. Digital project managers should be nimble and responsive to the market dynamics and to customer needs. Digital project managers should employ the following key best practices to adopt a customer-first vision:

- Understand your end users through surveys and interviews. Through these tools, you can gain insights into user expectations, wants, needs, access channels, and personalization needs.

- If user behavioral data is available, use it to analyze user groups (also known as personas). For each user group, analyze the user actions, page views, paths, and downloads.

- Map the user journey for each persona through journey maps (sometimes referred to as experience maps) to understand user behavior on the site and optimize the touch points during each step in the user journey.

- Involve a representative set of end users in various phases of the digital project execution. You can solicit feedback about the design, wireframe, and application features from end users in the early stages.

- Conduct beta testing of the final application involving the end users. Carry out A/B testing (alpha/beta testing) and multivariate testing to analyze and understand various design alternatives.

- Set up a robust monitoring infrastructure to monitor and understand the end user metrics (such as perceived performance, site availability, page load times, response times during peak load, user traffic metrics, and so on).

Strategic Business Engagement for Long-Term Business Relationships

Successful digital solutions can be designed through active engagement of all stakeholders. Business owners are another set of key stakeholders in this engagement. Digital project managers should look beyond the IT stakeholders to establish good connections with business stakeholders. This allows them to completely understand the business vision and align digital projects accordingly. The key best practices to actively engage and involve business stakeholders in the digital solution are as follows:

- Project managers should actively connect to and collaborate with all concerned business stakeholders to understand the key business objectives, goals, and overall vision of the program. This includes conducting requirement workshops, interviews, and application walkthrough sessions.

- Digital project managers can use business objectives and goals to devise metrics for the digital solution. The metrics should unambiguously define the business value derived from the program. Project managers should clearly articulate the business value (such as ROI, cost savings, etc.) to communicate the value of the digital projects. A properly articulated digital solution can guarantee long-term support and sponsorship from concerned business stakeholders.

- During the requirements elaboration phase, project managers should ensure that the user journeys and existing painpoints are fully analyzed. Project managers can explain the findings from the user journey modeling during business workshops to understand the business point of view.

- Digital project managers should proactively plan to do industry and competitive benchmarking to come up with the best of the breed digital technologies based on the industry standards. Benchmarking and competitive analysis help project managers select the right set of digital products and defend the technology choices to the business community.

- The project management office (PMO) should include representation from the business team so that they are updated about the progress and status updates. Business stakeholders also play active role in prioritizing the requirements, prioritizing the change requests in change control boards, and such activities.

Software as a Service Model

The cloud is gaining prominence in B2C applications and has been widely adopted for delivering digital applications. Using hosted solutions is a paradigm shift in the digital solution offerings and project managers should be equipped to execute projects involving cloud hosting. Deploying a digital solution over the cloud for B2C scenarios is preferred due to its elastic scalability, high availability, and optimal cost. During the initial stages, cloud adoption was impacted due to security concerns, cloud vendor lock-in, performance/latency issues, and data privacy concerns. Modern cloud providers, such as Amazon and Microsoft, address these concerns through mature offerings. On the project management side, the execution model of cloud-based application requires the following best practices:

- Identify and articulate various drivers for cloud deployment. In many cases, organizations are motivated by business goals such as infrastructure consolidation and cost optimization,. Similarly there will be technology drivers such as technology standardization, on-demand scalability, high availability, and improved monitoring and performance. Digital project managers should align project metrics and objectives to fulfill these business goals and articulate the business value of the digital projects to all stakeholders. Developing cloud-native applications or migrating on-premise applications to the cloud require a different set of execution methodologies and metrics. Digital project managers should be aware of this and use the appropriate project execution strategies.

- Evaluate various hosting options (such as on-premise/in-house deployment or cloud deployment). On-premise is preferred when the customer wants to maintain an application and its data within the organization and when there are strict data security and retention policies. Cloud-hosting options can be chosen based on the needed on-demand scalability and SLAs and to optimize infrastructure/deployment costs.

- Assess the cloud readiness of the digital applications. The assessment includes testing the integration scenarios from the cloud, using cloud-based storage systems and cloud databases, and validating performance/scalability and availability SLAs. Project managers should also assess the compliance to security requirements, data privacy requirements, and regulation policies. You'll read about a cloud adoption strategy at the end of this chapter.

- Project managers should monitor the cost, net revenue, return on investment (ROI), and other project metrics and SLAs for the cloud project.

Appendix A explains the cloud adoption strategy.

Agile Project Execution with DevOps

The digital project execution models should provide an iterative delivery to cater to demanding users and to maintain a competitive edge. A fast-evolving digital technology landscape and dynamic business models with ever-increasing customer expectations need digital solutions that are easy to use, can easily absorb changes, and can be deployed quicker to market. In order to enable these features, the digital project manager should use appropriate execution models, create change responsive development models, and roll out the digital solution quicker to market.

The Agile delivery model is most suitable to handle the key demands of digital customers and fast changing business dynamics. We discussed the Agile execution methodology in previous chapters. The Agile methodology provides a sprint-based approach to developing the capabilities through logically defined user stories and enables quicker time to market. It also can easily absorb changes. Time-boxed Agile releases need increased collaboration among team members and are geared toward meeting customer expectations by implementing the prioritized requirements in a timely way. Frequent code check-ins, rapid prototyping, stakeholder collaboration, fail-fast philosophy (a design philosophy that uncovers errors as early as possible so that they can be rectified in earlier iterations), continuous integration, and continuous testing are key tenets of Agile DevOps. Digital project managers should develop self-organizing teams that can handle responsibilities to implement the Agile model in an effective way.

DevOps brings in release management best practices and improves the delivery quality. DevOps mainly brings in the best practices and processes related to collaboration, automation, continuous delivery (continuous build, continuous integration, continuous testing, continuous deployment, and continuous monitoring) to all phases of the project lifecycle.

On the technology front, adopting DevOps in an Agile delivery model helps you bring digital solutions faster to market (through synergized processes) with enhanced quality (through automated testing and code reviews). It also achieves robust operations governance (with matured release management processes), enhances communication and collaboration among development and operations teams, speeds up deployment, and stabilizes the processes. On the business front, DevOps reduces operation cost (through automation of the build, test, and deployment processes), minimizes turnaround time (through the continuous delivery model), increases change responsiveness, reduces risk, and incrementally adds client value.

A typical DevOps process is depicted in Figure 13-1.

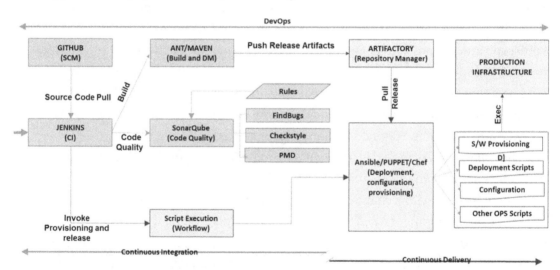

Figure 13-1. Typical Agile DevOps process

Figure 13-1 uses the Jenkins continuous integration (CI) tool. This tool checks out the code from a source control system (SCM) such as GitHub and builds the code. The build activity is usually executed by ANT (Another Nice Tool) or Maven and it would in turn be comprised of various other jobs, such as code quality analysis (through FindBugs, Checkstyle, and PMD). Once the build is complete, the code is deployed and provisioned to various environments.

The Mobile First Strategy

As mobile devices are becoming the de facto gateway to the web, it is imperative to target mobile devices for any successful digital strategy. Modern digital applications are designed and developed using a mobile first approach. The mobile first approach targets mobile platforms as the primary delivery channels. Various design activities such as user experience design, content design, and information architecture are designed for mobile devices first, followed by desktop designs. The mobile first approach uses techniques such as mobile web development using responsive web design, progressive enhancement, and adaptive content design.

The digital project manager can adopt the steps in Figure 13-2 for a successful mobile-first strategy implementation.

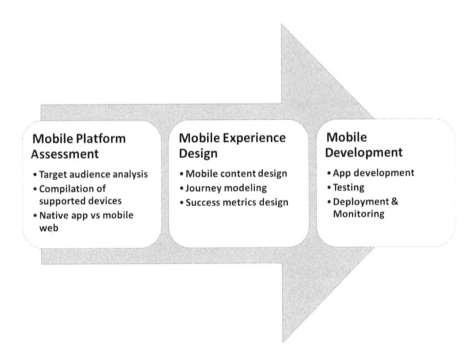

Figure 13-2. *Mobile first strategy implementation process*

During the Assessment phase, the project manager has to get the appropriate consultants to understand the target audience and their primary access channels. This survey would provide insights into the key mobile platforms, devices, and form factors you need to target. You should also look at exploiting any native mobile-specific features such as touch events and mobile device sensors that are appropriate for the digital application. For instance, many retail mobile apps push promotions and offers using the mobile device's geolocation data. You should also come up with an appropriate strategy for mobile platforms: native mobile apps or hybrid mobile apps or mobile web. Native mobile apps (such as mobile apps built on Apple iOS or Google Android platforms) offer rich user experiences and exploit the device-specific features with optimal performance. The native apps are ideal for gaming applications. On the other hand, mobile websites are preferred when quickly targeting the content to various devices and platforms. Each of these options needs to be carefully evaluated. Sample mobile strategy selection criteria is shown in Table 13-1.

Table 13-1. *Mobile Selection Process*

Selection Criteria	Native Mobile Apps	Hybrid Mobile Apps	Mobile Web
User experience	Rich, engaging, and highly responsive	You can develop a rich user experience	You can develop a rich user experience
Performance	Highly optimized	Less optimal than the native app	Can be optimized
Total cost of ownership	High, as you need to develop and maintain native apps for various platforms	Cost is less than native mobile apps	Relatively low cost, as the mobile web can be accessed by mobile devices and desktop browsers
Access to device features	Full access	Partial access	Very limited access
Mobile app ecosystem	Available through app store apps and marketplaces	Limited ecosystem	Not applicable

In the next phase, the digital project manager can engage the user experience designers to develop the user experience for the selected mobile platforms. This includes designing page layouts, journeys for the mobile user, content, navigation controls, and flows for mobile devices. You also define the success criteria, KPIs, and metrics during this phase.

In the final stage, the mobile app (or mobile web) is developed and tested on all supported devices and platforms. Once the mobile app is deployed, it is continuously monitored for performance.

Automation and Productivity Improvement

Digital projects—especially during the support, maintenance, and enhancement phases—have automation and productivity improvement as a key metric. Using automation and productivity improvement measures, you can achieve continuous improvements in effort and cost with each release.

You can achieve automation by closely looking at repetitive tasks and coming up with ways to automate them. For instance, a typical release management process includes a lot of repetitive manual tasks, such as building the deliverable, copying the file to a shared folder, and restarting servers. For such activities, you could develop a script to automate the build, file copy, and server restart tasks.

A high-level automation framework is depicted in Figure 13-3. Digital project managers can adopt this framework to automate various activities in their digital projects.

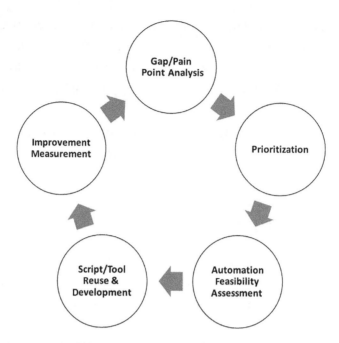

Figure 13-3. *Automation framework*

The first step in the automation journey is to identify the existing painpoints and gaps. This step typically involves analyzing existing business processes and other activities that are time consuming and that require a lot of manual effort. Some of the processes also impact business revenues; for instance, a time-consuming release management process with many manual steps is expensive and limits the ability of the enterprise to quickly deploy solutions to market. As a next step, you need to prioritize the gaps and painpoints based on their business impact and value. You can use metrics such as revenue generated, cost saved, and effort saved to prioritize your list. Once you have the prioritized list ready, you can assess the feasibility of automation for each process. Ideal automation candidates typically have the following qualities:

- Steps are repetitive and stable.

- Steps are structured and well understood, with well defined sequences.

- Steps are currently done manually and involve significant human effort.

- Steps are tedious in nature and involve minimal creativity.

Once you assess the automation feasibility of the activity, you can explore approaches to automate the activity. Two main ways to automate an activity are as follows:

- Search for any existing open source/commercial tool that can be used for automation.

- Develop scripts, tools, or frameworks to automate the activity.

You can measure improvements achieved through automation measures using the metrics defined (effort decreased, cost saved, productivity improvement in person days, reduction in testing effort, increase in test coverage, reduced maintenance cost, etc.). You then iterate this process several times until you exhaust all automation opportunities. Table 13-2 lists some ideal automation candidates.

Table 13-2. *Ideal Automation Candidates Across Project Lifecycle Stages*

Project Lifecycle Phase	Ideal Candidates for Automation
Development	• Usage of frameworks • Reusing libraries • Automated static code analyzers for checking code quality • Open source tools
Testing	• Automated testing tools • Defect tracking and reporting tool • Regression testing tools • Unit, web, and functional testing tool
Release Management	• Automated deployment tools and scripts • Continuous integration tools such as Jenkins
Project Management	• Tools such as Jira (`https://www.atlassian.com/software/jira`) for project planning, tracking, and reporting
Monitoring	• System and application monitoring tools

Other Trends in Digital Solutions

This section discusses other general trends in the digital solution space. Digital project managers can evaluate the applicability of each of these features in their digital solutions and plan/incorporate the trends wherever necessary. Key trends—such as personalized unified experience and platform philosophy—are used in almost all modern digital solutions.

- *Personalized, unified, responsive, and contextual user experiences*: Modern digital applications are user-centric and the user experience is designed to provide a holistic view of all the user activities. Customers expect consistent cross-channel experiences due to proliferation of mobile apps and multiple digital channels. Digital applications provide a unified view through personalized dashboards and landing pages with aggregated information from various sources. The aggregated information is personalized for the end user based on the user's preferences, permissions, and historical behavior. Digital dashboards not only provide unified views to the users, but they also help you analyze trends and patterns and provide a "single-stop-shop" experience. Personalization features provide targeted content to users based on the user's context (device, location, time, etc.), preferences (interests, implicit and explicit), and roles (profile attributes, security privileges, etc.).

- *Platform philosophy*: Normally, development of a digital platform for an enterprise requires implementation of multiple capabilities such as experience modules, personalization modules, content management system, digital marketing modules, mobile apps, services enablement, web analytics, search modules, and so on. In order to implement these features, digital project managers need to integrate multiple systems such as portals, CMS, web analytics, and all needed systems. Integration of multiple products adds to the overall cost and program effort. In order to address this, many vendors offer digital platforms that provide most of the needed features out of the box. These digital experience platforms provide full-stack capabilities that can help you build a holistic view of all customer activities across all channels through built-in features. This platform-based approach of building digital solutions is gaining momentum and digital project managers can evaluate the right fit of digital platforms suitable for their scenarios.

- *Business process optimization*: Underlying business processes are optimized through process automation and simplification. Products such as BPM (Business Process Management), message oriented middleware (such as Enterprise Service Bus—ESB, and API gateway), and rules engines are used to orchestrate the complex rules-driven business processes.

- *Internet of Things (IoT)*: IoT and sensors are used to get real-time information from various connected devices and report/predict the outcome. Connected and wearable devices are increasingly used in the health care domain.

- *Big Data analytics*: Applying analytical techniques to a massive volume of data will reveal the hidden patterns and trends and provide vital insights into the data. Digital solutions can leverage Big Data analytics for predicting outcomes, providing relevant recommendations, understanding the data, creating data visualizations, and making faster decisions. Big Data analytics is increasingly used in financial applications, digital e-commerce solutions, and in health care.

- *Touch- and gesture-based inputs*: As native mobile apps are gaining momentum for implementing the mobile-first strategy, touch-based features and location-based services are replacing traditional keyword/text based inputs.

- *Social integration*: Social and collaboration features (such as blogs, wiki, chat, community, forums, calendar, surveys, and message boards) and integration with social media platforms (such as Twitter and Facebook) are becoming a basic necessity in most modern digital applications. Enterprises are engaging their customers at various social touch points and carry out personalized and targeted marketing campaigns. Enterprises also use other advanced features such as social analytics, social listening, social media marketing, and sentiment analysis to gauge user sentiment about the organization's service and product.

- *Voice-enabled applications*: More and more B2C digital applications are becoming voice-enabled. Most of the digital applications, such as search, maps, mobile apps, and smart phone assistants, work based on voice commands.

- *Location-aware services*: As mobile devices are becoming primary access channels for users, more digital applications are exploiting the location-based services to push the notifications, offers, promotions, and services to actively engage with end users. Digital applications such as maps, games, navigation systems, and logistics systems use location-based services.

- *Gamification*: Gaming concepts such as point-based incentives, explorative themes, entertainment value, increasing complexity of challenges, using multimedia content, instant feedback, goal/task based UI design, and collaborative problem solving are used in the context of digital solutions. Gamification is widely used for digital marketing, e-learning, e-commerce applications, digital knowledge management, and question-answer systems. Gamification concepts actively engage users and help them use the digital content more effectively and comprehend the digital content easily. Digital project managers can explore gamification concepts for their digital solutions to enhance user engagement.

- *Augmented reality (AR)*: The AR-based systems augment the real world with digital world, thereby enhancing the end user experience. Augmented reality creates a virtual world and is mainly used in retail domain, gaming/entertainment, and e-commerce domains.

Innovations in the Digital Solution Space

This section looks at some core innovations that can provide a competitive edge to your digital solutions.

Design Thinking

The success of a digital solution largely depends on end user adoption and its effectiveness in reducing the end users' painpoints. The design thinking approach addresses these concerns.

Design thinking is a user-centric approach to problem solving that shows empathy towards end users. In a typical design thinking methodology, the focus is on the end users in various phases of the solution definition phase. The solution is iteratively defined to address the identified painpoints and end user needs. Digital project managers can use the design thinking methodology as an innovative tool to design and iteratively develop digital solutions. A digital thinking approach is used to deal with complex problems and while dealing with uncertain scenarios.

Typical steps of the design thinking methodology are depicted in Figure 13-4.

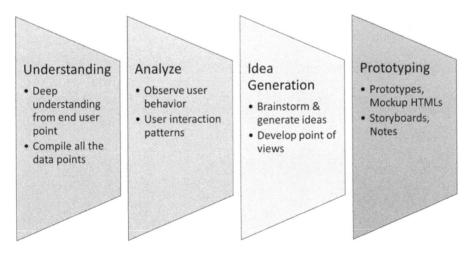

Figure 13-4. *Design thinking methodology*

During the Understanding phase, you thoroughly understand the problem from an end user standpoint. Explore the problem from multiple dimensions that are of concern to the end users. User persona modeling is one of the main activities during the analysis phase. In the Analysis phase, you seek more data points about user interaction and behavior. You seek to understand the gaps, metrics, key goals, and needs of the end users. The Idea Generation phase is a group activity wherein the solution designer and the team brainstorms and generates ideas to solve the identified problem. Other techniques such as white boarding and critical questioning can be used as well. The main intention is to explore the problem space through various points of view, leading to convergence of the problem space. Diverse ideas are encouraged without judgment. Any and all ideas/points of view should be focused on satisfying the intended end user goals. During the Prototyping phase, you evaluate the solution options and ideas discussed in the earlier phase. You generate the HTML mockups and prototypes to explain the solution concepts to end users and stakeholders to get early feedback. This phase is based on the "fail early and fail often" concept. You also use various other tools such as models, post-it notes, physical prototypes, role playing, and storyboarding to reflect the generated ideas. The solutions/ideas and prototypes are iteratively refined based on the feedback. The optimal prototype is chosen based on feasibility, viability, and desirability, as depicted in Figure 13-5.

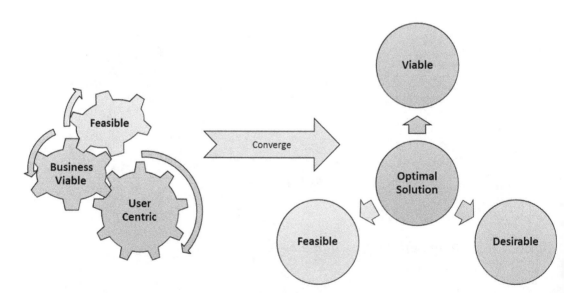

Figure 13-5. *Optimal solution selection in design thinking*

This section looks at a use case that elaborates on a design thinking led digital solution design. An organization wants to redesign an existing e-commerce web application. The design thinking approach is used in the redesign of the next generation e-commerce platform. During the Understanding phase, the solution designer emphatically looks at the problem from the end user standpoint. The solution designer models various user personas for the current e-commerce solution and defines the current problems. For the "customer" user persona, the key challenges identified are information discovery (finding the right products in the right place at the right time) and performance (page response time and search response time). Sample customer persona details are shown in Table 13-3.

Table 13-3. *Sample Customer Persona*

Persona	Details (Age, Demographics, Experience, Job Role, Competencies, etc.)	Goals	Painpoints	Needs
Customer	Average age 27	Shop for latest products	Finding the right products quickly, slow loading pages	A seamless multi-channel experience and a smooth checkout experience

During the Analyze phase, the solution designer models the user journey for all user personas. During this phase, the solution designer creates an activity map for the customer user persona and models the end-to-end customer journey for the e-commerce application. The activity map and user journey model provide deeper insights into the user's interaction and behavior with the application. It reveals the most frequently used functionality are product search and shopping cart features. During the Idea Generation phase, the team comes up with the following ideas to address the goals and fix the painpoints:

- Improve the search functionality to find the relevant products quickly.

- Provide a seamless personalized experience by using portal products.

- Develop mobile web and mobile apps for an improved end user experience.

- Optimize the flow of checking out and test it on all supported browsers and devices.

The main points of view generated during this phase are related to personalized user experience and performance.

During the Prototyping phase, the solution designer and the creative team develop clickable HTML mockups that depict an enhanced user experience. In the new design, enhanced smart search is used as a key tool for contextual and relevant product discovery and the user experience caters to all browsers and mobile devices for a seamless user experience.

Using Artificial Intelligence Tools and Techniques in Digital Platforms

Modern digital applications increasingly rely on machine learning and other artificial intelligence (AI) techniques to bring innovation to digital solutions. Some of the AI tools that are gaining popularity in digital solutions are listed here. Digital project managers can include these AI-based tools to enhance user engagement.

- *Chat bots*: Interactive chat bots provide useful information and respond to common and basic questions from users. Chat bots use natural language processing techniques to respond to users. Chat bots are mainly used in messenger applications, customer service domains, and for marketing/promotion purposes.

- *Virtual assistants or intelligent virtual agents (IVA)*: These are AI-based programs that can help users on variety of services by acting as online customer service representatives or as assistants in smart phones. IVAs provide voice-based responses through powerful search features. IVAs complement a range of digital applications such as e-commerce solutions, retail applications, and such.

- *Analytical and semantic searching*: Expert systems such as IBM Watson use a combination of machine learning, natural language processing, and semantic searching techniques to mine rich information repository. They extract semantic concepts from the information source to provide highly accurate search results. Such systems can be trained for functional domains (such as health care or legal domain) to assist the subject matter experts in making an informed decision. Expert systems serve as alerting systems, diagnostic assistants, pattern recognizers, interpreters, and more. In many functional domains, expert systems are used as powerful question-answering engines, for data-based reasoning, and for analytical predictions and recommendations.

- *Robotic process automation (RPA)*: RPA includes AI-based robot programs that can act as virtual users and mimic user activities. RPA can be used for simple, repetitive backend jobs such as form entries, testing, data entry, data processing, and operational activities. These programs can be trained for the business activity and can be deployed in business domains such as backoffice activities and IT support. They can greatly contribute to user productivity and enhance operational efficiency through reduced costs.

Collaborative Planning

In traditional project management planning processes, the planning is mainly a top-down activity. The project manager creates the project plan and assigns the ownership and timelines in a work breakdown structure. Some of the major drawbacks of this top-down planning approach are over-estimated or underestimated effort, late involvement of technical team (leading to lack of commitment and ownership), and absence of iterative releases. Modern digital solutions involve multiple SMEs, diverse teams, and various technologies, and they need to be rolled out frequently. In such scenarios, a digital project manager has to involve the whole team in the planning process to get their input and secure buy-in. Collaborative planning is an essential element of the Agile project methodology, wherein core team members have a say in planning, timelines, and milestones. Collaborative planning helps digital project managers roll out the solutions quickly with less risk.

Developing Domain-Specific Digital Platforms

Each business domain has a specific set of business drivers and a common set of business use cases. In such a scenario, digital strategists and digital project managers should plan to leverage preexisting digital platforms, which can be utilized for a given business domain. Domain-specific digital platforms give you a jump start to the digital solution development, as many of the core business use cases can be implemented through configuration or as-is reuse. Alternatively, an enterprise can plan to develop a digital platform for its future needs. The key business drivers and core business use cases are listed here for the insurance, banking, and utilities domains. They can be used to develop a digital platform. The home-grown digital platform serves as a framework for implementing future innovations. Essentially, the digital platforms address the main concerns of digital engagements: accelerated development, reduced integration overhead due to pre-integrated stack, and standardized development.

Domain-Specific Functional Use Cases and Key Business Drivers

Appendix B covers the key use cases across various business domains. You'll need to elaborate on these use cases during the requirements elaboration phase.

Common Integrations Across Various Enterprise Digital Solutions

This section covers the common enterprise systems that digital solutions will be integrated with for implanting domain-specific functionalities: CRM, SSO, web analytics, data warehouse/analytics, campaign and promotion, payment gateways, social sites, e-commerce engines, knowledge bases, core banking platforms, live chat tools, billing systems, search, order management, ESB, API gateways, survey tools, security systems (LDAP and security managers), CMS, database, reporting systems, and so on.

Summary

This chapter covered the recent trends and innovations that project managers can use in their own digital projects.

- The key trends in the digital space are the customer-first vision to a digital solution, strategic business engagement for long-term business relationship, software as a service model, cloud adoption, Agile project execution with DevOps, mobile first strategy, and automation and productivity improvement.

- The customer-first vision focuses primarily on the end users. All the design, experience, functionality, and content are created based on what users want.

- Strategic business engagements that encourage long-term business relationships need close connections with business stakeholders to align the digital project and fulfill the long-term strategic objectives.

- The software as a service model is related to moving the digital application to the cloud after determining if the applications are suitable.

- Agile project execution with DevOps is concerned with developing digital applications in iterations using continuous integration tools.

- The mobile first strategy involves targeting digital applications first for mobile users.

- Automation and productivity improvement involves adopting various productivity improvement measures, such as process optimization and automation, at various stages of the project.

- Other trends in digital space include creating a personalized, unified, responsive, and contextual user experience, business process optimization, the Internet of Things, using Big Data analytics, and incorporating touch and gesture based inputs. Other trends include social integration, voice-enabled applications, location-aware services, gamification, and augmented reality.

- Key innovations in the digital space are design thinking, collaborative planning, usage of artificial intelligence tools and techniques in digital platforms, and leveraging and developing domain-specific digital platforms.

- Design thinking is a user-centric approach to problem solving that shows empathy toward the end users.

- Using artificial intelligence and machine learning tools and techniques in digital platforms involves chat bots, virtual assistants, analytical and semantic searches, robotic process automation, and so on.

- Collaborative planning involves all teams and stakeholders in project planning in order to get robust commitment.

- Leveraging and developing domain-specific digital platforms includes developing a domain-specific digital platform.

CHAPTER 14

Post Production Support and Maintenance in Digital Projects

Robust operations and governance are essential to sustain the long-term success of digital projects. Once a digital solution is deployed to the production environment, the real litmus test for the solution begins. Nonfunctional SLAs and metrics related to performance, availability, security, and scalability will be put to the test in the real world.

During this phase of the project, development and validation teams take a back seat and the support and operations teams are actively involved. Support teams handle production incidents and minor enhancements, and admin teams look after maintenance activities such as patching, upgrades, and SLA monitoring. They also handle production outages.

This chapter mainly looks at the post production support and post production maintenance activities. We look closely at some of the processes and best practices in support and maintenance.

Project managers, system administrators, and production support personnel will find this chapter useful.

© Shailesh Kumar Shivakumar 2018
S. K. Shivakumar, *Complete Guide to Digital Project Management*,
https://doi.org/10.1007/978-1-4842-3417-4_14

Production Support for Digital Applications

As soon as the digital application goes live, production support processes come into play. The operations team starts monitoring the SLAs related to performance and availability for the web application on a continuous basis. As part of production deployment, we also define the production operation processes (sometimes referred to as "standard operating procedures") related to incident handling, outage handling, defect fixes, product patching, release management, etc. As a part of the process, the operations team also identifies all the necessary tools, framework, and scripts. During the "steady state support," the operations team implements the defined production operating processes, handles the production incidents, and monitors the SLAs. During this phase, the operations team is also involved in production bug fixes, releasing application enhancements and product patches, and other preventive maintenance activities.

Production Support Activities

In a normal production support scenario, we have various levels of support. Table 14-1 provides a list of these activities.

Table 14-1. *Production Support Activities*

Support Type and Brief Details	Activities
Level 1 (or L1) *L1 team does first level operational activities without needing in-depth technical or domain knowledge*	• Monitoring the digital applications for availability and performance • Providing first-level support, voice support, and call center based support • Responding to functional how to queries and basic questions • SLA monitoring of the application components • Initial response to production incidents • Maintaining and using knowledge base for support and incident response • Responding to tickets that have known problem patterns and that are related to common problems • Escalation to second level if the issue is not resolved

(continued)

Table 14-1. (*continued*)

Support Type and Brief Details	Activities
Level 2 (or L2) *L2 team has basic functional and technical knowledge*	• *Incident management:* Diagnose and provide known workarounds, root cause analysis of incidents (analysis of root cause of the incidents; the framework is elaborated in next section), handling infrastructure related incidents, trend analysis • *Preventive maintenance:* Patching, activity monitoring, software upgrade handling, performance analysis, data backup and restore, developing scripts for maintenance activities • *Documentation:* Develop and document standard operating procedure (SOP), adding lessons learned and best practices to knowledge repository • Release management for enhancements, new releases, patches, and bug fixes • Change management related activities such as analyzing the change request and the impact • Developing knowledge articles (such as best known methods, how-to guides, tutorials, user guides) and training materials • Batch job setup and management • Environment setup and capacity planning • Health check monitoring • Application configuration management and data updates (such as application and server configuration and data updates) • Escalation to third level if the issue is not resolved
Level 3 (or L3) *L3 team has deep technical expertise, in-depth functional knowledge, and work on code and product issues*	• Minor bug fixes related to core code modules (such as core libraries, framework components, base code) • Working on minor code enhancements such as minor look and feel changes and cosmetic UI changes • Performance improvements and optimizations • Preventive maintenance activities (activities related to quality improvement; detailed in the "Production Maintenance" section)

A typical support ticket flow is depicted in Figure 14-1.

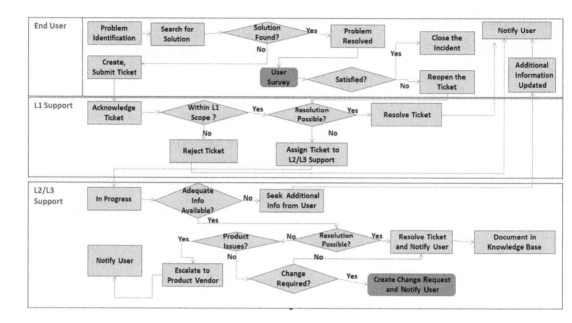

Figure 14-1. *Support ticket flow*

The user searches for the solution using the search interface and if he/she can get the required information through in-context searching, he/she will not log a ticket; otherwise, the user logs a ticket to get the solution. Hence, search and information discovery tools play a key role in avoiding and reducing ticket volume. The search will get the solution from a centralized knowledge base consisting of best practices and how-to articles. The centralized knowledge repository can be used as the Known Error Database (KEDB) to store all known issues and their solutions. Once the issue is resolved, users can optionally take a survey to rate the support experience.

If the solution is not obtained through searching, a ticket is created for the L1 team. The L1 support team analyzes the ticket. If it can be resolved through known solutions or, if the question is basic, the L1 team resolves it. Otherwise, the ticket is assigned to the L2/L3 team. The L2/L3 team can seek additional information from users if needed and then can resolve the ticket. If the issue is due to a product defect, it is escalated to the product vendor for further action. If the issue can be resolved without a change request, the L2/L3 support team fixes the incident and notifies the user. Otherwise, a change request is logged. Once the ticket is resolved, the solution details are added to the knowledge base for future reference.

Knowledge Transition Framework

The production support framework involves the knowledge transition process. The support and operations team transfers the know-how, established processes, and knowledge to new team members. A robust knowledge transition framework is needed for smooth support operations and for providing around-the-clock support. An efficient knowledge transformation framework enables smooth, comprehensive, and fast knowledge transition across teams, with minimal disruptions to business and operations. The knowledge transformation framework should also adhere to defined SLAs and it should provide continuous improvement of service to the team.

A knowledge transition framework is depicted in Figure 14-2.

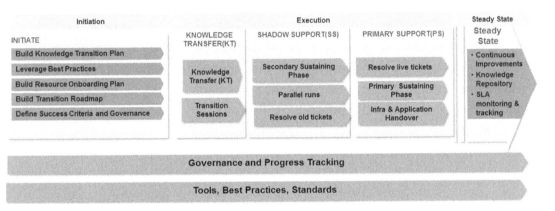

Figure 14-2. *Knowledge transition framework*

The knowledge transition framework is a three-phased approach. During the Initiation phase, a digital project manager defines the knowledge transition plan. The plan identifies the knowledge modules, associated documentation, ownership, and timelines for the knowledge transition. It also leverages all the lessons learned, best practices from previous incidents, and support tickets. Most of the time, the knowledge artifacts and best practices are stored in a centralized and secured knowledge repository. The digital project manager also defines the on-boarding plan for the new resources and defines the roadmap for the knowledge transfer. The knowledge transition roadmap defines various stages and maturity levels of the knowledge transition program. If new joiners need any functional or domain training, such trainings will be planned. The final step of this phase is to define the success metrics/KPIs and the necessary governance processes.

During the Execution phase, the knowledge transfer (KT) happens from the existing team to the newly on-boarded resources. Knowledge transfer is done through process documents, videos, diagrams, face-to-face sessions, web based trainings, online tutorials, and wikis. During KT sessions, the new joiners also learn about the existing services, SLAs, processes, incident trends, constraints, assumptions, high-level solution design, infrastructure, tools, and activities to perform the support activities.

Once the knowledge transfer is complete, the newly trained personnel shadows the existing support personnel in their support work. The newly trained personnel can solve old tickets and low priority/low complexity tickets under the guidance of the primary support team. Shadow support includes providing backend support, observing the methods and tools used by the support personnel, and other such activities. During the shadow support phase, the support team executes parallel runs, whereby the existing team and new team perform same job to assess the readiness of the new team. Based on this assessment, the training plan is fine tuned. Once the trained personnel have sufficient confidence, they provide primary support and handle all incidents. The incumbent support people hand over the application and infrastructure support responsibilities to the trained personnel.

During the Steady Stage phase, the support team performs continuous improvement activities such as minimizing incident resolution time and minimizing production outage periods. The knowledge and lessons are stored in the knowledge repository. SLA monitoring tools are used to track defects, support incidents, and track other defined success metrics to determine the effectiveness of support processes. Various activities that happen during the Steady State phase are depicted in the following table:

Activity Category	High-Level Activities During the Steady State Phase
Incident management	Handling incidents, SLA adherence, process adherence, knowledge management, root cause analysis
Operations management	Patching activities, application configuration, batch job management, application administration, monitoring, product upgrades, migration
SLA monitoring & reporting	Continuous real-time SLA monitoring, communication planning
Knowledge management	Adding best practices and lessons to knowledge repository

(*continued*)

Activity Category	High-Level Activities During the Steady State Phase
Continuous improvement	SLA improvement, automation, productivity improvement initiatives
Defect fixes	Code updates for defect fixes
Enhancements	Implementing simple enhancements

Service Level Agreement (SLA) Management Framework

SLAs are defined for a number of support related activities to enable effective tracking and monitoring. SLAs measure the overall effectiveness of the support process. This section defines an SLA management framework that digital project managers can use to define and maintain an SLA. The SLA management framework is depicted in Figure 14-3.

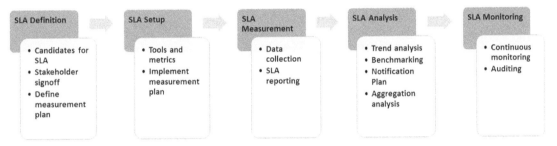

Figure 14-3. *SLA management framework*

The SLA management framework consists of five phases for end-to-end SLA management. During the SLA Definition phase, you identify all candidates for which SLAs need to be defined. Ideal candidates include incident management, voice support management, defect management, enhancements, and production outage handling processes. For each of the defined SLAs, you need to define the measurement plan and define the baseline values. The measurement plan elaborates on the parameters that will be tracked for the SLA, such as the measurement methods, the management and reporting of measurement data, and the details of the measurement data. For instance, for the incident management process, sample SLAs are that the priority 1 incident age should not be more than three days; maximum age for any incident type should not be more than 30 days. Similarly for the performance process, the SLAs are a page response time less than two seconds during an average load and a page response time less than five seconds during a peak load. The measurement plan defines the defect tracking tool to measure the defect age for measuring SLAs related to the incident management process and defines the web analytics tools used to measure the SLAs related to page performance. Once the SLAs are defined, they should be reviewed and signed off on by concerned stakeholders.

During the SLA Setup phase, tools and scripts are configured and set up to measure and track SLAs. All necessary configuration and steps are implemented as per the defined measurement plan. For instance, to monitor the SLAs related to the incident management process, the defect tracking tool is set up and configured to trigger notification e-mails when the defect age for priority 1 defects exceed three days. For tracking the performance SLAs, web analytics scripts are configured with the web page and monitoring tools are set up as part of the SLA Setup phase. A sample SLAs for defects are listed in Table 14-2.

Table 14-2. *Sample SLA for Defects*

Defect Category	First Response Time	Fix Time
Critical	5 minutes	60 minutes
High	60 minutes	240 minutes
Medium	120 minutes	420 minutes
Low	240 minutes	840 minutes

During the SLA Measurement phase, the data obtained from the tools setup process is aggregated, analyzed, and used for reporting. During the SLA Analysis phase, the selected, aggregated SLA data is benchmarked (compared against the baseline SLAs). For instance, the incident age trend is analyzed over a period of three months during this phase for key SLAs. The analysis reports are published to the support team to take appropriate action. During the SLA Monitoring phase, tools are configured for continuous monitoring. Reports are published and notified based on monitoring. The SLA reports and findings from the monitoring are then frequently audited to gain insights about SLA adherence.

Production Support KPIs

This section outlines the KPIs that are used in a typical digital support project. The digital project manager can use these KPIs to monitor the quality and responsiveness of support activities.

Here are the production support related KPIs:

- *Average response time (ART)*: This KPI indicates the response time for the support incidents. A lower ART is preferred for higher customer satisfaction.

- *Average total ticket resolution time*: This measures the total time to completely close the ticket. A lower number is better.

- *Average ticket age per ticket priority*: This KPI provides the average number of days since the ticket was opened based on ticket priority. High priority tickets have stricter average ticket age needs.

- *Ticket backlog*: This indicates the total number of tickets with an average age exceeding a specified duration. A smaller backlog is preferred.

- *Percent of tickets reduced*: The metric tracks the reduction in support ticket volume across releases. It measures the decrease in ticket volume over a period of months.

- *SLA adherence*: This metric indicates the percentage of tickets that were resolved within specified SLAs.

- *Number of reusable assets created*: This includes the reusable assets such as knowledge articles, how-to manuals, tutorials, or reusable scripts/tools that can be used to improve support response time.

- *Percent of tickets resolved at L1 and L2*: This metric indicates the effectiveness of knowledge artifacts such as workarounds, tutorials, how-to articles, and best practices used by the L1 support team for providing first-level support. Likewise, at L2, you measure the impact of preventive maintenance activities and root cause analysis that prevent the tickets from moving to L3.

Here are the production defect related KPIs:

- *First time right (FTR)*: This metric indicates the defects that are fixed completely after the first code fix for a given sprint release. It is the ratio of the total number of production defects that are fully addressed the first time (without being reopened) to the total number of production defects. Something close to 100% FTR is needed to ensure high standards in the production environment.

- *Root cause identification*: This metric tracks the percentage of root cause analysis done for recurring problem patterns. The goal is to ensure that root causes are identified for all recurring problems.

- *Production defect identified proactively*: This metric indicates the production defects identified during production smoke testing or through other measures. The goal is to identify any zero-day defects that are missed by the QA team.

- *Percent of test cases automated*: This metric is the ratio of automated test cases (test cases that can execute without manual intervention) to the total number of test cases.

Customer Related KPIs

The metrics in this category are collected for all customers during a given period of time.

- *Average customer satisfaction in tickets*: This metric provides the average customer satisfaction rating explicitly provided by customers in the tickets during a period of time.

- *Average customer complaints*: This indicates the average complaints/ defects logged by customers about a specific feature or over a period of time. The complaints indicate loss of functionality, poor usability, or deviation from the specific feature.

- *Average ticket reopens*: This is the average number of incidents reopened by a customer. Higher reopen rates indicate poor quality of defect fixing.

- *Uptime and availability*: The average availability of the applications. Higher availability leads to better customer satisfaction.

Business Continuity Plan (BCP)

A BCP (also known as a Continuity of Operations plan) is a comprehensive set of steps and processes used during emergencies to ensure continuity of business operations and to fulfill committed SLAs. The BCP is well documented, communicated, and tested to ensure the availability of critical resources and the continuity of business operations in the event of a disaster. A BCP is relevant to digital applications, where the application availability and performance are of paramount importance. The BCP typically covers the following topics:

- *Disaster Recovery (DR) process*: The DR process includes the mirroring of the primary site at a remote data center with regular data and code synchronization between the primary site and the DR site. It also details the process for switching the primary site to the DR site during emergencies.

- *Role responsibility matrix*: Defines the roles and responsibilities of various persons who handle the emergency processes.

- *Emergency governance*: Defines all the processes that need to be followed during an emergency, such as security processes, physical asset protection processes, data backup/recovery processes, information security processes, and communication processes. The governance process also covers synchronization of transactions and data updates that occur during the emergency into the primary data center, post recovery.

Production Incident Management

Production incidents (or tickets) are normally raised by end users or by the L1 team regarding production issues. The production incidents are usually categorized as critical (when production service is unavailable or when there is loss of critical functionality that has a high impact on the business without any known workarounds), high (a high impact on the business or degradation of a production service), medium (a medium impact on the business), and low (negligible impact on the business). For continuous improvement, you should perform root cause analysis for logged incidents and use the insights to avoid future incidents. The root cause analysis framework is discussed in the following section.

Root Cause Analysis Framework

Recall that root cause analysis (RCA) is an important tool for preventing defects proactively. The RCA framework involves the following steps:

1. Perform a historical analysis of the production incidents/tickets from the past 9-12 months based on priority.

2. Categorize the tickets in to a few common categories.

3. Pick up a representative ticket from each of the categories and identify the root cause. Repeat this exercise with a few more ticket samples from the same category to confirm the commonality of the root cause.

4. Define an approach to address the root cause. The approach involves thoroughly testing and fixing the problem that's causing the module/library or enhancing the usability of the web page.

5. Monitor the ticket volume to test for effectiveness. You can monitor the defect injection rate from the root cause in the future.

A sample root cause analysis framework is listed in Table 14-3.

Table 14-3. *Sample Root Cause Analysis Framework*

Ticket Volume Category (as a Percentage)	Root Cause for the Category	Approach to Address the Root Cause
14% - Performance related tickets	Not testing the performance of the application	Identify the areas causing performance issues Fix the performance issues and test Set up monitoring infrastructure to monitor the performance
7% - Usability related	Lack of usability testing Lack of user awareness	Provide context-sensitive help Conduct end user training Conduct usability testing Create self-help features
5% - Workflow related	Complex workflow Performance issues in the workflow	Optimize workflows Automate crucial workflow steps

Production Maintenance

Once the digital applications are deployed to production, the operations team will engage in production maintenance activities. The main business drivers and high-level goals of a typical digital project maintenance project are:

- *Continuous reduction of incidents and defect density*: Organizations aim to reduce the ticket and incident volume on a continuous basis.

- *Minimal code rework*: Enhancements should be achieved through minimal code changes using the configurations.

- *Strict adherence to SLAs and high service quality:* Organizations aim to adhere to the promised SLAs for performance and scalability.

- *High availability*: Organizations and end users expect maximum availability of the digital solution.

- *Increased user satisfaction*: This is a broad goal that factors in various issues such as user experience, performance, information discovery, etc.

- *Innovation*: One of the key business drivers is to use best of breed innovative technologies and tools. This includes state-of-the-art technologies such as artificial intelligence (AI), predictive analytics, and continuous improvement processes.

- *Improved business agility*: Used to respond to new changes and dynamic market needs. Reduction in operation costs in overall support and maintenance costs.

- Improved productivity in maintenance activities.

Hence, the maintenance activities and best practices should aim to address these key business drivers. Digital project management can select the activities for each maintenance category and adopt the best practices listed in Table 14-4.

Table 14-4. *Maintenance Activities and Best Practices*

Maintenance Type	Activities	Best Practices
Corrective maintenance	Defect fixes, data checks and updates, SLA adherence	Use defect monitoring and reporting tools, well defined governance process for defect handling and SLA adherence
Adaptive maintenance	Code enhancements, compliance to changes in requirements, regulations and other changes, software upgrades, product patching, process updates	Define standard operating procedure for software upgrades and product patching, define issue prioritization processes, define change management and configuration management processes, accurate effort estimation
Perfective maintenance	Proactive environment updates (changes to infrastructure sizing), monitoring setup, performance optimization, proactive code updates for future readiness, root cause analysis, metrics based improvements, proactive enhancements and set up of collaboration features	Use streamlined release management processes, define the key metrics and SLA related to defect age, performance, availability, etc.
Preventive maintenance	Proactive root cause analysis, defect prevention measures, analysis of common and recurring problems, optimizing incident handling process, productivity improvement measures, proactive reduction of production outages, code refactoring for improved maintenance, performance tuning, monitoring batch jobs, system upgrades	Establish a root cause analysis framework, proactive code optimization, establish centralized knowledge management system, perform enhanced code quality reviews, continuous improvement of design standards, continuous usage of best practices, enablement of self-service features

The Next Generation Digital Maintenance Framework

The next generation digital maintenance framework should address the business goals by adopting the state-of-the-art tools, technologies, and processes.

The key steps in the next generation digital maintenance framework are depicted in Figure 14-4.

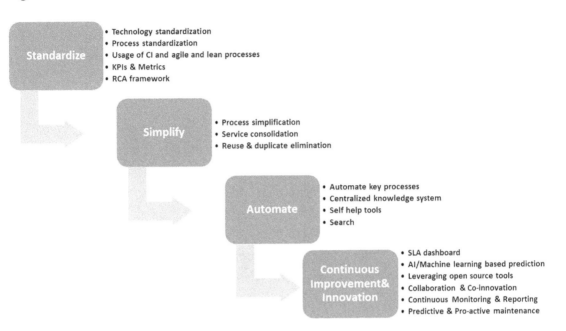

Figure 14-4. *Next generation digital maintenance framework*

The framework consists of four key phases to improve maintenance activities:

- *Standardization phase*: During this phase, all technologies and processes related to maintenance activities are standardized. This involves consolidation of standard tools. During this phase, you adopt continuous integration (CI) and lean processes to achieve business agility and accelerate maintenance activities such as release management, deployment, etc. The maintenance KPIs and metrics are baselined and the root cause analysis framework (RCA) is defined.

- *Simplification phase*: During this phase, you eliminate all the unnecessary and redundant steps in the maintenance processes. For instance, multiple manual approvals during release management process would be replaced by automated approvals.

- *Automation phase*: You identify the automation candidates during this phase. Automation is mainly applied to testing, impact analysis (to reduce SME dependency), automate service requests (such as password resets, user provisioning, access issues, account unlocks), and system tasks (such as restart, disk cleanup, etc.). A centralized knowledge base to help information discovery is created. Self-help tools such as FAQ, self-service portals, and unified view are created to eliminate incidents.

- *Continuous improvement and innovation*: During this phase, you perform the SLA and performance management. Create a unified dashboard for business users to track and monitor the key business metrics, such as application availability and SLAs and application performance in real time. The monitoring dashboard should provide insightful reports related to SLAs, performance, and performance improvement. Adopt AI and machine learning techniques to mine insights from the centralized knowledge base and use them for predictive analytics. Leverage chat bots for responding to how-to queries based on information stored in the knowledge base. Adopt collaboration tools such as wikis, forums, and communities for co-creation of the knowledge base.

Production Support Best Practices

This section describes the generic best practices during the production support and maintenance phase. The digital project manager can adopt these proven best practices for achieving optimal efficiency during the support phase.

- *Process automation*: Automating the repetitive activities during the support phase is key to achieving process optimization. This removes manual intervention for a clearly defined set of steps. You can plan for automation for release management, synchronization jobs, and recovery jobs that greatly improve quality. In a digital content management solution, a bulk publishing process is an ideal candidate for automation.

- *Integrated knowledge management*: Document the lessons, best practices, methods, standard operating procedures (SOP), training documents, and know-how into a centralized knowledge repository and make it accessible to all support personnel. Centralized knowledge management should contain all artifacts related to functional/domain and training content to enable the support executives to quickly resolve the incidents. A centralized knowledge base consists of tickets, complaints, documents, articles, and processes. Each artifact in the knowledge base is tagged with relevant metadata to aid in information discovery. Provide search tools to access the information from the knowledge base. Use artificial intelligence and machine learning techniques to mine the knowledge repository to analyze, gain insights into, and predict future metrics.

- *Shift left strategy*: A shift left strategy advocates that the incident/ticket should be resolved in the nearest location to the end user. The most effective shift left is to have a self-service website that addresses most of the end user problems at the source. The next best option is to resolve maximum problems at the L1 support level.

- *Governance*: Define the processes for handling incidents, defects, and production outage scenarios with clearly defined roles and responsibilities.

- *Process optimization*: Leverage tools and frameworks to optimize the process. Reduce the number of process steps and introduce automation and self-approvals wherever possible.

- *Continuous improvement*: Plan for continuous improvement measures with each release. Continuous improvement includes reduction in ticket volume, improvement in key SLAs, improved customer satisfaction, and improved delivery quality.

- *Improved documentation*: Document the details of the incident, enhancement, or defect for better understanding.

- *Problem analysis*: In order to minimize the support incidents and defects, it is imperative to understand the root cause and related trends. The root cause of recurring problems needs to be analyzed to identify any trends and patterns. For instance, a common library module could lead to various defects. In such cases, you can rewrite the library module to improve its quality. If multiple factors lead to failure, you could use correlation analysis (in which the relationship between various events are analyzed to create a consolidated snapshot of critical events) to identify the key contributors to the failure.

- *Problem prevention*: Provide self-help features to enable end users to resolve the problem quickly. Use preventive maintenance and root cause analysis techniques to avoid the problem. Identify the common problem using root cause analysis and take steps (such as thorough testing and code refactoring) to prevent potential future defects. Enhancing the site usability and improving the user experience also prevents tickets; this includes providing help/training content, FAQ content, self-help features, collaboration features, etc. Identify the areas causing high ticket volume and take steps to address them to eliminate potential future tickets. Provide self-help features for access requests and account lockout to prevent tickets. Adopt root cause analysis to eliminate remaining defects.

- *Support-centered experience*: Most of the digital applications provide online support features to collaboratively solve the problem with a support analyst. The support page/screen should provide intuitive features such as "click-to-call" and virtual collaboration tools such as video sharing, video chat, and white boarding, as well as other collaboration features such as desktop sharing and uploads. For a support engineer, the incident dashboard should provide vital information such as incident age and priority-based ordering, and it should highlight incidents that need immediate attention. The system should also allow the support engineer to create virtual sessions with points of contacts from development and business for faster issue resolution.

- *Support center of excellence*: Digital project managers can set up a center of excellence (CoE) that can look into thought leadership activities leading to continuous improvement. The CoE team actively works on identifying and evaluating productivity-improving tools and frameworks that can be used in the support and maintenance activities. The CoE team is constantly engaged in applying and documenting the best practices and lessons across all support activities.

- *Skill development*: Support people should be cross-trained on various technology areas and functional domains so that they can handle a wide variety of incidents.

- *Robust monitoring*: Set up and configure real-time monitoring tools for application performance monitoring. Set up a monitoring dashboard that provides a holistic view of all parameters and highlights deviations from specified SLAs/metrics.

Summary

In this chapter we discussed various aspects of support and maintenance:

- Production support mainly consists of L1, L2, and L3 support.

- L1 is the first level of support and consists of voice support, monitoring, ticket initial response, and responding to basic queries

- L2 support includes activities such as incident management, preventive maintenance, documentation, release management, batch job setup, and application configuration.

- L3 support involves the development team and they are involved in activities such as defect fixes, minor code enhancements, and preventive maintenance activities.

- The knowledge transition framework is a three-phased approach consisting of an initiation phase, an execution phase, and a steady state phase. During the Initiation stage, you define the transition plan, the on-boarding plan, and the transition roadmap activities. During the Execution phase, you provide knowledge transfer, shadow support, and primary support. During the steady state phase, you do continuous improvements, monitor the SLAs, and improve knowledge repository.

- The SLA management framework consists of five steps: SLA definition, SLA setup, SLA measurement, SLA analysis, and SLA monitoring. During the SLA definition step, you identify SLA candidates and define the measurement plan. During the SLA setup phase, you identify the tools and metrics and implement the measurement plan. During the SLA measurement phase, you collect the data and report the SLAs. During the SLA analysis phase, you perform the trend analysis, benchmarking, notification and data aggregation analysis. You perform continuous monitoring during the SLA monitoring phase.

- The main production support KPIs are average response time (ART), average total ticket resolution time, average ticket age per ticket priority, ticket backlog, percent of tickets reduced, SLA adherence, number of reusable assets created, first time right (FTR) , root cause identification, production defect identified proactively, average customer satisfaction in tickets, average customer complaints, average ticket reopens, and uptime and availability.

- A business continuity plan (BCP) is a comprehensive set of steps and processes used during emergencies to ensure continuity of business operations and to fulfill the committed SLAs. A BCP includes a disaster recovery (DR) process, a role responsibility matrix, and an emergency governance plan.

- A root cause analysis framework includes historical analysis, ticket categorization, and identification of the root cause. It involves addressing the root cause and monitoring effectiveness.

- The main maintenance types are corrective maintenance, adaptive maintenance, perfective maintenance, and preventive maintenance.

- The key best practices in production support are process automation, integrated knowledge management, shift left strategy, governance, process optimization, continuous improvement, problem analysis, problem prevention, support-centered experience, and support center of excellence.

PART IV

Digital Project Management Scenarios and Case Studies

CHAPTER 15

Key Digital Project Management Scenarios

Digital project managers encounter a variety of challenging scenarios during the execution of a digital project. Based on our experience with a variety of digital projects with varied degrees of complexity across various industry domains, this chapter lists the important digital project management scenarios. It includes the background of each scenario to set the context and common challenges and common root causes of each scenario. This chapter also provides the proven best practices to handle these scenario and address any gaps.

This chapter serves as a ready reference for digital project managers to get to know the best known methods (BKM) and proven best practices of a given scenario. The chapter attempts to cover a wide variety of scenarios in digital engagements, such as change management, stakeholder coordination, scope creep handling, etc. Each scenario is like a mini use case, covering the scenario's background, challenges, best practices, and lessons.

Practicing project managers and program managers will find the content in this chapter useful.

Addressing Scope Creep in Digital Projects

This is one of the key risk factors in any digital project. Due to the dynamic business environment and demanding customers, project managers often get requests for software enhancements after the requirements are finalized. Normally in a traditional project execution methodology (such as the waterfall or iterative execution models), any requirement that deviates from the agreed upon and frozen requirements is categorized as a change request, leading to scope creep. Handling scope creep is a key skill that every digital project manager needs to have, as it is very common. Mismanaging scope creep can result in schedule slippage, dissatisfaction among stakeholders, budget issues, and more.

© Shailesh Kumar Shivakumar 2018
S. K. Shivakumar, *Complete Guide to Digital Project Management*,
https://doi.org/10.1007/978-1-4842-3417-4_15

Challenges of Scope Creep

Here are some of the challenges with scope creep:

- Scope creep is one of the major reasons for the schedule slippage and cost/effort escalation.

- Unmanaged scope creep can eventually lead to project failure.

- If the change requests are critical to business revenue, not absorbing these change requests will lead to dissatisfaction among business stakeholders and could lead to poor adoption.

Root Causes of Scope Creep

There can be a variety of reasons for scope creep; some of the common ones are listed here:

- The project starts with a fluid set of requirements. The requirements keep evolving based on interviews and requirements sessions with stakeholders. Without firmed up requirements, scope creep is inevitable.

- The dynamic nature of the business domain and demanding end users are potential contributors to scope creep.

- Changes to the business environment or a legal regulation can introduce unexpected change requests.

Handling Scope Creep in Digital Projects

Here are the key rules and best practices for handling scope creep:

- Plan the project effectively using the proper estimation model and with signed-off requirements.

- Define the scope items, out of scope items, and assumptions properly. Having a baselined scope document and a frozen requirements document help project managers effectively manage scope creep. Any deviation from the finalized requirements can be categorized as change requests and you can accordingly apply the change management process.

- Track each change request and analyze the impact of the change request and its business priority. Any request deviating from the baseline scope should be categorized as a change request. Establish the change management process in which the change control board (CCB) considers the impact of the change request and prioritizes it for implementation. For all absorbed change requests, the impact on the schedule, cost, and effort should be incorporated into the project plan.

- Adopt an Agile execution model whereby you can address the change request as part of the next sprint.

Strict Project SLAs

Many digital projects have strict SLAs for key project metrics, such as effort, quality, timeline, and cost. Deviation from these SLAs not only impacts the revenue targets but also has adverse impacts on customer expectations. Such projects need to be closely monitored. In many scenarios, organizations cannot afford to miss the timeline targets, as doing so could drastically impact their revenue and digital strategy. In other scenarios, the project cannot exceed the agreed upon budget under any circumstances. Managing these strict project SLAs is the key to project success.

Challenges

Here are some challenges you'll face with strict project SLAs:

- Niche and unproven digital technologies may lead to effort and schedule escalation if they are not managed properly. Constant changes to scope and requirements impact the project SLAs.

- A high volume of defects impacts the delivery timelines.

- Dependency on third-party SMEs and external teams could impact the overall project SLAs.

- Inadequate skillsets on the team and high attrition both impact the delivery schedule.

Root Causes

Here are some of the root causes to consider:

- In most cases, the schedule constraints and timeline-related SLAs are driven by business demands.

- Cost SLAs are dictated by the IT budget of the organization.

- Effort and quality SLAs are internal targets for a digital project manager and they impact project profit margins.

Handling Strict Project SLAs

Meeting strict SLAs requires an experienced project manager who can proactively anticipate the challenges and be ready with mitigation options. Project managers must apply project management best practices and proven guidelines.

The proven guidelines and rules needed to maintain strict project SLAs are as follows:

- Comprehensive requirements elaboration and verification. A project manager has to ensure that requirements are obtained from all relevant stakeholders. All scope items, deliverables, and assumptions should be unambiguously documented. The program objectives and requirements should be stated unambiguously, following the SMART (Specific, Measurable, Achievable, Realistic, and Time-Bound) principle. All stakeholders should review the requirements and scope documents and the project manager should get sign-off from them.

- A dedicated project management office (PMO) should be set up. The key directives for the PMO are to actively monitor the project and handle any contingencies such as scope creep management and escalation management. The PMO must have representation from all stakeholder groups and engage all relevant stakeholders. It must align the program to achieve the desired goals.

- The project manager has to develop a checklist of all project management related best practices and lessons learned from previous projects. The project manager should conduct a few initial sessions with the team to explain the best practices and lessons learned. This ensures that the team will not repeat the same mistakes from the past.

- The project manager has to define a comprehensive traceability matrix. The traceability matrix should map the requirements and use cases to the code artifacts, test cases, and deployment modules. This ensures coverage of key requirements.

- Regularly conduct project health check assessments that comprehensively cover various metrics such as code coverage, code quality, automation percentage of test cases, root cause analysis of recurring defects, effort/schedule adherence, backlog defects, and so on.

- All risks should be identified and a mitigation plan should be defined. All risks and their mitigation plans should be communicated to all concerned stakeholders to secure their commitment wherever needed.

- Appropriate estimation models should be used to estimate the effort to incorporate each functionality. This helps in correct staffing and arriving at an accurate project plan.

- Any deviations from the plan should be appropriately communicated to all relevant stakeholders. The project manager should appraise stakeholders about possible risk, risk impact on project SLAs, and mitigation options.

- The project plan should cover resource on-boarding, resource training (to address the skill gaps), testing and deployment efforts, user training, and work breakdown structure (WBS) assigned to all team members to take care of all aspects of project. The WBS should capture a modular work package with clear ownership and timelines. The WBS deconstructs high-level requirements into manageable pieces that can be accurately estimated and scheduled. Project health check dashboards keep close track of milestones, schedule progress, code quality, etc. The project manager has to create cross-functional teams to work on critical items simultaneously. Estimation and planning should be fine-tuned to fit the organization's culture and shared values to avoid any potential conflicts in the future.

- The team should consist of the right mix of people with good knowledge and the right skillsets needed for the project. A training plan that trains across job roles should be used wherever needed.

- The project manager has to closely watch the activities on the critical path. Wherever possible, the activities on the critical path should be reduced, fast tracked, and prioritized to minimize the impact on other activities. For instance, if authentication module development is on the critical path, the project manager has to identify ways to expedite this activity (for instance, through reuse of open source authentication module or by allocating more resources to finish the activity).

- The project manager has to plan for proof of concept (PoC) to assess the feasibility and validation of complex solution elements. This will mediate any scope creep or performance issues in later stages.

- A project manager must use the proven estimation model, the project management tools, and reporting tools to better control the project SLAs.

Dealing with Frequent and Late Changes

Project managers often get frequent change requests from business stakeholders and end users. Although each of these change requests independently might seem small and can be apparently absorbed into the project, over time, these changes will accumulate and certainly can impact the effort and timeline SLAs. However, all such change requests cannot be rejected, as some of them will have high business value. Change requests coming in during the end stages of the project have a drastic impact on the project schedule.

Another variant of this scenario is dealing with uncertain requirements. If the requirements are not clearly defined or if they are constantly evolving, this can lead to scope and requirement changes.

Challenges with Late Changes

Here are some challenges you'll face when dealing with these kinds of changes:

- Unscheduled changes impact on the planned cost, effort, and timelines.

- Development and testing must undergo rework due to changes in requirements.

- Consistent cost and effort overrun can lead to decreased team morale.

- If the changes are not managed properly, they can cause dissatisfaction among business stakeholders who requested for the change.

Root Causes of Late Change Requests

Here are some root causes of such changes:

- The main root cause of this problem is an improper requirements management process. When all the functional and non-functional requirements have not been fully elaborated and signed off on by the stakeholders, this leads to requirement gaps and defects.

- A missing traceability matrix can lead to gaps during development and testing that later appear as defects or change requests.

Handling Frequent and Late Changes

Here are the generic rules for handling frequent and late changes in a digital project:

- Establish a robust change management process that's reviewed and signed off on by all project stakeholders. The change control board or change advisory board perform change management governance by deciding on the final set of prioritized change requests.

- Every change request must go through a change management process. The impact on the cost, effort, and schedule should be clearly defined. Based on the priority of the change request, it can be implemented in an upcoming sprint. Here are some of the prioritization techniques for change requests:

  - Change requests need to be prioritized based on their business impact. If there are any change requests that will directly impact revenues or user experience, they need to be prioritized over others.

- Change requests should be categorized using the MoSCoW method (a requirement prioritization technique based on the importance of the requirement), wherein each change request is categorized as Must Have, Should Have, Could Have, and Won't Have. The Must Have and Should Have change requests should be prioritized over others.

- Sometimes logged defects actually turn out to be enhancement requests or change requests. In such cases, the project manager should clearly distinguish between a defect and a change request with the help of baseline requirements and treat it accordingly.

- The Agile execution approach with sprint-based releases and the iterative execution model are good ways to absorb frequent changes. The project manager should use these execution models if he anticipates frequent change requests or if the requirements are in flux.

- Early release of the product and prototypes help the project manager showcase the end product to the concerned stakeholders. Mockups, high fidelity wireframes, and prototype screens are very effective tools for communicating the design, navigation, and information architecture to the stakeholders. This information reduces the risk of last-minute defects and change requests.

- All business processes should be modeled through process and flow diagrams and the business rules should be clearly documented.

- Contingency plans and buffers (related to cost, timeline, and effort) should be defined to handle some of these unavoidable change requests without impacting the overall cost and schedule.

- The project manager should identify if there is a recurring theme or pattern related to the change requests. If there is a well-defined pattern to these change requests, the project manager can explore avenues for automating it or creating an extensible framework to easily implement the changes. For instance, if the majority of the change requests are related to creating new web pages, you can create reusable page templates that can be easily and quickly modified to create a page. If there are a large amount of change requests related to creating a localized version of an English web page for example, the project manager can create an automated translator utility to create a translated version of the web page.

- The project manager can negotiate with the client business stakeholder to either extend the timeline or increase the cost to accommodate the changes.

Efficient Stakeholder Management Scenario

Various stakeholders support a project. Anyone who has a vested interest in the project qualifies as a stakeholder. All key stakeholders need to be actively engaged to ensure the success of the overall program. A fully engaged stakeholder will act as a champion of the digital program and create awareness of end users while securing the funds needed for the initiatives.

Challenges with Managing Stakeholders

Here are some challenges you'll face:

- Mismanagement of stakeholders can lead to project failure.

- In many cases, business stakeholders do not quantitatively understand the benefits of the digital program.

- Adoption of the new digital application will be impacted.

Root Causes

Due to the wide impact of digital projects, there are numerous stakeholders from various departments.

Handling Various Stakeholders

To handle stakeholders from diverse departments, consider these points:

- Identify all the stakeholders who have an interest in the project or who will be impacted by the project. Create a stakeholder matrix and assign roles, importance, and responsibilities.

- Develop a communication plan to actively engage all the stakeholders. The communication should cover status updates, risks, project metrics, and any action needed from stakeholders.

- A digital project manager should conduct workshops to explain the changes and impact.

- Clearly define the key metrics for business stakeholders. The common business metrics are return on investment (ROI) and increase in revenue. The metrics should clearly and unambiguously articulate the business value of the project.

- A project manager has to secure a project sponsor. A project sponsor with stake in the project plays a key role in securing the needed resources and removing any hurdles in the project.

Human Resource Churn

Motivation levels, aspirations, and career goals vary from person to person. In the dynamic world of digital projects, resources with a niche skillset are always in demand. People with good domain expertise also have ample opportunities. Resource churn is a huge risk to the project.

Unfortunately, resource churn is a hard reality when dealing with digital projects. Hence, project managers must plan for proper resources to handle this issue.

Challenges with Churn

Here are some of the challenges with resource churn:

- Delayed project execution.

- Loss of application and domain knowledge.

- Project incurs overhead to on-board new resources.

Root Causes

Some of the common root causes of resource churn are as follows:

- People pursuing better career opportunities

- Lack of incentives and motivations in the current job

- Team atmosphere missing positive energy

- Too many controls and lack of flexibility

- Repetitive nature of the job

- Lack of learning opportunities

Handling Resource Churn

The key best practices to prepare for and handle resource churn are as follows:

- The project manager has to create a core group in a project consisting of a select few individuals who have core domain and technology expertise and SMEs without whom the project cannot run smoothly. The project manager has to select second line resources based on their performance and potential. The core group should groom the identified second line resources actively. The second line resources shadow the core group members and are actively involved in the knowledge transfer, code reading, and related support activities to help the core group. This model creates a pool of knowledgeable resources that comes in handy if any of the core group resources leave.

- The project manager has to define a training plan for all the team members on a frequent basis. Resources should be trained across various modules and job roles. The project manager has to plan for regular knowledge-sharing sessions across the team. Every team member should have sufficient knowledge to handle a wide variety of responsibilities.

- The project manager should frequently rotate the roles and resources within a team. Resources can be rotated across jobs such as deployment, development, testing, and so on. This not only helps sustain motivation of team members, but it also minimizes the risk due to resource churn.

- The project manager should create a centralized knowledge repository consisting of domain artifacts, process documents, how-to documents, troubleshooting tips, business rules, and code documentation. This centralized knowledge repository minimizes the dependency on knowledgeable SMEs.

- The project manager has to implement the performance-based rewards/recognition program. Based on the quantitative and objective analysis, top performers should be suitably rewarded and their contribution should be recognized in team meetings. This will motivate top performers and inspire other team members.

- The project manager has to earn the trust of the team so that the team adopts the program objectives.

- A project manager has to provide independence and flexibility to the top performers.

Dealing with a High Volume of Defects

During system testing and UAT (user acceptance testing), encountering a high volume of defects has a serious impact on the project timelines. Business users will be rightfully concerned about the quality of the digital application in this scenario.

Challenges

Here are some of the challenges when dealing with a high volume of defects:

- Drastic impact on project schedule and cost

- Rework of application modules leading to effort overrun

Root Causes

Causes include the following:

- Missing quality processes such as checklists and code reviews

- Missing testing processes such as unit and integration testing

- Missing regression test cases

Handling a High Volume of Defects

Use these points to handle a high volume of defects:

- Leverage the root cause analysis framework to identify the root causes of recurring defects. In many scenarios, 80 percent of defects can be attributed to 20 percent of root causes, as defined by the Pareto principle. Addressing the inherent root cause will fix a majority of such defects.

- Re-examine the traceability matrix and define the reasons for missing the defects in the early stages of the project. The corrective actions include enhancing test coverage, automated regression testing, and automated unit and functional testing to reduce the defect volume in the later stages. Enhanced test coverage covers all scenarios, code conditions, and business processes, thereby increasing the probability of detecting defects early in the project stages.

- Develop automated test suites that perform regular automated regression testing of the application. Automated regression testing identifies the regression issues across new releases.

- Maintain a quality dashboard to track the key project quality health check parameters such as test coverage, code quality, reopen rate, and so on.

- Use code quality checklists, industry best practices, and lessons from previous engagements as the key gating criteria for code promotion from one environment to another.

- Set up a continuous integration (CI) process to automate key release management and deployment activities, such as code review, unit testing, functional testing, and so on.

Achieving Productivity and Continuous Improvement in the Support and Maintenance Phase of Digital Projects

During the support and maintenance phases of digital projects, the main activity involves handling incidents, fixing defects, or implementing minor enhancements. Normally, a production support team (consisting of L1, L2, and L3 support personnel) and a small development team are involved in such phases. Over time, the digital applications become stable enough that they need minimal maintenance and enjoy a reduced ticket volume. The digital project manager has to come up with productivity improvement plans and continuous improvement plan during this phase. The continuous improvement plan should adhere to agreed upon SLAs and improve on earlier SLA metrics.

389

Challenges

Here are some of the challenges you'll face during these stages:

- Support coverage spans across geographies to provide around the clock support. A continuous improvement plan should consider this factor.

- The team might tend to become complacent during the maintenance phase and may also lose motivation. Hence, the project manager faces challenges in maintaining team motivation.

Root Causes

A high percentage of support and maintenance activities are fairly repetitive. Business stakeholders expect operational efficiency and cost efficiency during this phase.

Implementing a Continuous Improvement Plan

Here are the proven best practices for implementing continuous improvement during the support and maintenance phases:

- Project managers should adopt the "shift left" policy. Typically, production support consist of the L1 team providing the first level support. The L2 and L3 teams then handle unresolved issues from the L1 team. In a shift left model, the team uses a number of tools (such as search, knowledge management, training, automated jobs, batch jobs, and such) to solve problems in early stages. For instance, the incidents that are typically handled by L3 teams can be moved to the L2 team by creating an automated job. Similarly, some of the L2 jobs can be moved to the L1 team through how-to articles in a centralized knowledge base. This movement of solutions to the left is achieved by using the shift left model, which reduces cost and the average ticket resolution time.

- The project manager has to analyze the production incidents and tickets to get insights into the nature of the problem. This includes root cause analysis, ticket trend analysis, SLA analysis, average ticket resolution time, and periodic ticket volume analysis. Based on the insights gathered from these activities, the root cause (such as defective code module leading to high volume of tickets or a process gap leading to SLA violations) should be corrected. Track the change in the metrics through regular monitoring and report improvements to the business stakeholders.

- The digital project team can identify the key nature of the incidents and develop self-service tools and applications to avoid the issue. For instance, if the incidents are mainly related to the data, you could develop a reporting application that provides various views of the data to the users. Similarly, other self-service applications like password reset, user administration, user registration, knowledge base, collaboration, etc. can be used to avoid tickets. This also improves the user experience. Automated application monitoring and notification jobs can ease the job of the maintenance teams. Batch jobs, release management tools, automated regression testing tools, and file copy jobs can significantly reduce the cost and workload of the maintenance teams.

- The project manager should create a centralized knowledge repository to store all the lessons, best practices, how-to articles, and process documentation. All production teams should be cross-trained using this knowledge base so that they can be deployed to various jobs.

- Traditional pricing models such as fixed pricing can be replaced by work unit based pricing models and revenue sharing models to achieve cost optimization. The fixed pricing model provides a fixed cost for a specified duration irrespective of the workload. Work unit based pricing model charges a predetermined cost per every work unit. (A unit in the case of production support could be based on the number of production incidents.) Revenue sharing models are used for transactional systems wherein the revenue of a successful transaction (such as items sold) is shared among all parties.

Proactive Identification of Digital Opportunities

The project manager has to constantly look out for ways to improve the user experience and the business outcomes. When a digital project is stable, the team has a good understanding of the client ecosystem, the business processes, and the key metrics. These insights should be used to come up with digital opportunities. This can lead to increased opportunities and revenue as well as to strategic partnerships with other business.

Challenges

Here are some of the challenges:

- Lack of continuous innovation can ultimately lead to low adoption of the digital applications.

- Without proactive account mining, it is not possible to engage the customer in long-term strategic initiatives.

Root Causes

Here are some of the root causes:

- Complacency in support and maintenance

- Insufficient bandwidth and resource constraints prevent other opportunities

Ways to Mine Existing Digital Client Accounts

Here are some of the ways to mine existing digital accounts:

- Digital projects are all about bringing in business value and sustainable competitive advantages. Identify the growth opportunities for the client's business domain by leveraging the latest digital technologies. This can include niche digital technologies such as AI-based automation, IoT technologies, segmented marketing, and so on.

- Common digital opportunities in large enterprises are application consolidation, cloud deployment, automation of business process activities, and legacy system modernization.

- Leverage the center-of-excellence expertise to bring innovation and thought leadership to the business domain. This includes proactive proposals for mobile commerce, exploring new markets, launching loyalty programs, and so on.

- Continuous innovation and thought leadership. The execution team has to constantly try to leverage emerging technologies and trends and identify opportunities to leverage them for the business domain. Accelerators, solutions, and points of views from the center of excellence (CoE) can improve the business model and add business value to the organization.

Summary

In this chapter we discussed various project management scenarios:

- You can address scope creep by effective project planning, scope management, change request management, and adopting an Agile execution model.

- You can maintain strict project SLAs through comprehensive requirements elaboration and verification, dedicated project management office (PMO), using checklists for project management, creating a comprehensive traceability matrix, regularly conducting project health check assessments, managing risk appropriately, estimating effort appropriately, having a good communication plan, incorporating robust planning, building the right mix of the project team, managing activities in the critical path, and performing PoC based validation.

- You can handle frequent and late changes through a robust change management process, an Agile execution approach, prototype demos, and contingency planning.

- You can manage stakeholders efficiently through proper identification of all concerned stakeholders, having a communication plan, and properly articulating metrics based business value.

- You can minimize human resource churn by developing core group and second level resources, having training and knowledge management plans, rotating resources, and providing incentives and rewards for top performers.

- You can minimize a high volume of defects through root cause analysis framework, a traceability matrix, development of automated test suites, a quality dashboard, quality checklists, industry best practices, and CI processes.

- You can achieve productivity and continuous improvement by using the shift left model, incident analysis, self-service tools, and a good knowledge management system.

- The digital project manager has to identify digital opportunities to enhance the business value and leverage the center-of-excellence expertise. This will bring innovation and thought leadership to the business domain and add business value.

CHAPTER 16

Digital Project Management Case Studies

Case studies provide insights into detailed project management scenarios. Project managers can use case studies as reference points while dealing with similar projects. This chapter covers various scenarios related to project management. The case studies are closely modeled on real-world scenarios and include the background, challenges, project management practices adopted, and lessons for each of these case studies. We intentionally chose case studies across various business domains and that span across various digital technology scenarios to provide wide coverage. The case studies are designed to highlight the project management aspects without going too deep into the technical details so that you can understand the case study from a project management standpoint.

Digital project managers can use this chapter to understand and apply the lessons to various real-world scenarios.

End-to-End Execution of a Digital Consolidation Project

Consolidation of various digital applications and capabilities into a centralized digital platform is a common theme in digital projects. Consolidation and migration of data and functionalities are one of the primary best practices for the success of digital projects. This section looks at a detailed case study involving a digital consolidation scenario.

© Shailesh Kumar Shivakumar 2018
S. K. Shivakumar, *Complete Guide to Digital Project Management*,
https://doi.org/10.1007/978-1-4842-3417-4_16

Project Background

The organization is incurring high maintenance and operations costs for maintaining multiple applications. The legacy applications were developed in legacy technologies 15 years back and it is increasingly becoming difficult to add new features to these legacy systems. Additionally, the legacy applications are not scaling to increased user traffic and data volume. There are more than 20 legacy applications that are marked for this project.

The project involves consolidation of various legacy technologies and applications into a single digital platform. The key program objectives are:

- Create a common set of standards and a uniform technology stack.

- Migrate content and data and rewrite the legacy code in the new digital platform.

- Redesign the user experience to conform to the latest standards.

- Develop a scalable and extensible digital platform to cater to future needs and growth.

- Develop the digital platform based on open standards.

- Redesign existing business to make it more efficient and improve productivity.

- Ensure minimum business disruption during the migration exercise.

- Leverage latest digital technologies related to automation and self-service enablement.

Challenges Involved in the Project

Here are the key challenges involved in this project:

- There are multiple diverse and sometimes incompatible technologies in the current ecosystem. Combining them into a common set of standards and technologies requires careful assessment and planning.

- The project manager has to define the migration process to cause minimal disruption for the business. This involves various challenges related to design and development of migration jobs, synchronization jobs, design of various fallback mechanisms, etc.

- Continuously changing requirements and adding to the scope creep needs to be managed.

Project Execution Details

A successful execution of this project involved these aspects. We discussed the detailed migration approach in Chapter 12. The migration approach defined in Chapter 12 is further explained in this section. We discuss the various aspects of successful project execution in this section.

Elaborate Project Planning

Based on the priorities, the project manager has to categorize more than 20 applications into three categories: *Needs Migration* (the applications that need to be migrated along with its code, data, and content), *Needs Redesign* (the applications that need to be fully revamped and rewritten using the latest digital technologies with minimal migration), and *Retire* (for legacy applications that need not be migrated).

The migration and execution plans will be designed based on these categories. The applications that add high business value under Needs Migration and Needs Redesign will be taken up for the initial release iteration.

Proof of Concepts (PoC) for Solution Approach Validation

PoCs are mainly used for two main purposes: to select the most appropriate digital technology and to validate the solution approach. Candidate products were selected based on the detailed product evaluation framework (consisting of technology criteria, functional criteria, and operational criteria) we defined in Chapter 12. The top three products were used to carry out PoCs to finalize the product.

Robust Migration Process

For the applications that need to be migrated, the project manager needs to define a robust migration process. The high-level steps of the migration process are depicted in Figure 16-1.

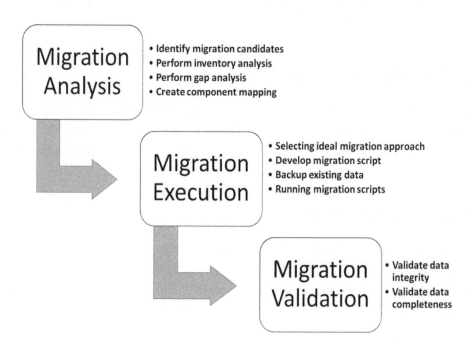

Figure 16-1. *Migration process steps*

Figure 16-1 provides the key phases in the migration. During the Migration Analysis phase, the existing inventory of components is identified. We pick the main modules, libraries, data, and content from the 20 legacy applications that are sorted into the "Needs Migration" category. We also identify any existing gaps and challenges with the existing functionality so that they are addressed during migration. For instance, removal of any redundant web pages, consolidation of libraries, and removal of duplicate functionality are marked as gaps so that they can be addressed during migration. During this phase, the source components will be mapped to their counterparts in the target system.

During the Migration Execution phase, we select the ideal migration approach (delta or complete migration) and develop the migration script for automated migration. Before executing the actual migration, the code, data, and content needs to be backed up. The last stage is the Migration Validation phase, wherein we test migrated data for various scenarios such as integrity checks and completeness checks to ensure that complete and correct data is migrated.

During the digital consolidation exercise (the exercise to consolidate the legacy applications), the business data was distributed across various systems. One of the key exercises of this project is to consolidate the data as well. The various steps of the data migration process are depicted in Figure 16-2.

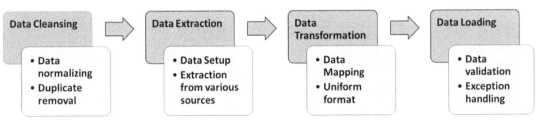

Figure 16-2. *Data migration steps*

During the Data Cleansing stage, the source data is prepared for migration. This includes normalizing any tables, removing duplicates, removing invalid data, etc. The data from various systems is then extracted during the Data Extraction phase. The extracted data is transformed and formatted into a uniform format to suit the target system. Normally, XML is the preferred intermediate format for the data. During data transformation, the formatted source data is mapped to the target data. Once the data transformation is over, the data is loaded into the target system. After data loading, the data is validated for completeness. The exceptions during data loading are logged into a log file for further analysis.

Lessons and Key Takeaways

The main lessons from the project are listed here:

- Develop reusable migration scripts and leverage available tools in the migration project. Although this exercise needs initial investment, it improves productivity in future migration phases.

- Prioritize the applications that need to be migrated based on their business importance.

- Execute migration in iterations and continuously fine tune the migration strategy.

- Validate the migrated applications and data using a comprehensive test suite to ensure that there are no regression issues.

The next section looks at a digital transformation case study.

Large-Scale Digital Transformation Project

This case study is about the execution of a large-scale digital transformation project. The overall project costs more than 3 million USD and spans more than 18 months. The peak team size is more than 50 people.

Chapter 17 takes a deep dive into a digital transformation exercise and defines its drivers, challenges, and best practices.

Project Background

The digital project involves building a B2C e-commerce digital platform for a retailer. The e-commerce platform was rolled out in more than 50 locations and catered to 300K peak user traffic. The main business drivers for the e-commerce platform are as follows:

- Gain competitive edge by using niche digital technologies.

- Reduce total cost of ownership (TCO) and optimize operation costs.

- Enjoy a faster time to market for launching new products and services.

- Optimize business processes across various geographies.

Challenges Involved in the Project

Here are the key challenges of the e-commerce digital project:

- The e-commerce platform has to be integrated with more than 30 systems, which poses challenges with performance and transaction management.

- There is a vast set of requirements and a huge number of business rules that need to be fully captured.

Project Execution Details

The salient features of successful execution of this e-commerce project are listed in the following sections.

Elaborate Discovery Phase

Due to the vastness of the project, the execution team has to engage various stakeholders to understand the requirements from all dimensions. An elaborate and multi-dimensional discovery phase covers the following aspects:

- Requirements elaboration meeting and workshops with all stakeholders and SMEs. Interviews and surveys with sample user population are also conducted to understand the expectations from the new platform. The captured requirements are elaborately documented in the requirements document and reviewed and signed off on by concerned stakeholders.

- All existing documentation is carefully reviewed to understand the process flows and business rules.

- The integration requirements with various interfaces are carefully documented. Various integration options are evaluated before selecting the recommended option. A separate integration architecture document is developed.

- A technical architecture team is formed to select the products, tools, and technologies and to design the platform.

- The project manager creates a detailed risk and mitigation plan to detail potential risks, probability of occurrence, and impact along with a mitigation plan. The project manager also develops the training plan for the identified tools and technologies. The project manager estimates all functional modules. A 10% buffer is added to effort to address any contingencies and execute the risk mitigation plan.

Well Defined Acceptance Criteria and Metrics

Due to the volume and variety of requirements, the project manager has to clearly define and communicate the acceptance criteria and in-scope items for all the functional and nonfunctional requirements. The SLAs, metrics, and test criteria should be quantified to ensure proper testing. Here are good examples of quantified acceptance criteria:

- *Scalability*: The e-commerce platform should be scalable for the peak user load of 300,000 users per hour.

- *Performance*: The average page load time across all geographies should not exceed two seconds.

All assumptions (related to scope, staffing, resources, dependencies, etc.) and constraints should be documented and validated with all stakeholders.

Independent Execution of Multiple Tracks

The development of the e-commerce platform is subdivided into numerous logical modules. The iterative execution model is selected for the project execution. In the first iteration, the core platform components such as the platform framework, essential building blocks, initial integrations, and login functionality are developed. The project manager identifies modules such as the payment, inventory, experience, and services modules that use the platform components. Each module is developed in subsequent iterations.

Enterprise Integration Track

Due to the complex nature of the integrations, the enterprise integration architects have to develop an enterprise integration architecture document covering all details of the integration. This includes the selected integration methodology, data formats, SLAs, exception handling, localization handling, fallback handling, and more. The QA team has to iteratively test the integration aspects for every iteration.

Robust Quality Practices

The project manager has to define multiple quality gating criteria to ensure robust quality across all tracks. Here are the proven quality gating criteria at various levels:

- Each developer has to use the published coding best practices and checklists as references during code development.

- Developers should also use code quality analyzer tools (such as PMD and SonarQube) to analyze the code's quality before checking in the code to the source control system.

- The project manager has to define a peer review process wherein the module leads review the code manually on periodic basis.

- A continuous integration (CI) setup has to run the code analyzers, unit test cases, and functional test cases automatically on a daily basis to assess the overall quality of the project.

- The validation team has to develop test cases to cover all key functional scenarios to perform end-to-end testing for every iteration. With each iteration, the validation team has to execute regression testing.

- The project manager has to create and maintain an end-to-end traceability matrix to track the implementation of requirements. The traceability matrix should be updated on a periodic basis.

Lessons and Key Takeaways

Here are the key lessons from the project:

- With a large digital transformation project, it is important to capture all non-functional requirements related to security, performance, availability, and scalability. You need to define SLAs based on these nonfunctional requirements and test the deliverable and application against these SLAs.

- All the dependencies on external systems and SMEs should be clearly documented and communicated to the respective owners. The project manager has to clearly communicate the SLAs and requirements from the dependent systems.

- Associated risks should be identified up front and the project manager has to define the risk mitigation plan. All the high-priority risks should be carefully monitored and all the stakeholders should be notified on a regular basis.

- Domain consultants and functional SMEs should be on-boarded for large programs to elaborate and fine tune the domain-specific requirements and business rules.

- The project manager has to maintain a knowledge repository that can be used by all team members. This repository should store the domain artifacts, requirement documents, and process documents. The induction kit consisting of training documents and other resources can be used to train the team members. Individual team members can contribute to the knowledge base articles and best known methods (BKM), and can collaborate through blogs and the community wiki to share knowledge.

- Due to the diverse nature of the teams involved in large engagements, the project manager has to establish open communication channels across cross functional teams.

- The project manager has to focus on increasing productivity by using tools and open source frameworks and automating the activities involving high manual effort (such as using automated deployment scripts for release management activity).

- The project manager has to define a robust change management process to handle and absorb the change requests coming from stakeholders.

The next section looks at a legacy modernization case study.

Legacy Modernization Project

Legacy modernization is another common scenario in digital projects. When organizations want to consolidate, retire, or modernize their legacy applications into modern digital platforms, they must execute legacy modernization projects. In this case study, we look at various aspects of a typical legacy modernization project.

Project Background

This case study discusses the legacy modernization into a digital platform. The organization has more than 10 legacy applications (mainly using mainframes) and they must bring the capabilities of the legacy applications into a modern digital platform. The main goals of this project are listed here:

- Redesign legacy code (COBOL based) into modern web technologies.

- Develop service-oriented architecture for the overall application.

- Develop flexible and modern architecture that can easily absorb changes.

- Reduce the number of systems through consolidation of systems and redesign of system landscape.

- Migrate the monolithic application into a layered architecture adhering to the separation of concerns concept.

- Migrate legacy data into a new web application.

- Retire and decommission most of the legacy systems.

- Combine disparate systems into an uniform platform and eliminate systems that are not adding business value.

- Increase responsiveness to changes through systems consolidation and integrated systems.

- Develop a forward-looking, scalable platform.

Challenges Involved in the Project

Here are the challenges with this project:

- On-boarding people with varied skillsets who would understand the legacy code and design the modern layered architecture.

- Identification and design of services for the new platform.

- Managing multiple stakeholders to define the accurate scope and goals.

- Training existing team on new technologies and managing changes in the organization.

- Lack of in-depth understanding of legacy systems and business domain.

- Executing the legacy modernization in a non-disruptive model.

Project Execution Details

This section provides the details of executing the legacy modernization project.

Define the Design Principles of the Modern Digital Application

Based on the business drivers and program objectives, you must clearly define the design principles of the modern digital application to which the legacy application will be migrated. Here are the key design principles of the modern digital application:

- Develop the application using a layered architecture to create loosely coupled components.

- Use service-oriented design for integration with external and internal systems.

- Use lightweight presentation components and lightweight services for faster response.

- Enhance user experience through a responsive and interactive user interface.

- Enable faster production rollouts by using DevOps.

- Reduce total cost of ownership) through automated processes and optimized business processes.

Create the Legacy Modernization Strategy for Legacy Applications

Design the appropriate legacy modernization strategy for each of the legacy applications. There are two main ways for legacy modernization:

- Migrate the legacy application data and content into a new digital platform. With this approach, you redesign the user experience in the digital platform and rewrite the business logic in the new platform. The old legacy application will be retired.

- Service-enable the existing legacy application and consume the service in the new digital application. In this case, the existing legacy application will be maintained and new services will be built around the existing capabilities to enable point-to-point integration. Alternatively, you can leverage middleware systems (such as ESBs and API gateways) for developing a service-oriented infrastructure.

Define the Robust Migration Strategy

The project manager has to define the migration plan for modernizing the legacy application. The key steps in defining the migration strategy are as follows:

- Identify the critical business functions in the legacy applications. Define a detailed business model elaborating the business flows in the model diagram. Identify the associated datastore for each of the business functions. In a retail domain, business functions include user enrollment, payment, product information management, inventory management, price management, and so on.

- For each of the business functions, identify the best legacy modernization approach (such as migration or service enablement). Accordingly migrate the data and rewrite the business logic in the new digital platform (for migration option) or develop a service for the existing functionality (the service enablement option).

- Consolidate the data sources during the migration process.

Early and Continuous Engagement with Business Stakeholders

The digital project manager has to proactively set up the workshops and "show and tell" demo sessions with concerned stakeholders on a regular basis. The "show and tell" demo workshops are mainly used to demonstrate the refined business processes, web page prototypes, and early releases. The early feedback received in such sessions were addressed in subsequent iterations. These early stakeholder engagement sessions also helped the project manager identify the gaps quicker and address those gaps. As end-to-end process involves multiple teams and SMEs, the project manager has to involve all the related teams and SMEs while redefining the process related requirements.

Lessons and Key Takeaways

The key takeaways from the legacy modernization project are as follows:

- Understand the main business drivers and motivations for the legacy modernization. This is essential to designing the new digital platform.

- Draw a clear boundary on the scope of items for legacy modernization. Elaborate the use cases and business flows to the last level of detail and get signoff from all stakeholders so to avoid any ambiguity and rework in the future. Leverage the expertize of the business domain consultants to understand the existing business processes and business rules.

- Evaluate the product and technology thoroughly to identify the most appropriate product and technology suitable for the technology migration.

- Plan a proof of concept (PoC) to validate the migration approach for each of the business functions.

- Due to the nature of the legacy application, the project manager has to manage the dependencies. All the dependent applications, services, and SMEs should be notified and be available for the migration effort.

- The project manager has to establish a strong project governance structure. The digital project manager has to define processes for change management, quality assurance, functional and non-functional testing, and so on. A project management office (PMO) and steering committee need to be established to manage the program objectives and scope, prioritize issues, handle escalations, and set the program direction.

- When the project involves multiple teams and stakeholders, the project manager has to clearly define the roles and responsibilities of all the stakeholders in the RACI (Responsibility, Accountability, Consulted, and Informed) matrix format. Each stakeholder/SME is assigned the role of responsibility, accountability, consulted, and informed for the key activities.

The next case study examines the details of implementing a digital knowledge platform.

End-to-End Implementation of a Digital Knowledge Platform

A digital knowledge management platform is widely used as a collaboration tool in digital solutions. This case study looks at the details of implementing a digital knowledge platform.

Project Background

The project involves creating a large-scale digital knowledge management platform for internal and external stakeholders. The organization wants to develop a centralized robust knowledge management ecosystem with a knowledge portal, knowledge repository, and knowledge services. The main drivers for this project are listed here:

- Minimize dependency on individual SMEs and process experts and store the structured and searchable knowledge in a centralized knowledge base.

- Leverage the digital technologies to develop the next generation knowledge management platform and provide easily accessible contextual content.

- Develop reusable artifacts for training, competency and productivity development, customer service, and knowledge transfer and management purposes.

- Provide secured access to the content.

Challenges Involved in the Project

The key challenges of this project are as follows:

- The knowledge artifacts are in various formats (documents, web content, videos, web pages, and images) and are distributed across various systems. Consolidating various documents into a uniform and consistent format and migrating all content into a single location is a challenging task.

- Lots of tacit knowledge and business process knowledge is with SMEs and domain experts and there is no documentation. Extracting knowledge into a centralized knowledge base is a challenge. There was a heavy dependency on few SMEs, as the knowledge was not well documented and understood by the team members.

- Lack of existing knowledge management processes is another challenge. There are no processes defined for capturing, storing, searching, and distributing the knowledge artifacts. The digital project manager has to define the knowledge management governance as part of this project.

- The complex security requirements pose additional challenges with filtering the documents.

Project Execution Details

The sample best practices for successful project execution are covered in the following sections.

Define Knowledge Management Processes

The project manager has to define the end-to-end knowledge management processes to build a robust next generation knowledge platform. The key knowledge management process steps are detailed in Figure 16-3.

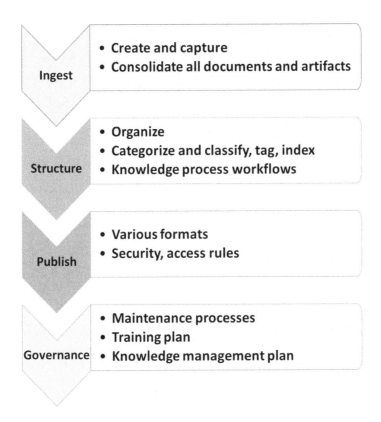

Figure 16-3. *Knowledge management process*

The knowledge management processes are mainly centered around four key steps: Ingest, structure, publish, and governance.

During the Ingest phase, the knowledge artifacts are created. This process involves creation of knowledge artifacts, converting expert knowledge into process documents, and consolidating various documents distributed across multiple sources into a single repository. During the Structure phase, the knowledge artifacts are organized and categorized into logical categories. The artifacts are tagged so that they can be easily searched and discovered. The knowledge management processes, such as archiving, publishing, authoring, deleting, and versioning are created during this stage. During the Publish phase, the knowledge artifacts are published to various destinations in the appropriate formats (such as HTML, JSON, and XML). The Governance stage is an ongoing phase where the knowledge artifacts are maintained and used to train the team. A knowledge management plan is designed to continuously update the knowledge artifacts and make them more effective.

Lessons and Key Takeaways

The key takeaways from this project are listed here:

- Define processes and governance structure to address the current painpoints and to implement the business objectives.

- Critically analyze the gaps in the existing knowledge management processes and come up with a plan to fill those gaps.

- Tag the content with meaningful metadata so that it can be easily discovered.

- Develop a search function to provide secured and contextual access to relevant information.

- Provide self-service features centered on knowledge services. For instance, you can provide content recommendations, solution suggestions, personalized searches, and so on, which increase the productivity of the end users.

Summary

In this chapter we discussed case studies about project management:

- Consolidation of various digital applications and capabilities into a centralized digital platform is a common theme in digital projects.

- The main objectives of the consolidation project case study are content migration, technology standardization, UX redesign, and scalable platform development.

- The main challenges are absence of standards, business disruption, and scope creep.

- A successful consolidation project needs elaborate project planning, proof of concepts (PoC) for solution approach validation, and a robust migration process.

- The main business drivers for the digital transformation project are gaining a competitive edge, cost optimization, obtaining faster time to market, and optimizing business processes.

- The main highlights of the digital transformation project are elaborate discovery phase, well defined acceptance criteria and metrics, independent execution of multiple tracks, enterprise integration, and track and robust quality practices.

- The key goals of the legacy modernization project case study are redesign of the legacy code, developing a service oriented architecture, developing a flexible and extensible architecture, and retiring existing systems.

- Main challenges with the legacy modernization project are availability of legacy skillsets, services design, and domain experts.

- The key execution highlights of the legacy modernization project are to define the design principles of modern digital application, create the legacy modernization strategy for the legacy applications, define a robust migration strategy, and gain early and continuous engagement with business stakeholders.

- The key drivers of the digital knowledge platform case study are to reduce SME dependency, leverage digital technologies, and develop reusable artifacts.

- The main challenges with the digital knowledge platform case study are the wide variety of document formats, minimal documentation of tacit knowledge, and lack of KM processes.

- The goal of the digital knowledge platform case study is to define knowledge management processes with a well defined governance process.

CHAPTER 17

Digital Transformation: A Project Management Case Study

Digital transformation is a quintessential element of the digital journey. Every organization embracing digitization undergoes digital transformation in various phases. Some of the most common digital transformation scenarios are re-design/reimagining the user experience, legacy modernization, and digitizing business processes. As digital transformation is the most common scenario faced by digital project managers, this chapter takes a deep dive of various digital project management concepts and provides a detailed case study.

This chapter explores the project management aspects of digital transformation. To start with, you will look at the main concepts of digital transformation, such as common drivers, challenges, and trends. Then you will look at a detailed case study involving the digital transformation of a banking solution.

Chapter 16 briefly looked at digital transformation for the e-commerce digital platform. This chapter explains the digital transformation in greater detail, by discussing the business drivers, project management aspects, etc. The case study mainly focuses on the project management topics of digital transformation, as the primary focus area of the book is about project management.

The case study serves as a project management reference for executing large-size complex digital transformation projects.

Project managers and account managers will find the content in this chapter useful.

Digital Transformation Overview

Digital transformation projects leverage digital technologies to redefine business models, creating newer and more collaborative engagement models and optimizing operational cost to improve performance. This section looks at common drivers, challenges, best practices, trends, and other aspects of digital transformation.

Common Drivers of Digital Transformation Programs

Here are the key business motivations for digital transformation programs:

- *User experience enhancement*: Organizations that want to transform the user experience must have a thorough understanding of painpoints, experience touch points, social marketing needs, and business metrics (such as ROI, loyalty improvement, conversion improvement, campaign management needs, promotion needs, etc.). Organizations aim to provide user-centric, forward-looking, interactive, engaging, personalized, and responsive web experiences through modern web technologies such as HTML5, SPA, and Responsive Web Design (RWD) and develop a modern, forward-looking digital platform.

- *Digitization of business*: Organization wants to transform business models and enable business processes with digital technologies. Enterprises aim to bring agility to the business process and scale the existing systems for business expansion and future growth. Enterprises also like to leverage various new opportunities and possibilities that are made possible because of digital technologies.

- *Operation optimization*: Organizations want to optimize the operations and maintenance through initiatives such as process digitization, automation, productivity improvement measures, self-service, collaboration, customer service improvement, real time performance management, etc.

- *Consolidation*: Many digital transformation programs are driven by the need to consolidate technology, data, infrastructure, service, and functionality. Consolidated data provides efficient insights about customer behavior. Organizations aim to standardize systems, technologies, and products acquired through mergers and acquisitions. Consolidating multiple disjoint user experiences into an integrated digital platform is one of the key drivers of a digital transformation.

- *Active user engagement*: Organizations want to engage users on all channels to establish long-term relationships. As a result, the modern digitally-enabled organizations involve end users in crucial stages of the solution development through collaborative channels. Organizations use digital capabilities such as analytics, gamification, machine learning, and Big Data analysis to engage users effectively. Organizations also like to have a deeper understanding of their customers through data consolidation and by using analytics technologies.

- *Business agility*: Organizations pursue digital transformation to become more responsive to change. Organizations want to quickly adapt to market dynamics and fast-changing customer demands and expectations to retain a competitive edge.

Common Challenges in Digital Transformation Programs

The common challenges in executing the digital transformation programs are listed here:

- *Niche digital skillsets*: Due to the variety and continuous evolution of digital technologies, it is challenging for organizations to on-board the right skilled people, especially with niche digital skills.

- *Resistance to change*: As digitization brings in changes to existing business processes and business models, the existing staff might resist the change due to fear of the unknown. This resistance needs to be addressed through orientation workshops, training, and other such initiatives.

- *Governance changes*: Digitization of business models, automation, self-service, and such changes bring in changes to governance processes. The governance changes pose challenges due to organizational culture, need for accurate tracking metrics, and people mindset.

Common Best Practices in Digital Transformation Programs

The main best practices for digital transformation programs are listed here:

- *Enable services*: Expose key business functionalities through services. This can be done by developing new services or wrapping services around existing functionalities (usually done in legacy modernization).

- *Platform approach*: The digital solution should build a scalable and easily extensible platform to add capabilities in the future. A platform should provide much of the needed capabilities out of box.

- *Process optimization*: The digital consultants should carefully analyze the existing business processes to identify opportunities for process optimization, process automation, or redefining the process through digital capabilities.

- *Customer touch point optimization*: Understand customer needs and user journeys to optimize the user experience at every touch point.

- *Iterative transformation*: Lay out the digital transformation roadmap to progressively enable the needed capabilities for the enterprise.

- *Harnessing collective intelligence*: In the world of Big Data and social media, create collaborative features to harness and involve end users in the digital transformation journey.

- *Success metrics tracking*: Define and track the success metrics (such as ROI, conversion rate, site traffic, online revenue, customer satisfaction, order value, online cost, and productivity improvement) relevant to the business domain.

Recent Trends in Digital Transformation Programs

As the digital technology ecosystem is continuously evolving, an organization needs to constantly look out for modern digital technologies to realize their digital vision. The main current trends in the digital space are given here:

- *Location-based analytics*: Using location-based services, organizations want to push personalized, relevant, and effective campaigns and services.

- *Social channel utilization and touch point optimization*: Organizations want to engage their customers at all touch points (web, offline, kiosk, mobile, social media, IVR, etc.). Due to increased popularity of social media platforms, organizations use them for the voice of customer channels, brand marketing, campaigns, etc.

- *Mobile-first and cloud-first strategies*: Digital platforms are built with mobile devices as their primary delivery platforms. The applications are deployed increasingly on the cloud to realize the "software-as-service" model.

- *Intuitive user experiences*: Seamless and integrated cross-channel enabled content with dashboard views, unified views, 360-degree activity views, and rich, real-time visualizations are becoming the norm in the user experience space. Good customer experiences bring trust and loyalty.

- *Digital marketing*: Organizations are leveraging social media platforms to market their products and brands. Peer recommendations and peer approval play a major role in influencing customers.

- *Analytics*: Real-time analytics of user actions and analysis of historical data will be used for contextual recommendation and for personalizing the experience.

- *Domain-specific trends*: Each functional vertical has its own set of digital transformation goals. The main digital transformation goals for some of the verticals are as follows:

  - *Banking*: Digital banking, omni-channel experience, personalization, dashboard experience, virtual branch, self-service tools, social media engagement, analytics, mobile apps, digital payments, and digital wallets.

  - *Retail*: Virtual assistant, AI-based smart recommendations, chat bot, augmented reality, mobile apps, Big Data, IoT, wearables, cloud delivery (SaaS), social media marketing, social listening, user enablement, targeted marketing, loyalty management, digital marketing, customer segmentation, and voice of customers.

  - *Utilities*: Dashboard experience, self-service, process automation, real-time monitoring, dashboard view, and analytics.

  - *Life sciences*: Business intelligence, mobile apps, CRM, ERP applications, wearables, IoT, and reporting.

  - *Automobile*: IoT and telematics.

- *Other digital technologies*: Organizations are increasingly investing in Big Data, IoT, and wearables for applicable use cases.

Project Activities During Digital Transformation

This section looks at various activities of a typical digital transformation project.

Table 17-1 explains in detail the different phases, key milestones, activities, and deliverables. The activities might vary based on the type of the digital transformation (such as UI redesign, data migration, process re-engineering, etc.) and execution model (Agile, iterative, etc.).

Table 17-1. *Project Activities in a Typical Digital Transformation Project*

Phase	Activities	Deliverables
Planning & Requirements Elaboration	• Requirements and scope definition, including functional and nonfunctional requirements through requirements workshops and stakeholder interviews • Understanding business processes, tools, and business rules • Set up environment and needed infrastructure • Detail integration requirements • Detail UI details, including navigation design, information architecture design, and journey modeling • Develop environment setup and infrastructure setup plan	• Project plan • Validated system requirements specification • Software architecture document • Validated UI standards and specification • Communication plan • Risk management plan • Quality management plan • Release management plan • Configuration management plan • Integration specification document
Architecture and Design	• Create a high-level solution architecture document • Develop test plans for unit testing, system testing, functional testing, and integration testing • Design UI visual design, information architecture, and wireframes • Define architecture patterns, standards, reusable frameworks, and tools for the project	• Software architecture document • Sequence diagram(s) • Detailed design document • Test plans and scripts • Visual design

(continued)

Table 17-1. *(continued)*

Phase	Activities	Deliverables
Build	• Develop code • Unit testing • Functional testing • Integration testing • Integration with interfaces	• Source code • Test report • Updated requirement traceability matrix
User Acceptance Testing	• Defect fixes • Support UAT • User training	• UAT defect reports • Training manuals • Implementation plan
Post Go-Live	• Production incident handling • System maintenance (patching, backup, and upgrades) • Application monitoring	• SLA reports

Guiding Principles for Digital Transformation

The key guiding principles for a sample digital transformation are depicted in Figure 17-1. A project manager should provide crucial inputs in governance, project monitoring and control, program quality assurance, and other operations aspects of the project execution.

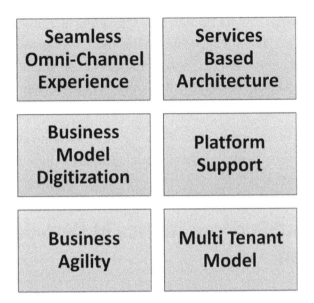

Figure 17-1. *Guiding principles for digital transformation*

A typical digital transformation project adheres to these main principles:

- *Seamless omni-channel experience*: Users should experience consistent personalized experiences across all channels and all devices. The user journey should be seamless across all touch points.

- *Focus on services*: The business functionality should be available as services and should be the preferred method for integration. Micro-services provide granular, lightweight models for services-based integration that enables you to create highly scalable systems.

- *Digitization of business models*: Business models should be automated and driven to enable business self-service. Rules and policy-driven business processes and process automation should be adopted.

- *Platform reusability*: The platform should provide out-of-box capabilities and configurations to implement the needed functionality. Developers should reuse/extend out-of-box functionality and leverage product configurations to minimize customization.

- *Business agility*: The digitization of the business model should reduce the time to market and make businesses more responsive to change. Continuous integration (CI) and continuous deployment (CD) are key enablers of business agility. They facilitate faster product launches and quicker defect fixes.

- *Support for multi-tenant model*: The digital application should be able to support the multi-tenant model through skins and white labeling options.

Capabilities and Success Metrics of Next-Generation Digital Platform

The next step is to map the business goals and organization into capabilities needed in the digital platform. A sample capability diagram is depicted in Figure 17-2.

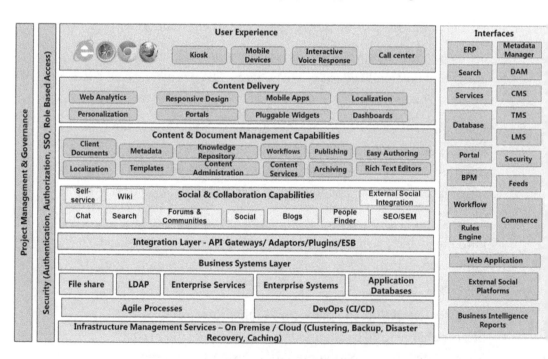

Figure 17-2. *Capability view of next generation digital platform*

Figure 17-2 depicts the layer-wise capabilities for the next generation digital platform. We identified various components of the user experience design layer that include device specific user journeys. The Content delivery layer includes various forms of content rendition capabilities such as Responsive Web Design (RWD), portals, mobile apps, and such. The integration layer consists of ESB (enterprise service bus) and API gateways for enabling service-based integration with the business systems layer. The business systems layer includes various systems of records, such as CRM (customer relationship management), ERP (enterprise resource planning), billing systems, payment systems, etc. DevOps (with CI and CD), infrastructure services, project management, governance, security, and end-to-end testing are the horizontal components of the digital platform.

The Interfaces layer consists of various enterprise interfaces such as search, commerce, the BPM (business process management) platform, LMS (learning management system), DAM (digital asset management), CMS (content management system), TMS (translation management system), rules engines, social platforms, web applications, reports, and collaboration systems that will be integrated through services.

Success Metrics

The metrics are closely aligned to the functional domain and business goals. For instance, the key metrics for digital transformation of customer service domain are Customer Satisfaction level, reduction in service calls, and number of customers retained/lost from a business standpoint. They also include metrics such as overall resolution time, satisfaction index, and efficiency from a customer standpoint.

Digital Bank Digital Transformation Case Study Details

This section discusses the digital transformation of a bank, mainly focusing on the project management aspects. This case study also looks at the main planning activities such as the communication plan, project management plan, risk management plan, change management plan, and configuration management plan, which was discussed in Chapter 3.

Case Study Background

The banking ecosystem has undergone a massive transformation in recent years. Traditional banks are trying to catch up with modern digital technologies to stay ahead of the competition. In this elaborate case study, we examine the digital transformation journey of a bank and the various processes involved.

Digital Bank Vision

The bank has identified the following vision elements for developing a next generation digital bank:

- *Digitization of existing banking processes*: Leverage digital technologies to simplify and optimize existing banking processes such as user registration, funds transfer, payments, etc.

- *Development of next generation online banking platform*: The bank wanted to leverage modern digital technologies that provide robust transactions and service experiences by maintaining client relationships.

- *Omni-channel personalized user experience*: Completely revamp the traditional user experience with next generation, responsive and mobile-enabled user experience. Mobile app and mobile web are needed to provide personalized seamless anytime, anywhere user experiences.

- *Digital bank*: Launch new digitally-enabled banking capabilities such as digital bank office, virtual branch, digital wallets, etc. Provide other enablers and decision-making tools.

- *Increased connections, reach, and engagement*: Engage customer on social media platforms and create participation-driven collaborative platforms. Move away from transaction-oriented to relationship-oriented engagements with customers.

- *Flexible and scalable next generation banking platform*: The bank wanted to build a lean, flexible, and maintainable architecture to accommodate growth and accelerate innovation.

Challenges with the Existing Banking Platform

Table 17-2 depicts the challenges with the existing banking system.

Table 17-2. *Challenges with the Legacy Banking System*

Challenge	Brief Description
User experience	<ul><li>Too many product offerings are adding to the overall technology complexity.</li><li>Absence of modern web technologies with responsive design.</li><li>Absence of mobile apps and social engagement.</li><li>Existing style guides and UI templates are not customer friendly.</li><li>Existing mobile app is rendering off the mobile site in a container and has no additional capabilities.</li></ul>
Performance and availability issues	<ul><li>Too many integrations are also causing performance and availability issues for the banking website.</li></ul>
Productivity issues	<ul><li>The inherent complexity of the online platform leads to a greater time to implement.</li><li>Missing common, reusable component and frameworks. No reusability and automation during migration.</li></ul>
Not aligned with overall digital strategy	<ul><li>Existing system was missing certain functionalities such as two-factor authentication and web chat.</li></ul>
High Maintenance cost	<ul><li>High software licensing and support costs due to multiplicity of products and technologies involved.</li><li>High development, testing, and skill cost involved.</li><li>Many of the legacy technologies were nearing end of life and end of support.</li></ul>
High Infrastructure cost	<ul><li>Heavyweight packaged product requiring high server configurations.</li><li>Missing a single, modern product offering combining functionalities in an overall digital space.</li><li>Dedicated infrastructure required needs for current online platform.</li></ul>

Implementing Digital Bank Vision

During digital transformation, new digital technologies were leveraged to implement various vision elements. The details are discussed in the following sections.

Digitization of Existing Banking Processes

Many of the key banking processes were digitized and simplified. User registration and account opening processes were fully digitized, which means bank customers don't have to visit an actual branch. Simplified one-step registration is easier for customers. The forms used for these two processes are shorter and the underlying business processes for approvals were simplified. Many stages in the account opening processes were auto-approved for existing customers, thereby reducing the overall account opening time. The customer support function was supported by digital capabilities such as collaboration platform and chat bots. The new banking platform offered Facebook and LinkedIn based login to ease the authentication process along with additional security measures such as 2FA (two-factor authentication).

Omni-Channel Personalized User Experience

The redesigned user experience provided a simple yet responsive user design. The user interface provided a personalized dashboard or all user transactions in a unified view.

   The online banking website was redesigned with modern web technologies such as HTML5, CSS 3, and Bootstrap 3.0, and used responsive web design (RWD) principles. The revamped user interface provided rich, responsive, and personalized experiences for the customers. Mobile apps with a subset of banking features were introduced to the selected geographies.

Digital Bank

The revamped banking platform provided decision-making tools such as loan calculators, product comparators, financial planners, intuitive visualizations, analytics reports on spending patterns, etc. The new banking platform also supported a virtual branch, where the users can closely collaborate with a banker and exchange information.

Increased Connection, Reach, and Engagement

The new banking experience platform (XP) leveraged niche and innovative digital technologies to engage the customers at various touch points. Using predictive analytics banking, the XP recommends various banking products after analyzing past behaviors. Newer digital technologies also leveraged social media platforms for marketing purposes and to engage with and get feedback from customers. Introduction of self-service and knowledge base reduced customer tickets and call center call volume.

Digital Transformation Themes and Solution Design

The digital transformation themes are depicted in Figure 17-3.

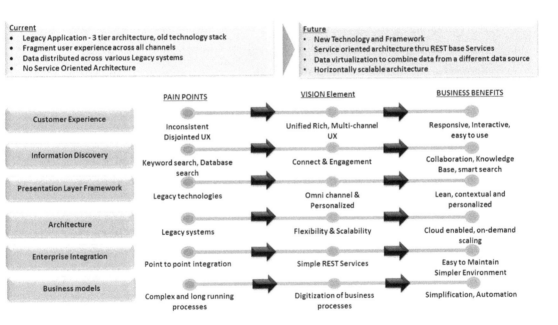

Figure 17-3. *Digital transformation themes*

Aligned to the digital bank vision, the existing legacy systems were transformed based on various themes such as customer experience, information discovery, presentation layer framework, overall architecture, enterprise integration, and business models. The following sections discuss these core solution tenets and solution elements.

Key Solution Tenets

The main solution tenets to realize the solution are listed here:

- *Security and single-sign-on (SSO)*: This is essential, as the banking platform needs to seamlessly link to and communicate with lots of other backend systems. Although the application provides authentication flexibility using Facebook and LinkedIn-based logins, additional security constraints such as 2FA (two-factor authentication) were used to provide additional security measures.

- *Standards based design and development*: All component design and implementation will be based on industry standards. UI standards will be based on HTML5 and other standards.

- *Services based integration*: As integration is one of the main motivations of a consolidated platform, it needs to be designed so as to be extensible and scalable while meeting the performance SLAs. A services based integration approach will be prioritized over other forms of integration whenever possible, owing to the flexibility offered by this approach. This includes integration with data access services, business services, reporting system services, and others. Services-based integration includes SOAP over HTTP(S) and REST.

- *Performance, availability, and scalability*: Performance is an issue starting with the component design stage all the way through the performance testing stage. In addition to performance-based design, other performance optimization techniques will be adopted, including:

  - The solution will also be tested iteratively to ensure that the desired performance SLA is met.

  - Scalability can be achieved by using the appropriate infrastructure and hardware.

  - Incorporation of monitoring governance model to proactively check the heartbeat of the systems (portal and other applications) ensures system availability and uptime. In case of any outages or performance issues, the monitoring systems trigger automatic notifications to the system administrators, who can take immediate action.

- *Reusability and automation*: Reusing existing components/ frameworks will contribute to quicker time to market, increased developer productivity, and better overall quality. The digital architects need to create a reusable framework, reusable components (such as service integrators and utility libraries), and reference architecture that can be used by the development team.

Digital Solution Elements

The key solution elements shown in Figure 17-3 are described in Table 17-3.

Table 17-3. *Key Solution Elements of the Solution*

Category/Vision	Solution Elements	Benefits
Customer experience: unified rich and responsive	Use experience platform and provide unified dashboard experience, intuitive information architecture, and iterative rapid prototype-based requirements gathering workshops. Involved solution architects to create framework components to bring about a uniform and rich user experience.	Increased customer engagement and higher satisfaction, better user engagement, responsive and easy-to-use experience, increase in revenue.
Presentation layer framework: omni channel, personalized experience	Web technology upgrade to Angular JS and lean frontend technologies, usage of powerful JavaScript based MVC framework, reusable UI component widget library, enhanced UX with data sorting, data filtering, contextual help, UI controls, async screen refreshes, and responsive web design (RWD).	Optimal performance, increased user satisfaction, delivery of personalized and contextual content, and reduced maintenance costs.
Architecture	Layered loosely coupled architecture, infrastructure sizing, and standards based open architecture.	Technology upgrade to make application easily scalable and extensible, maintenance of SLAs at peak load.

(continued)

Table 17-3. (*continued*)

Category/Vision	Solution Elements	Benefits
Enterprise integration	Service-oriented architecture (SOA), preference to lightweight REST-based services, and using message oriented middleware such as ESB or API gateway for centralized integration management.	Future readiness for other application integrations, easy to on-board future integrations, and centralized security and governance of integration concerns.
Business models	Process simplification, process automation, self-service models, and process digitization.	Operation agility and higher operation efficiency, faster time to market, and reduced IT dependency.
Information discovery	Using collaborative tools such as forums, blogs, and chat bots.	Promote contextually relevant content and optimized information discovery.

Project Management Plan

This section discusses the various aspects of the project management plan, such as project execution details and sprint activities.

Project Execution

The digital transformation is planned using the Agile mode. Various activities are depicted in the Figure 17-4.

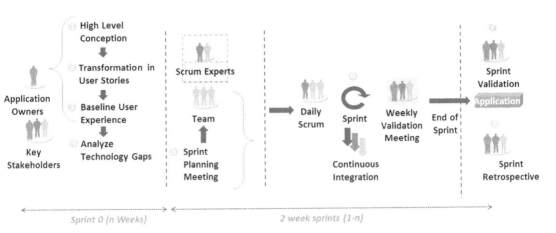

Figure 17-4. *Activities of Agile execution*

Details about the activities in various sprint phases are depicted in Table 17-4.

Table 17-4. *Sprint Activities*

Sprint Phase	Activities
Sprint 0: Conception, Story Transformation	• Converting requirements to user stories. Based on the nature and complexity of the project mapping of requirements to user stories, this may take more time.
	• Define and baseline the user experience.
	• Maintain healthy product backlog for projects across next three-four sprints.
	• Identify gaps in and challenges with existing systems.
	• Keep the engineering teams engaged with forthcoming requirements and changes.
	• Create requirement traceability matrix for all functional and non-functional requirements.
	• Prioritize the backlog for each sprint.

(*continued*)

Table 17-4. (*continued*)

Sprint Phase	Activities
Sprint Planning	• Arrive at an understanding with IT on exact features to be delivered in the sprint. • Define the stories and finalize the success criteria. • Create the wireframes, visual design, navigation model, information architecture, and content needed for the sprint pages. • Define the acceptance criteria.
Sprint Execution	• Hold daily scrum meetings. • Understand day-to day progress. • Reprioritize features/stories per customer requirements. • Design, build, integrate, test, and deploy. • Perform continuous integration.
Sprint Validation and Retrospection	• Clarify what's delivered in the sprint. • Perform scrum validation and testing. • Perform ROI measurement and metrics tracking.

Phase 1 of the digital transformation project execution was done for 10 months, as depicted in Figure 17-5. Seven sprints were executed, followed by UAT and production support. Each sprint had the necessary integrations, sprint planning, and QA for the sprint deliverables. Production rollout happened after UAT in month seven, followed by production support. Continuous feedback from business stakeholders was prioritized and implemented in future sprints.

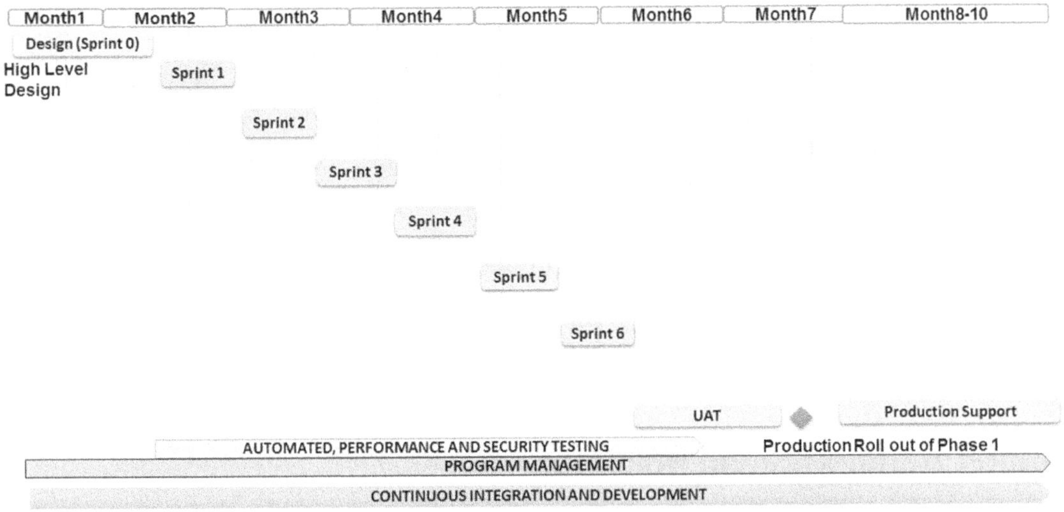

Figure 17-5. *Sprint based execution*

Continuous integration, program management, and automated security/performance testing were all used throughout the entire program execution.

Main Tools Used for Project Execution

The Jira tool was used for Agile service delivery. The Jira tool accurately tracked activities, progress, product backlogs, backlog distributions, and dashboard views of all the activities.

Digital Marketing and Content Management Plan

For marketing content creation, the digital marketing SMEs developed a four-phased strategy:

- Planning phase wherein the user personas and journeys were modeled and analyzed through a series of requirements workshop and stakeholder interviews. Reusable content and content layouts were modeled.

- During the design phase, the style guide (consisting of UI guidelines, standards, and UI specifications) and wireframes were developed. The content design includes messaging, tone, brand values, business goals, and intuitive information architecture . Authoring, review, and tagging processes were defined. Various campaigns needed by the bank were designed during this stage.

- During the build phase, the content, templates, static assets (images, videos), UX prototypes, editorial calendar, interactive widgets, and apps were built and tagged.

- During the execute phase, they published to various destinations and integrated with the final HTML. Translation workflows were developed to create localized content. The effectiveness of the created content is then monitored based on predefined metrics.

Digital Transformation Roadmap

During project management, the project manager created a roadmap for the overall digital transformation, as depicted in Figure 17-6. The digital transformation roadmap consisted of the foundation phase followed by three phases. The foundation phase and Phase 1 are taken up for first delivery, which takes about 10 months. The remaining two phases will be taken up for the next delivery.

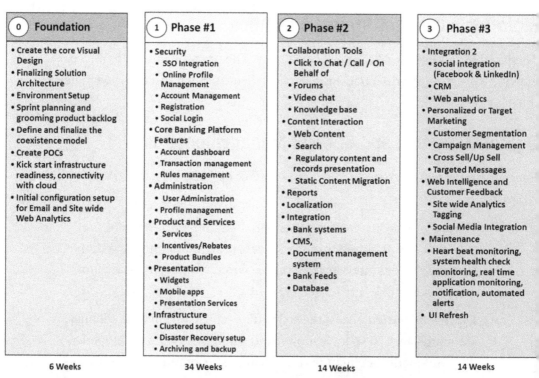

Figure 17-6. *Digital transformation roadmap*

The foundation release consisted of various core capabilities such as solution architecture, sprint plans, visual designs, infrastructure setup, and configuration setup. Phase 1 consists of business-critical capabilities such as security, core banking platform functionality, administration, products and services, presentation components, and infrastructure setup.

Subsequent phases are planned to implement other capabilities, such as collaboration, content management, reports, integrations, personalization, and maintenance.

Agile Success Factors

Here are the main best practices followed for a successful Agile execution:

- *Cohesive team*: One team for each sprint was formed consisting of various SMEs and functional experts for close coordination. Cross-functional roles and responsibilities were defined to ensure active participation from all team members. This reduced the friction across teams and ensured smooth integration and sprint execution.

- *Self-organizing team*: Instead of "instruction-led" teams, self-organizing teams were created. The team was self-sufficient with all needed skillsets and had sufficient authority to make the quick decisions. This led to increased delivery agility and faster time to market.

- *Stakeholder commitment*: The project manager got the buy-in and commitment from all business stakeholders to execute the project using the Agile model. This ensured the timely resolution of dependencies and secured any needed culture changes within the organization.

- *Usage of tools*: The Agile team heavily used tools (such as code generators, code validators, code analysis) to automate build, deployment, and quality activities. This led to enhanced quality, increased productivity, and faster deliveries.

- *Continuous improvement*: A feedback loop was used to continuously improve the delivery quality to match the stakeholders' expectations. Continuous integration and automated security and performance testing led to reduced delivery timelines.

Communication Plan

The communication plan is designed to fulfill the following objectives:

- Provides a structured and action-oriented notification to all stakeholders.

- Details status or various activities, deliverable, and milestones.

- Assigns ownership to any key action items along with timelines and dependencies.

Table 17-5 shows the sample communication topic, frequency of update, and audience in a sample communication plan.

Table 17-5. *Communication Plan*

Communication Topic	Method	Frequency	Audience
Daily stand-up meeting	Formal meeting	Daily	Product owner/project manager project manager UX lead
Status report	Formal meeting	Weekly	Product owner/project manager project manager
End of sprint meeting	Formal meeting	End of weeks (end of sprint)	Product owner/project manager Project manager UX lead
Project review	Formal meeting	Monthly	Relationship manager product owner/project manager project manager
Senior management review	Formal meeting	Quarterly or as needed	Senior management engagement manager

Risk Management Plan

Effective risk management includes early identification and a proactive risk response approach. Risks can arise from sources such as technical issues, resources, dependencies, culture, etc. During every stage in the project, risks are identified and documented. Project risks are identified at the proposal stage based on this risk, thus facilitating early identification and ample lead time to take proactive measures.

Risk management best practices are explained here:

- *Risk identification*: Proactively identify all the risk in the project initiation stage. Risks should be categorized into logical categories such as requirement-related risks, resource related risk, scope related risk, etc. Risk identification is a continuous process that happens throughout the project duration.

- *Risk mitigation*: For each of the identified risks, the project manager has to specify the mitigating options.

- *Risk quantification*: The project manager has to quantify the impact of the risk using risk probability and risk impact parameters. Risk scoring helps project managers prioritize the risks and their mitigation measures.

- *Risk monitoring*: All identified risks should be monitored on a continuous basis and the risk mitigation status should be communicated to all the stakeholders.

The focus of the project manager is to help identify risks early and monitor the risk status continuously during the engagement with a view to help projects succeed by mitigating high and critical risks.

As part of this project, some of the risks identified are mentioned in Table 17-6.

Table 17-6. *Risk and Mitigation Measures*

Risk Category	Risk Description	Mitigation Plan
Infrastructure	The requisite infrastructure not being available in time during various stages of development/ testing may impact the schedule (such as QA environment not ready prior to UAT).	The solution provider provides advance notification of infrastructure needs for development/ testing to plan the infrastructure team and arrange for infrastructure setup in advance.
Roles and Responsibilities	The roles and responsibilities are not clear among the team.	Well-articulated support plan with details of: • Support process flow • Roles and responsibilities matrix • Contact details • Infrastructure/license details • Governance structure • SLAs
Web Services Dependency	No standards or customized web services needed for mobile app will lead to schedule slippage.	The bank has to identify the required web services by the end of the design stage and communicate to the backend team. The backend team develops the web services and makes them available during the build phase.
Ticket Volume	High ticket volume post releases	There should be a mutual agreed upon SLA penalty relaxation for a specific period after a major release for impacted applications (due to release). Early involvement with the testing team to understand the defect trends in the testing environment. The support team should be involved during system testing for any major/minor enhancements as part of releases.

(*continued*)

Table 17-6. (*continued*)

Risk Category	Risk Description	Mitigation Plan
Stakeholder Availability	Lack of right SME/stakeholder during various phases of project may lead to delay in ensuring requirement clarity, delay in sign off and reviews, and can impact the schedule.	The project manager has to communicate the requirements of the stakeholder or SME availability and ensure the same during project execution.
Scope Changes	Change in scope during development phase will result in rework and schedule changes.	The scope changes are addressed based on their priority in subsequent sprints.
Integration	Performance and specification mismatch risk during integration.	Bank needs to provide sample request and response. Explore early integration and iterative integration testing.
Performance Testing	• Absence of documentation for existing applications. • Inadequate number of test machines and software licenses to run performance test exercise. • Performance test results obtained in non-production like test environment may not reflect the true application behavior. • Significant application or architectural changes during the performance testing or estimation phase may impact the correctness or timeliness and lead to rework. • Non-availability of test data for performance testing.	• Document information, architecture, etc. with help of performance test requirements to be accessed initially and communicated to in advance. • Workload and environment is like production as much as possible. • Minimize the architectural, design, and configuration changes during application test runs. • Use tools to create test data as much as possible. • Share the testing schedule with the teams to give them time for the set up. • Proper number of test machines and licenses are procured for performance testing.

Change Management Plan

The Change Management plan treats change management as a continuous and iterative process. Key steps in the change management process are detailed here:

- A project change request will be generated when a proposed change impacts the project plan.

- Project change requests may be generated for the following reasons:

  - Scope changes

  - Schedule changes

  - Requirements/functionality/architecture/design changes

  - Dependencies not being met timely/reconciliation work with baseline teams

- The project manager will assess the impact on time estimates and the estimated costs for the change and raise a change request. The change request will highlight the following:

  - Description of the change

  - Impact of the change on project cost

  - Impact of the change on project schedule

- Change requests will be submitted to the CCB (change control board) for review and approval.

- On approval, the change request will be incorporated into the project plan and executed.

Configuration Management Plan

The configuration management plan defines the process steps, guidelines, and standards for controlling project artifacts (such as source code, project documentation, requirements document, etc.). In this plan, you detail the process for naming conventions, artifact versioning, artifact check out, artifact labeling, artifact tagging, artifact locking, artifact merging, and so on.

Naming Convention and Version Numbering Scheme

A consistent/unique, structured naming convention will be followed to identify the artifacts.

- Example: Project Name_Module Name_Artifact Name

- Example: Version: 1.0 →1.1......→2.0

Version Control

Version control is an important activity for managing different versions of an artifact. It supports multiple versions of a file, a locking facility to prevent two or more people from modifying a file at the same time, and recovery of any previous versions of a file. This will help you identify respective changes in the file, as each version caters to the specific set of requirements or changes. For every change (irrespective of whether it is a major or minor change) or group of related changes, there is a change in the version of the artifact.

1. The current code version will be saved in a manifest file (or any other property file).

2. Each time a new functionality is released or issues are fixed, the version should be increased for defect fixes, feature enhancement, branching, versioning, etc. The trunk typically contains the latest code and you then create branches for maintenance and defect fixes.

Branching

Branching (see Figure 17-7) is done to create a separate path for file changes. Normally branching is done for defect fixes or for maintenance activities. Branching is also used for multiple checkouts of the same file.

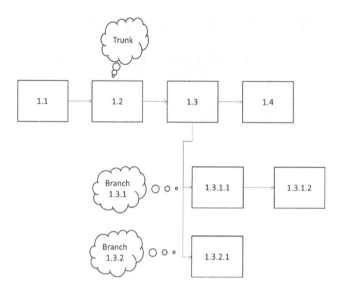

Figure 17-7. *Branching in configuration management*

Checkout

If the developer/team member wants to update the file, she must check out the file from the code base repository before making any changes so that other team members will not be able to modify the file at the same time.

Checkin

Once the developer is done with the changes after validation, she must check the file in to make the changes persisted onto the file and the changes will be available to all.

Locking

The locking mechanism ensures that only a single person can work on a file at any given point. Locking is used to avoid source code conflicts and integration issues.

Merging

Merging mainly involves synchronizing the code in one branch to another branch or to the trunk. For instance, if you need to release the enhancements along with major release, the maintenance branch is merged with the release branch to reconcile the contents of both branches.

Tagging

When the source code is stable in the developer's workspace and ready for deployment, the code should be checked in and tagged in the CM system. The same code will be moved to subsequent environments in the hierarchy for further deployments.

Whenever there is an issue in the code in the higher environments like SIT and UAT, it has to be fixed in the DEV environment. The code should be tagged again and deployed in other environments. The main purpose of this exercise is to ensure that the CM system always has stable and executable code. While tagging, there should be some proper comments that explain the high-level changes to the code. A consistent approach should be followed to name the tag. Preferably a timestamp approach is used.

Release Notes/Release Management

Whenever there is a new deployment or release, release notes should be there to identify the changes to the new release. Release notes should capture the database, configuration, or other changes in order to support the code changes in the new release. Any known issues or problems should be captured in the release note as well.

Summary

This chapter covered a case study involving project management and touched on the following points:

- Common drivers for digital transformation are user experience enhancement, digitization of business, operation optimization, consolidation, active user engagement, and business agility.

- Main challenges in digital transformation are niche digital skillsets, resistance to change, and governance changes.

- Common best practices in digital transformation programs are enabling services, platform approach, process optimization, customer touch point optimization, iterative transformations, harnessing collective intelligence, and success metrics tracking.

- Guiding principles for digital transformation are seamless omni-channel experience, focus on services, digitization of business models, platform reusability, business agility, and support for the multi-tenant model.

- The case study discussed has the following vision elements: digitization of existing banking processes, omni-channel personalized user experience, digital bank experience, increased connections, reach and engagement, and a flexible and scalable next-generation banking platform.

- Key solution tenets of the solution are security and single-sign-on, standards-based design and development, services-based integration, performance, availability and scalability, reusability, and automation.

- Agile success factors included cohesive team structure, self-organizing teams, stakeholder commitment, using the right tools, and continuous improvements.

Cloud Adoption Strategy Checklist

You learned in Chapter 13 that the cloud has become the mainstream phenomenon for running digital applications. Digital project managers need to understand the cloud's suitability for digital applications and define the steps for enabling digital applications on the cloud. This appendix defines a sample checklist for determining how digital applications fit on the cloud and includes the key steps for enabling these applications on the cloud.

The following table shows a sample checklist for determining the cloud suitability of a digital application. You assign a score to each parameter. This example uses a three-scale scoring model, with 1 indicating a negative or minor fit, 2 indicating a medium fit, and 3 indicating a strong fit. A high total score implies that the application is well suited to cloud deployment.

Category	Parameter	Comments
Infrastructure	Is the existing infrastructure fully utilized?	High score if existing infrastructure is less utilized.
	How much of the existing hardware is virtualized (servers abstracted through use of virtual machines)?	High score for high degree of virtualization.
	Is dynamic scalability (on-demand allocation of resources to serve the request) needed for the application?	High score if dynamic scalability is needed.
Application	How mission-critical is the application?	High business criticality means a low score.

(*continued*)

© Shailesh Kumar Shivakumar 2018
S. K. Shivakumar, *Complete Guide to Digital Project Management*,
https://doi.org/10.1007/978-1-4842-3417-4

Category	Parameter	Comments
	What is the amount of integration needed with enterprise applications?	High degree of internal applications means a low score.
	Are there any privacy needs or compliance and regulatory policies about security and data sharing?	Stricter compliance and regulatory policy mean a low score.
	Does the application need consistent high performance and maximum availability?	Stricter performance needs and stricter availability needs (such as 99.999%) mean a high score.

Steps for Cloud Deployment

Here are the detailed steps involved in moving digital applications to the cloud:

- *Infrastructure analysis*: Analyze the dependencies of the application on various infrastructure components, such as enterprise interfaces and internal systems.

- *Analysis of quality parameters*: Compile the list of SLAs for non-functional requirements, such as security, scalability, availability, and performance. The SLAs are usually specified by the business during the requirements elaboration phase. You then use these SLAs for evaluating the cloud plans.

- *Evaluation of cloud options*: During this stage, you identify the applications and services suitable for a public cloud, a private cloud, or a hybrid cloud (which is a combination of a public and private cloud). Applications and services accessed by the general public and by Internet users are best suited for a public cloud. Applications and services that are accessible to a larger community are best suited for a hybrid cloud, and applications and services that are accessible only to internal users and intranet users qualify for a private cloud.

- *Digital application deployment*: Digital applications are deployed and hosted on selected cloud environments. Security and monitoring policies are set up.

- *Governance*: Once the application and services are deployed, they are continuously monitored using the defined SLAs.

Domain-Specific Functional Use Cases and Key Business Drivers

The appendix provides functional domain-specific business use cases and business drivers. These insights can be used by a digital project manager to build domain-specific solutions and accelerators to speed up development. The tracking metrics and KPIs can also be designed based on the business drivers.

- Insurance domain

  - *Key use cases*: User registrations, claims processing, premium calculator, quote processing, policy purchases, claim tracker, office locator, customer dashboards, searches, grievance redresses, policy renewals, social integration, collaboration (chat, blog, wiki, community), FAQs, premium payment and policy recommenders, and product management

  - *Key business drivers*: Unified experiences, effective information discovery, and decision making tools

- Retail Banking domain

  - *Key use cases*: User enrollment, account opening, loan processing, product comparator, complaint handling, branch locator, virtual digital banking, card processing, fund transfer, service request handling, e-statements, personalized dashboard, bill payment, reports downloading, and mobile banking

  - *Key business drivers*: Providing industry leading digital experiences and multi-device enablement

451

© Shailesh Kumar Shivakumar 2018
S. K. Shivakumar, *Complete Guide to Digital Project Management*,
https://doi.org/10.1007/978-1-4842-3417-4

- Utility domain

  - *Key use cases*: Plan comparators (for comparing various service plans), plan recommendations, bill payments, searches, usage history reports, end–user collaboration (blog, wiki, community, and forums), user profile management, plan switching, enterprise integration (billing system, inventory management, order management ERP—Enterprise Resource Planning, and CRM ERP), customer self-service, digital marketing, campaign management, case/incident management, and personalization

  - *Key business drivers*: Revenue increase in business channel, enabling self-service, maintenance cost optimization, and increased collaboration

- Manufacturing domain

  - *Key use cases*: Information consolidation, searches (such as parts finder), user registration, omni-channel access, user administration, single-sign-on, services based integration, web analytics, SEO (search engine optimization), localization, social integration, personalization, knowledge management, content management, taxonomy management, and responsive and interactive user experience development

  - *Key business drivers*: Business self-service, efficient information discovery, single-stop-shops through a unified view, consolidation, business process optimization, and process automation

- Healthcare/lifesciences domain

  - *Key use cases*: Member preference management, claims management, analytics management, provider integration, records management, payment integration, reporting, workflow management, and personalization

  - *Key business drivers*: Business self-service, efficient information discovery, provide single-stop-shop through a unified view, consolidation, and business process optimization

- Financial Services domain

  - *Key use cases*: Virtual branches, enterprise integration (with core banking systems, CRM, email servers, risk management systems, card systems, payment gateways, reporting systems, wealth management), transaction management, social integration, authentication and authorization, mobile app experience, collaboration (such as chat, co-browsing), and alerts and notifications

  - *Key business drivers*: Customer self-service, increase customer lifetime value, enhanced customer support experiences, and holistic dashboard experiences

APPENDIX C

Exit Criteria for Testing Phases

This appendix explains the exit criteria for various testing activities. Project managers can use it as a checklist and as acceptance criteria during testing phases.

Test planning phase:

- All requirements/use cases/user stories are finalized and the integration, data, and migration requirements are finalized.

- Testing metrics and SLAs such as defect resolution time, along with code coverage, are agreed upon and finalized with stakeholders.

- Test planning document is created, reviewed, and signed off by all stakeholders.

- All needed testing tools are identified and set up in the appropriate environments.

- All test scripts are developed.

Unit testing phase:

- All unit test cases are executed successfully.

- Test case coverage meets the specified criteria.

- Unit test cases are automated and are part of the continuous integration process.

© Shailesh Kumar Shivakumar 2018
S. K. Shivakumar, *Complete Guide to Digital Project Management*,
https://doi.org/10.1007/978-1-4842-3417-4

Integration testing phase:

- All system test cases are executed successfully.

- Integration defects with a severity of 1 and 2 are fixed and successfully closed.

- Integration defects with a severity of 3 and 4 are either deferred or closed.

- The impact analysis of deferred defects is published.

System testing phase:

- All system test cases are executed successfully.

- System defects with a severity of 1 and 2 are fixed and successfully closed.

- System defects with a severity of 3 and 4 are either deferred or closed.

- The impact analysis of deferred defects is published.

- System test report is published and signed off on.

Performance testing phase:

- All performance test cases are executed successfully.

- All defined performance SLAs are met during performance testing.

- The system's health check parameters (CPU utilization, memory utilization, and disk utilization) are verified to meet the SLAs.

APPENDIX D

Project Scope Document Template

This appendix provides the structure of a typical Project Scope document. It briefly explains each section of the document. A digital project manager can use this as a reference when creating a Project Scope document.

The Project Scope document should include the following items:

- Introduction

    - *Opportunity details*: This section provides the financial details of the project, such as expected revenue, project duration, and such.

    - *Context and background*: This section summarizes the key business drivers and current challenges. The section also provides brief details about the critical success factors, business KPIs, and metrics.

    - *Executive summary*: The summary highlights the business themes, proposed solutions, high-level timelines, and cost. The summary is presented to business stakeholders.

- Project scope

    - *Technical scope*: This section provides the high-level technical scope that will be further detailed in technical documents such as the architecture document and the design document.

    - *Business/functional scope*: This section provides the high-level business requirements that will be further elaborated on in the business requirements document (BRD).

© Shailesh Kumar Shivakumar 2018
S. K. Shivakumar, *Complete Guide to Digital Project Management*,
https://doi.org/10.1007/978-1-4842-3417-4

- *Operations scope*: This details any in-scope operations work, such as incident handling, server maintenance, etc.

- *Success criteria*: This defines the key success criteria and the desired end state.

- *Metrics*: This section details the main metrics and KPIs that can be used for tracking and monitoring.

- *Assumptions and constraints*: This section details all the technical and requirement assumptions and constraints.

- *Non-functional/quality criteria*: This section details the non-functional requirements related to performance, scalability, availability, security, etc.

- Execution approach

  - *Project execution methodology*: In this section, the project manager details the execution model (such as Agile, iterative, waterfall, etc.).

  - *Project timelines*: This section provides the phase-wise delivery and schedule plan.

  - *Project milestones*: This section describes the major milestones and corresponding payment details.

- Others

  - *Stakeholders*: This section lists all the key stakeholders along with their roles and responsibilities.

  - *Compliance standards*: This section provides a list of all compliance standards related to technology.

  - *Legal and regulation rules*: This section lists all the regulations applicable to the digital program (such as data sharing, data storing, data archival, and more).

  - *AS-IS landscape*: This section provides a high-level overview of current systems, processes, and workflows.

CMS Product Evaluation Scorecard

This scorecard provides a list of capabilities needed for a typical content management solution. Solution requirements are grouped into three categories—functional capabilities, technology capabilities, and miscellaneous. Each of the solution requirements should be ranked on a score of 1-10, with 1 denoting full customization and 10 denoting full reuse of out-of-the-box features. The score is the weighted value of the rating. For instance, if the rating is 5 and the weight for that requirement is 50%, then the weighted score is 2.5.

This example scorecard includes three categories. The first level category is divided into three high-level capabilities related to functionality, technology, and operations. Each of these high-level categories includes second-level and third-level categories. The weights have been distributed based on their business importance.

The final score for the CMS product is calculated by taking the total of all the weighted scores. The final score is used to rank the candidate products.

Requirement#	Evaluation Parameter	Weights	CMS Product 1		
			Rating (1 - 10)	Score	Rationale
Functional Capabilities		50%			
1	Content Targeting	10%			
1.1	Tag content for targeting	5%			
1.2	Search optimization (support for SEO)	5%			
2	Publishing and workflow	10%			

(continued)

© Shailesh Kumar Shivakumar 2018
S. K. Shivakumar, *Complete Guide to Digital Project Management*,
https://doi.org/10.1007/978-1-4842-3417-4

Requirement#	Evaluation Parameter	Weights	CMS Product 1		
2.1	Publishing features (support for staging publishing, support for various publishing formats)	5%			
2.2	Workflow features (support for complex workflow modeling)	5%			
3	**Multi Device Support and Responsive Design**	**5%**			
3.1	Multi-device support	2%			
3.2	Responsive site design	3%			
4	**Versioning and Archival/Legal Discovery**	**5%**			
4.1	Versioning	2%			
4.2	Archival/legal discovery	3%			
5	**Access Control**	**5%**			
5.1	Access control lists	5%			
6	**Separation of Content and Presentation**	**5%**			
6.1	Ease of content authoring (support for templates, rich text editors, tagging support)	2%			
6.2	Multi-lingual capabilities	3%			
7	**Content Management**	**10%**			
7.1	Content standards (support for XML, JSON, HTML, and DITA)	2%			
7.2	Content reuse	3%			
7.3	Digital asset management	3%			
7.4	Layouts/components	2%			

(continued

Requirement#	Evaluation Parameter	Weights	CMS Product 1		
Technology Capabilities		**40%**			
8	**Integrations**	**15%**			
8.1	Integration with portal	10%			
	Integration with other applications	5%			
9	**Architecture**	**25%**			
9.1	Product architecture	5%			
9.2	Customization/APIs	5%			
9.3	Component library	5%			
9.4	Hosting (support for cloud)	5%			
9.6	Installation/configuration	5%			
Miscellaneous		**10%**			
10	**Operational**	**10%**			
10.1	Product roadmap alignment	3%			
10.2	Analyst ranking	2%			
10.3	Licensing costs	5%			

461

APPENDIX F

Digital Project Process and Governance Best Practices

This appendix looks at the best practices of digital project processes and governance. It covers security, employee engagement, knowledge transition, and code quality.

Security Governance

Based on the functional domain of the application, security gains prominent importance. As a part of robust security governance, the digital project manager has to cover the following aspects:

- *Application security*: Security issues in code, black box and white box testing, secure code reviews, system security, secure design, security checklists, and best practices adherence.

- *Testing*: Penetration testing and vulnerability assessments.

- *Security compliance*: Security audits, security policy setup, and compliance to standards such as Data Security Standard (DSS), Open Web Application Security Project (OWASP), Payment Card Industry (PCI), Common Weakness Enumeration (CWE), and System Admin, Audit, Network, Security (SANS).

- *Operations security*: Secure operations, security related monitoring, and system patching.

463

© Shailesh Kumar Shivakumar 2018
S. K. Shivakumar, *Complete Guide to Digital Project Management*,
https://doi.org/10.1007/978-1-4842-3417-4

- *Data security*: Data encryption, data masking, secure data storing and transmission, and rights management.

- *Infrastructure security*: End point security, setting up virus scanners, server hardening, and any applicable organization-specific security guidelines.

The following table provides various security-related activities that can be carried out in various SDLC phases.

SDLC Phase	Security Best Practices
Requirements elaboration	Gather security requirements
Architecture and design	Define security principles and create security checklist
Development	Security reviews and usage of security checklist and secure coding guidelines
Testing	Security testing, vulnerability testing, and penetration testing
Maintenance	Security monitoring and system patching

Best Practices During Knowledge Transition

Here are some of the best practices in performing knowledge transition:

- The project manager has to collect all the needed information related to systems such as the technical ecosystem, the incident patterns, and the needed documentation.

- Establish the processes related to knowledge transition such as training, documentation, etc.

- Trained persons to provide reverse knowledge sharing sessions with the team to validate their understanding.

- The project manager has to clearly define the success criteria that includes feedback assessment.

- Develop and use centralized knowledge repository.

- During ticket handling, trainees can provide shadow support by contributing to the ticket handling, issue resolution, and developing enhancements.

- Project manager has to clearly define the SLAs based on the priority of the defects, enhancements, and incidents.

- Identify and define gaps and opportunities for continuous improvement.

- At the end of knowledge transition, the trainees should be evaluated based on performance assessments.

Best Practices During Employee Engagement

Here are some of the best practices in employee engagement:

- Regular interaction of leaders and senior management with employees through open house sessions, all hands meet, live chats, and quarterly town halls.

- Establish open communication channels with employees by enabling employees to freely express their concerns about the organization practices.

- Conduct frequent skill set and technology-related training programs so employees can upgrade their skills.

- Encourage the culture of innovation through various initiatives such as coding challenges, rewarding IP creation, etc.

- Project managers need to provide frequent feedback to employees and understand their concerns and aspirations.

- Conduct "brown bag lunches" with senior management and high-performing employees.

- Conduct employee engagement surveys, whereby employees can freely participate and express their opinions.

System Quality Attributes in Quality Governance

System quality is the key component of the overall project quality governance. The following table includes system quality attributes along with questions that can be used to understand the metric values. Digital project managers can use the tools and questions listed here to track and monitor the overall code quality.

System Quality Attribute	Capturing the Attribute Value
Reliability	Defect rate, availability, and mean time to failure (MTTF)
Maintainability	Incident rate, production outage frequency, and mean time to repair (MTTR)
Usability	Average time needed for a new user to learn the system, UI defect rate
Portability	Compliance to standards Test results on supported platforms
Fault tolerance	Error handling rate Mean time to failure (MTTF)
Performance	Average response time and perceived response time
Testability	Ease of testing the system, presence of test cases, and availability of automated test setup

Index

467

© Shailesh Kumar Shivakumar 2018
S. K. Shivakumar, *Complete Guide to Digital Project Management*,
https://doi.org/10.1007/978-1-4842-3417-4

Get the eBook for only $5!

Why limit yourself?

With most of our titles available in both PDF and ePUB format, you can access your content wherever and however you wish—on your PC, phone, tablet, or reader.

Since you've purchased this print book, we are happy to offer you the eBook for just $5.

To learn more, go to http://www.apress.com/companion or contact support@apress.com.

Apress®

CPSIA information can be obtained
at www.ICGtesting.com
Printed in the USA
LVHW101602180219
607900LV00008B/245/P